TO THE
AND BACK

The Stories of Bobby Moegle's 40 Years as Baseball Coach at Lubbock Monterey High School
AS TOLD BY HIMSELF, HIS PLAYERS AND HIS COACHES

"To the road and back." That was Coach Moegle's attention-grabber. If there was a need to get our undivided attention, he would send us to the road and back.

– Mark Griffin '72

BY MIKE GUSTAFSON

Amanda Sneed, graphic designer
Cari Caldwell, graphic designer
Hartsfield Design

Copyright 2020 by Mike Gustafson

All rights reserved, including the right to reproduce this book, or portions thereof, in any form.

First printing: June 2020

Library of Congress Control Number: 2020908081

Thank you to all who participated in the interviews that made this book possible, whether in person, by phone or by email.

Thank you to the staff of the Southwest Collection/Special Collections Library at Texas Tech, in which Coach Moegle's scrapbooks, the locker room signs and his oral histories are housed. Their work remains a valuable part of our lives in West Texas.

A "last but not least" thank you to Lubbock ISD-TV, who conducted some of the interviews essential to this book.

CONTENTS

Introduction	7
The Cast	13
The Foundation	17
Preparation and Off-Season	53
Philosophy and Gameday	71
Success and Tradition	151
Friend, Mentor and Family Man	203
The Funny Stuff	233
The Impact	245
Reference	270
About the Author	273

Introduction

My earliest sports heroes played for Paul "Bear" Bryant's mid-1970s Crimson Tide football teams.

My mom had worked as a student in the University of Alabama athletic department. Her job was to interview out-of-state Alabama football players, write an article about each one and send it with a photo of the player in his uniform to his hometown newspaper. They were "local boy does good" stories, but for me they were the voices I listened to when mom brought her interview tapes home.

The interviews were peppered with the players' stories of Coach Bryant. Whether they were quoting him or relaying a tail-chewing, they had something to say about him.

As a kid, I had gotten his autograph on a slip of paper at an Alabama pep rally once and had also stood in line with my parents at the local mall to get him to sign a copy of his autobiography. When we went to Bama games, my eyes were constantly checking the sideline for his trademark houndstooth hat. I lack the eloquence to properly describe how revered he was.

Our family moved to Lubbock from Tuscaloosa late in the summer of 1978, which was the summer prior to 6th grade for me. Family legend has it that we were in Lubbock looking for a house and the realtor (not Mrs. Moegle) learned that I had made the local little league baseball all-star team in Tuscaloosa. She turned that car toward the Monterey district and that was that.

I attended Wheatley Elementary as part of Lubbock's busing program and loved it. I had missed the baseball season when we moved here, so my first interactions were as the "new kid" in school. One day, Wheatley brought in some athletes to speak to the kids, and among them were former Plainsmen Gary Ashby and Larry Horn, who then were playing minor league baseball. Also with them was Texas Tech quarterback Ron Reeves.

Later, I played YFL (Youth Football League), MOB (Monterey Optimist Basketball) and eventually Little League baseball, and that was where I learned about Bobby Moegle's Baseball School. I had been told I should attend, and did, and there I received my first formal baseball instruction. Jeff Harp and Reeves helped Coach Moegle with baseball school that summer. Harp was a player at Texas Tech by then, and I learned that both he and Reeves had also played baseball at Monterey High School. In future years as I attended the camp, Bob Fannin joined the group of instructors, and years later I served as an instructor.

As Pony and Colt Leaguers, and especially during All-Stars, we knew what it meant when Coach Moegle's very distinct late '70s conversion van turned in to the parking lot during our games. I can remember playing in the field and seeing that van. I would turn to whoever I was playing with who was headed to MHS and get their attention, then shoot a glance and a nod up at the parking lot so they knew Coach Moegle was watching.

The program was rolling when my class arrived at Monterey in the fall of '82. The state championships of '72 and '74 had long been in the books, and the '78 team was the state runner-up. When I was an 8th grader, the '81 team won Coach Moegle's third state title.

My time at Monterey was no different than many of the stories you are about to read. I spent a year on the JV under Coach Crutcher, and then a stretch early in my junior year in which I fought for and lost and fought some more and finally kept a starting job. To succeed at the level it took to keep a starting spot in those years often meant all-district and all-city honors.

I was very fortunate to play on two state tournament teams at Monterey. Our 1984 team was better than our 1985 team, which was my senior year. But both had the same fate, which was a season-ending loss in the state semifinal.

We endured the tail-chewings, the running and the daily mental grind that all of Coach Moegle's teams dealt with. I had heard those stories from Coach Bryant's players about sacrifice and teamwork and tradition, and later about the impact that playing at Bama had on their lives, and now I was living my version at Monterey.

Years later as a husband and father of two in the mid-2000s, I attended a celebrity golf outing at Texas Tech's Rawls Course. There I met Texas A&M legend John David Crow. His son, the late John David Crow Jr., had played running back at Bama when we lived in Tuscaloosa, so I thought I had enough conversation in my arsenal to approach Coach Bryant's only Heisman trophy winner. I also had my signed copy of the Bear's autobiography with me.

The resulting conversation with Mr. Crow was so great. We talked about Coach Bryant for 15 minutes before it was time for him to head out to the course. He had asked about my book and I showed him the Bear Bryant autograph from 30 years prior. He was flattered when I asked him to sign on that page. He had earned it.

As I reflected on his memories of playing and coaching for Coach Bryant, my experiences with Coach Moegle came back to me.

Mr. Crow talked about his days as a player and goofing around in the locker room. The noise of the door opening and closing when Coach Bryant entered the room was the sign to straighten up; the sound of him entering was just a little different than when everybody else entered. For us, that was the sound of Coach Moegle's office door closing.

Like Coach Bryant's football players, we wanted Coach Moegle to notice us, but we also knew what that meant if there was a slip up. And there was no nonsense … ever. I've always loved a story told by Jerry Duncan, a mid '60s player from North Carolina who had moved around to several positions during his time at Alabama. One day Coach Bryant came down from his iconic tower from which he oversaw practice. It was never a good thing when he came down to deliver a message in person. He headed for Duncan and said, "I'm moving you to tackle today. And if I have to move you again, it will be back to North Carolina."

The other obvious similarity between the two coaches was that their earliest teams had taken the full brunt of them installing their programs. What that means is, the stories of Coach Bryant's "Junction Boys" teams are well told, and we had heard of the long hours and toughness demanded by Coach Moegle's teams from the early 1960s. Both were much less vocal and animated as older coaches with so much success and tradition in place, but there was still no shortage of respect paid by their players.

Sylvester Croom, an outstanding center for Coach Bryant and later the first African American head coach in the Southeastern Conference, once said, "My dad taught me how to be a man. Coach Bryant forced me to put it into practice." Gary Ashby said it similarly about Coach Moegle. "He ran off as many good players as other teams had. I really think a lot of the success that the people who came through his regime had is that they were 'strung well' and were capable of enduring."

Croom also said, "Coach Bryant was always talking to us about what our lives were going to be 10-20 years down the road, and the lessons we were going to learn from the game. If you can discipline yourself to get through these practices. If you can discipline yourself to come back from a loss. If you can discipline yourself to keep fighting in the fourth quarter when you're behind, then those lessons will carry you later on when your wife gets sick, if you have a child die, or if you're out of a job. Then you'll know how to fight."

Keller Smith said about Coach Moegle, "The sustenance that was provided in the baseball world went way beyond that in life. Even though I couldn't play a lick of baseball today, I still carry with me the lessons that he provided me during the three years I was so intimate with him."

In the process of my conversation with John David Crow, the seeds of this book were planted. It would be years for the book to come to fruition, but the inspiration was there. Great coaches inspire great stories.

Travis Walden said, "My brother says if you meet a guy who was a Marine, you'll know within 5 minutes that he was a Marine. If a guy played baseball for Coach Moegle, you'll know within 5 or 10 minutes of a conversation, because something will happen and the guy will tell a story about playing baseball for him."

When Coach Moegle's players are together, the stories are told, and I wanted to capture those stories so they could be shared and kept forever.

This book would not be in your hands without source material provided by Lubbock ISD-TV and the Southwest Collection/Special Collections Library at Texas Tech.

Coach Moegle did two interviews with the Southwest Collection. One of those was a lengthy oral history that took place in 2006. The other was a much shorter interview conducted by David Murrah at Coach Moegle's house. That interview took place in the weeks following the 1972 state championship. When material from the 1972 interview is referenced in this book, I point that out.

Lubbock ISD-TV did several interviews with Coach Moegle, several of his former players – mostly from his first 15 years at Monterey – and longtime local media members Jack Dale and Burle Pettit. Those interviews were dated around 2008.

I added several more interviews which were conducted between 2015 and 2018. Others responded around that time to email requests and my Facebook posts.

I certainly appreciate everyone's words and time, whether spent with me in person or through their recorded voice.

I recall countless hours sitting at my favorite table at Rudy's BBQ in Lubbock transcribing interviews and putting the text for this book together. I also did a couple of my interviews there, in addition to a high school classroom, Judge's chambers, coffee shops and several offices. Thank you to all for their accommodations and patience.

The inspiration for the book came from my conversation with Mr. Crow in the mid-2000s, and you can do the math on how long it took to get here. There were surges of activity, often around the holidays when the pace of everyday life and work slowed, followed by stretches of inactivity.

In 2009, while on a jury in Judge Jim Bob Darnell's courtroom, he told me he had heard I was working on a book about Coach Moegle and wished me well. After my interviews with so many of the people in this book, their good wishes were added to the list of those offering encouragement to finish.

Throughout the project, Mark Griffin has been a confidant. I wish his father, Rip, was here to talk baseball and enjoy the stories just one more time.

In late 2016, I met with Coach Moegle's daughter, Sherri, at Rudy's (of course) to tell her of my intentions and show her a summary of the interviews and raw material. At that point, she was added to my list of "encouragers." She then became my official point of contact with the Moegle family. I see Coach Moegle around town and enjoy our occasional lunch, but the book was never a topic of discussion.

It was a great day in December 2019 when I was able to give the very first draft to Sherri to give to Coach Moegle as a Christmas gift.

I have one other publication – my doctoral dissertation. The number of people who actually read it might be counted on one hand, as it goes with most dissertations. Among those readers are my parents, who both took turns at editing this book. My mother, a journalist and editor by trade, took on the Herculean task of not only editing this book, but being my "Chief Encourager" to get me to finish the project when life sometimes slowed me down.

Mike Gustafson, MHS '85
April 2020

The Cast

The following people generously contributed recollections and information used in this book:

GARY ASHBY – played 1st base on the 1971-73 teams and later played at Texas Tech and in the Padres organization. He is an inductee of the Lubbock ISD Athletic Hall of Honor and the Texas Tech Athletic Hall of Fame. He resides in Lubbock.

SCOTT BRAND – played on the 1993-94 teams and later pitched in the Yankees organization. He lives in Lubbock.

CLINT BRYANT – played on the 1990-92 teams and later was a two-time Smith Award (national player of the year) finalist at Texas Tech. His number 23 is retired by the Red Raiders and he is an inductee of the Lubbock ISD Hall of Honor. His home is in Frisco.

DUSTY BUCK – played on Coach Moegle's final three teams at Monterey and later pitched at Texas Tech from 2000-03. His home is in Frisco.

DONNIE BUMPASS – pitched on Coach Moegle's first two teams at Monterey. He then pitched for four years at Oklahoma State. He has a doctorate in economics and spent his career in academia. He lives in Huntsville, Texas.

JEFF CHASE – pitched for Coach Moegle in 1990. He later pitched at Lubbock Christian for four years. His home is in Lubbock.

MIKE CRUTCHER – played catcher for Coach Moegle from 1966-68 and later served as Coach Moegle's assistant for 10 seasons, the most of any of his former assistant coaches. He continues as a history teacher and assistant football coach at Wylie East High School near Dallas.

JACK DALE – a career broadcaster in Lubbock from the 1950s until his death in 2011. His career included covering high school sports amid his many duties over the decades. He was the longtime voice of the Texas Tech Red Raiders.

JIM BOB DARNELL – played for Coach Moegle from 1964-66 and later briefly at Texas Tech. He graduated from Texas Tech University and Texas Tech School of Law. He lives in Lubbock.

JOHN DUDLEY – was on Coach Moegle's first three teams at Monterey, then played for four years at Texas Tech. He was Coach Moegle's first full-time assistant coach before moving across town to Coronado, where his number was retired after a 30-year head coaching career.

BOB FANNIN – played for Coach Moegle from 1976-78, and later at Ranger Junior College and Lubbock Christian. He was a player on the 1983 Lubbock Christian NAIA national championship team and was an assistant coach on the 2009 Lubbock Christian NAIA national championship team. He lives in Lubbock.

MARK GRIFFIN – was on Coach Moegle's 1972 state championship team. He attended The University of Texas and played for the Longhorns for four years, including the 1975 College World Series championship team. He is a graduate of the Texas Tech School of Law and lives in Lubbock.

JEFF HARP – played for Coach Moegle from 1976-78 and for four years at Texas Tech. He has spent his entire career as a high school teacher and coach. He currently resides in Lubbock.

STEVE HARR – pitched for Coach Moegle from 1971-73. He is a graduate of the Texas Tech School of Law and lives in Dallas.

LARRY HAYS – was the baseball coach at Lubbock Christian and Texas Tech from 1971-2008. His number 27 is retired at both schools. He is one of only 11 college coaches in history with at least 1,500 wins, and he was a 2015 inductee of the National College Baseball Hall of Fame. He currently resides in Colorado.

JEFF HORN – played for Coach Moegle from 1994-96. He is a graduate of Texas Tech and is a business owner in Lubbock. His home is in Graham, Texas.

GARY HUGHES – pitched for Coach Moegle from 1963-65. He is a graduate of Texas Tech and resides in Anna, Texas.

HUNTER LANKFORD – was a catcher for Coach Moegle on the 1985-87 teams. He is a graduate of Texas Tech and lives in Austin.

FRED OLIVER – succeeded Coach Moegle as the head baseball coach at Monterey. He coached the Plainsmen for 10 years and led them to eight playoff appearances and the 2005 state tournament.

BURLE PETTIT – worked in the newspaper industry for half a century, first as a sportswriter and later as editor of the Lubbock Avalanche-Journal.

TUEY RANKIN – played at Midland Lee under Coach Ernie Johnson in the mid-'80s but later served as Coach Moegle's final assistant coach from 1997-99. He lives in Lubbock.

RON REEVES – played for Coach Moegle from 1976-78. He played quarterback at Texas Tech, Canada and in the USFL. He is an inductee of the Texas Tech Athletic Hall of Fame and lives in Lubbock.

SHANE SALYER – was an infielder for Coach Moegle from 1983-85. He is a graduate of Texas Tech and is a business owner in Lubbock, where he resides.

JIMMY SHANKLE – played for Coach Moegle from 1972-74. After playing parts of five seasons in the Red Sox organization, he graduated from Texas Tech. He later served as head baseball coach at Lubbock Christian University, UT-San Antonio and Abilene Christian. His home is in Dallas.

KELLER SMITH – played on Coach Moegle's first three teams at Monterey. He is a graduate of Texas Tech and lives in Dallas.

NATHAN SWINDLE – played for Coach Moegle from 1979-81 and pitched at Texas Tech from 1982-86. He resides in Lubbock.

TRAVIS WALDEN – played for Coach Moegle from 1979-81. He pitched at Lubbock Christian before playing in the Phillies organization. He was Coach Moegle's assistant from 1989-94 before moving on to several college coaching positions. He lives in Lubbock.

BRAD WALKER – pitched for Coach Moegle from 1983-85. He is a graduate of Texas Tech and lives in Kingsville.

JIMMY WEBSTER – played for Coach Moegle in 1984-85. He is one of the few to ever be cut from the program then return to make the team and flourish. He later played catcher at Lubbock Christian and Texas Tech. He has spent his entire career as a high school teacher and coach. He currently resides in Grapevine.

And I, **MIKE GUSTAFSON**, played for Coach Moegle from 1983-85 and was an infielder at Texas Tech from 1986-89. I live in Lubbock.

The Foundation

When I first came to Monterey, I said the one thing I was going to do was work with a lot of kids and give them the opportunity to be a winner by the hard work they put in.

— *Coach Moegle*

COACH MOEGLE:

I was born on June 30, 1933, in Taylor, Texas. I very seldom ever got out of the county back in those days. I graduated from Taylor High School and played football, baseball, basketball and tennis there, but baseball became my best sport of all of them because of my arm strength and my ability to hit the ball a long way.

I didn't really have a mentor, but there was an old guy in Taylor, the only person who had played baseball at a professional level. He tried to help us kids. His name was Bob Sloan and he worked for the railroad. He set the example for me and caused me to be committed to baseball.

When I finished 2nd grade, the school changed from an 11-grade system to a 12-grade system, so all of us kids skipped the 3rd grade and went on to the 4th, which caused me to graduate when I was 16 years old.

My high school coach wasn't a great teacher of athletics, but he was a great person for motivating the kids and making us do things right. His name was Gilbert Conoley. He was our coach. I was a pretty good high school player so he made an approach to Bibb Falk when he was at The University of Texas. Bibb came over one day and saw me. He told me I wasn't good enough to play for him and to consider playing at a small school.

It was the first time I had been told that I wasn't good enough to be with The University of Texas. That perpetuated my desire to try and achieve something that was a little bit beyond what I really wanted. I pushed harder when Bibb told me I wasn't good enough to play at Texas. Which I wasn't at the time. I wasn't mature enough.

I had the opportunity to watch Texas play. They had some really good athletes, including Kal Segrist. Certainly, the level at that time was way beyond me, but it was a motivating thing to watch.

I had a cousin who had gone to Blinn Junior College. My mother and dad had enough money for me to go to one semester of college, so I went to Blinn with the idea that I would letter in a sport and get 1/3 of a scholarship. At Blinn I lettered in basketball and baseball

Coach Moegle - US Army baseball

and got my second semester of school paid for. The next year I came back to Blinn and played football, basketball and baseball, and just for fun I played in the state junior college tennis tournament and finished second in that. In two years at Blinn I got my scholarship paid for except for the first semester.

From the fall of 1950, my coach at Blinn was Frank Butler. He had been an All-Conference football player at Southwestern. At Blinn, I could throw hard, but I was wild. Several good people tried to teach me control.

Coach Butler contacted a man at Southwestern College named Randolph Medley, who gave me a full scholarship to play basketball and baseball. Georgetown was only 20 miles from Taylor. I attended there from 1952 to 54. It was a good thing for me to play both sports. We were just a bunch of ol' country kids playing baseball. We didn't win any championships. Southwestern was in the Big State Conference. Texas Lutheran was one of the better teams in the country at that time. Texas Wesleyan, East Texas Baptist, we didn't get down to Lamar or Pan American – that was a little too far for us. We played Concordia and St. Mary's, who were very good.

Of the coaches I played for from high school on, I didn't get much from their styles or philosophies of training athletes, but they were good Christian men. They were involved in Christian situations, which was good for me. They didn't know a lot about the sport of baseball. Frank Butler knew about football, but he didn't know anything about basketball or baseball. I never really had a baseball teacher but what I got from my coaches was how to be a good person.

After getting my degree, I went into the Army on August 26, 1954, and stayed for two years. I was in the 39th Infantry. After basic training at Fort Bliss, I ended up in Germany and played baseball with a good bunch of players, a couple of former All-Americans, a couple of college players and a couple in class C and D ball. We won the European Championship in 1955 and got to come back to the United States to participate in the All-Army Tournament. The next year we were winning it, but most of us were discharged and came home.

My brother, Dick, was playing for the 49ers at the time. He had been an All-American football player at Rice University, and he had some contacts with the Houston Buffs, which was a AA minor league ballclub that was affiliated with the St. Louis Cardinals. The general manager, Art Routzong, listened to my brother and they signed me.

I went to spring training with Harry "The Hat" Walker as my manager and stayed there two weeks before they sold my contract to the Cardinals.

I was 23 years old before I learned anything about baseball. I used to tell my high school kids that they were learning things that I didn't learn until I was 23.

That's where I started learning about baseball and how to play it well. I was older than most of the other kids and had a degree. Most of the others were first- or second-year pros. So I made up my mind to learn every aspect of the game. I attended every instructional session I could get to, infielders, outfielders, all of them. I spent a lot of time just watching and learning things.

George Kissell was a coach and instructor in the St. Louis Cardinals organization. He worked as a minor league instructor until 2008, when he was 87 years old. He was the finest baseball man I'd ever been associated with. Every time he spoke, I went to the session, whether in Albany, Georgia, or Daytona Beach, Florida, just to listen to him talk. This is where I developed a lot of knowledge. Watching him work and then playing for Al Unser, a former major league catcher for three years, helped me gain some insight. I picked up on how to pitch, the philosophy of pitching, and how to handle people from some knowledgeable baseball people. They had a real good background.

(In an August 1959, Associated Press newspaper article, Unser described Moegle as "the most underrated player in the Carolina League, a manager's ballplayer ... He was a real student of the game and an inspiration to the club.")

I was an outfielder and started my pro career in Decatur, Illinois, and had a really good year. The next year, I went to Winnipeg,

Canada, and had another good year. Then Winston-Salem, North Carolina. This was a little bit harder. We played in a bigger park and dealt with a lot of rain.

I was doing graduate work with The University of Texas in the off-season. Bully Gilstrap had been a teacher of mine there.

I hadn't thought about coaching, but with the young talent in front of me in the Cardinals organization, many of them bonus players who would be projected into the big leagues in three years, I knew I couldn't have a good enough year to get ahead of them.

I told Bully when I was about to leave for spring training in 1959 that it might be best that I start looking for a job. I told him if he heard of one somewhere, I'd consider ending my playing career and taking a job teaching and coaching.

One day in Raleigh, North Carolina, I got a phone call from Bully. He said he had two baseball jobs available – one was in Lubbock and one was in Odessa. I told him that I'd hardly been out of the county and didn't know where they were. I asked him for some information on which one he thought was best for me, and he suggested Lubbock because I was single and it was a younger, more progressive town with a university.

He told me to call Eck Curtis, the Lubbock ISD Athletic Director. I went to the desk at the hotel and got a pocketful of quarters and went to a phone booth. I dialed the number and started dropping quarters in the phone. I didn't know how to make a collect call. Once he found out I was calling on a pay phone and using a bunch of quarters to ask about a job, he gave me a stern lecture on how to operate a phone. He told me with Bully's recommendation I could have the job. I left North Carolina on August 15 for Taylor, Texas, and then on to Lubbock.

MARK GRIFFIN '72:

They must have had a sound upbringing where they learned right from wrong, with a high level of expectation for him and his brother. It's evident when you look at how they handled themselves in their professional lives that he had a mom and dad who loved him very much and expected him to do the right things at the right time, and to be a good citizen.

COACH MOEGLE:

I think I had a calling when I was a youngster. Work was really hard to find when I was a kid, and we did a lot of different stuff, but I always enjoyed teaching and I was always a good enough athlete that I could pass it on to somebody else who looked up to me a little bit. I enjoyed the teaching part, whether it was teaching swimming in the summer or whatever form of recreation we did. I had great admiration for my high school coaches. In fact, when I was about to get the job out here, I couldn't wait to get to my high school coaches at Taylor and tell them I was going to get the opportunity to coach. I never thought I wanted to do anything else.

GARY HUGHES '65:

I know his military training prepared him for a very difficult situation in handling a bunch of young guys who were going a hundred different directions. I think he decided early on that there was only going to be one voice and it was going to be his, and that we were going to do things according to his plan, that we were going to be superbly conditioned and that we were going to spend the time practicing and preparing.

COACH MOEGLE:

I didn't know anything about coaching high school baseball. My experience at Taylor was very limited. But after being a part of Army baseball with guys that had played professionally, and then playing professionally myself, I had developed my own ideas.

KELLER SMITH '63:

Coach Moegle's makeup, like it was for a lot of us, was a product of his life. Certainly, his upbringing, the experiences he had when he was growing up, were more difficult than it is for kids today who have everything. I think that his military service probably gave him a firmer backbone than he already had. I think in his minor league baseball career, they didn't coddle the players. So surely a combination of his own upbringing, his parents, his military exposure and the type of treatment he got as a pro ballplayer all went into formulating his character and his own approach to the game, with most of that being exemplified by discipline and toughness and "my way or the highway."

COACH MOEGLE:

I was also going to be assisting with the football team, and that was OK. I had a good background in football because of my brother being with the 49ers. Being around football all the time and playing at Blinn, I had a good knowledge of the strategies of the game.

Eck Curtis at Lubbock ISD was great to me. He latched onto the Moegle name because he had been offensive coordinator at Texas. They tried to recruit my brother out of high school. Dicky chose Rice, instead of Texas, but they knew what Dicky had done in football, the Cotton Bowl, making All-American, and in the NFL.

Eck latched onto me like I was one of his. Later on, he and his wife even gave me and my wife, Carolyn, who was teaching over at Roosevelt, a wedding party. That would be unheard of nowadays.

During the drive to Lubbock, I was thinking about how I would set up my baseball program. My idea was to run it like spring training. That was my objective.

JACK DALE, BROADCASTER:

Before the late '50s and early '60s, what was happening in high school baseball, at least in West Texas, was the baseball program would be turned over to an assistant football coach. He would be told, "By the way, you're the head baseball coach, too." That football coach didn't know the game of baseball like Bobby Moegle did.

COACH MOEGLE:

When I first came to Lubbock, people didn't know anything about how to play baseball. They got to see pro ball, watching the old Lubbock Hubbers, but they didn't know how to get down and dirty with the fundamentals. There was nothing being done to teach kids the fundamentals of the game like I had learned going to all the instructional sessions and playing with good people. I knew there was a difference between just playing baseball and learning how to play.

In my baseball program, I was going to take a bunch of high school kids and we were going to go through spring training. We did fundamentals, we did fundamentals and we did fundamentals until we got through the fundamental part, and then we went to the offensive part, which was batting practice and stuff like that. That's what we did in spring training – in the morning sessions we did all defense. When we came back in the afternoon, we worked on the offensive skills, like swinging and running.

Dale Grimes was my predecessor at Monterey. We first met in 1959. Dale had a ranch in Seymour. He was a good man and was highly respected.

I really didn't have a goal. I was never a goal-setter. My objective was just to do the best job we could do every day. We were going to compete so hard and we expected to come out on top. I instilled in the kids that discipline was the way to go, and that they had to be in control of themselves and be a man and assume responsibility for their actions.

KELLER SMITH '63:

Ironically, the Lubbock High baseball job came open at the same time as the Monterey job. My information is that Earl Parker was hired by the school district without assignment, but he was the coach of the Bell Red Cheks, which was the American Legion team that won the state championship in the summer of 1959. The guys on the team developed a lot of appreciation for Earl's coaching because of that championship, and they naturally assumed he would be the new coach at Monterey. But that wasn't how it worked out, because Bobby Moegle became the coach at Monterey and Earl Parker was given the job at Lubbock High. There was a sizeable amount of anger among that Monterey team going into the '59-'60 school year because they got a coach they didn't know anything about. But as the season developed, they realized that the right decision had been made.

COACH MOEGLE:

When I got to Monterey, I inherited a bunch of kids that could really play. They had won the American Legion state championship. I had a good portion of those kids back. They had some talent, they really did. I inherited one really good pitcher in Donnie Bumpass and a lot of kids who were so hungry to get to the next level that it really made it easy. I could throw out things, like show them how to grip a bat, how to sit it on your shoulder, just everything. It was the same way during the summer. I took them all by myself and we put in hours and hours of practice. Those kids in 1960 were workers and they believed everything I told them.

It was my idea that we would take these youngsters who had good skill and we were going to hone them to a new level. With me being single and not knowing a soul in Lubbock, they became my family. When I first got those kids, I loved them to death – they didn't know it. We spent all our time together. Any time I had free time, we would work out. In the summer, I would encourage them to go to church on Sunday, but at 1 o'clock we would hit the field and stay there until church at night. This was my approach and I never took a day off.

KELLER SMITH '63:

He was 26 or 27 at the time and he had no life other than coaching. He and Carolyn weren't married yet and coaching was his focus and his commitment.

COACH MOEGLE:

I was running around with an active, pro-Texas Tech person named Bill Dean, both of us single at the time. He asked if I would like to have a blind date with a Tech girl, a beauty. I said I would. So Bill and I and our dates went to play Putt-Putt golf. Carolyn was the first person I had seen who would cheat you. I liked that competitive spirit she had. We kept on dating and finally got married. She was a beautiful young girl, and I met her when she was a junior in college. She went ahead to get her degree and taught a year before we got married (in December 1963).

We have two real beautiful daughters. They inherited their mother's looks. My oldest is Sherri. She has two boys and works for Southwest Airlines. Melinda, who is a teacher, is married to a very good cotton farmer and has two kids. I am very blessed. I have two daughters who are well-situated and married well, so it's real easy.

JOHN DUDLEY '62, ASSISTANT COACH 1968-'72:

After playing a little pro ball and being in the military and not being married when he got out here, he had plenty of time to devote to baseball. And that's why we were on the field for all those hours.

COACH MOEGLE:

The first thing you've got to have is the respect of your players. You've got to get their attention to be a successful coach. I look back at when I first started coaching and those kids were hungry to learn.

DONNIE BUMPASS '61:

I was at Monterey in 1960 (as a junior) when Coach Moegle arrived. Our baseball group had some successes (American Legion state championship in summer of 1959, regional championship in American Legion in 1958), but there was a general belief that we had underachieved. Coach Moegle brought a higher degree of professionalism, focus and spirit to our baseball group. We believed we could be better. Perfect is a strong word, but he was "perfect" for our group of athletes.

COACH MOEGLE:

My real challenge was to teach them to win at a level higher than they thought they could go.

KELLER SMITH '63:

I think we were his family for a period of time, until he got married and had his own family. There was probably an obsession to do well, to excellence and an obsession to win, and to pass that on to the players. He's one of those unique human beings who never lost that obsession and passion even after he married and had his family. By the way, he was a great husband and a great dad. He has two wonderful daughters. He was able to juggle his family obligations and keep the same focus that he always had on the performance of the baseball team.

COACH MOEGLE:

In those years, there weren't any two-hour rules or limits on practice during the school year, other than no work on Sundays. Our practices typically ran four hours. I had a rule that when the sun went down, we went in. Out here in West Texas you're almost at the edge of the time zone. Boy, that sun went down pretty late sometimes. But we'd stay until the sun went down regardless.

TUEY RANKIN, ASSISTANT COACH 1997–'99:

He told me that in the '60s he worked them long and hard, and when that water tower to the west of the school was finally casting a shadow that got to the field, it was time to end practice.

COACH MOEGLE:

I probably saw those kids more than their parents did. I was with them from 2:30 until 6:30 or 7 at night. Their mother and dad didn't get to see them a lot. They would say "goodbye" to them in the morning and "hello" at night, so I became important in their lives just by being consistent.

KELLER SMITH '63:

There were parents like my dad, who were applauding at all times for him taking on the responsibility of policing these ragknots that, otherwise, they would be having to police. So what's wrong with that plan? You send your kid off to school at 7:30 in the morning and he comes home at 7 at night, and he's so tired he can't do anything but eat dinner, do a little homework and go to bed. The chances of getting in trouble are minimized substantially. And here came the weekend and we were typically playing baseball on both Friday and Saturday. Saturday night was about the only night that we really had off. So, "ol' Coach Moegle" became the parent to a great degree. Again, I think most parents were celebrating.

COACH MOEGLE:

We didn't care if there was snow on the ground or the wind was blowing or what. We worked with snow banked up on the backstops, or dirt blowing so bad we couldn't see. There just wasn't a day that we took off because we never knew what kind of weather we might have to play in. I always told the kids that the other teams had already gone home in weather like that, and we were still working and the reason for that was that the conditions weren't going to dictate how we played. If we had an opponent, we were focused on that opponent and not the wind, or cold or whatever, because we had been there. That was just how stubborn I really was.

We mostly played schools from Lubbock north, which was an advantage for us. The weather in Lubbock was an 8 to 10 degrees difference than Amarillo in the spring – here, we didn't have the real chilling temperatures. If it was 45 or 50 degrees here, those teams couldn't get outside up there. Of course, everyone in Midland and those schools had the weather advantage over us.

Monterey was an upper middle-income school, so the kids didn't have to worry about working. It was an ideal situation for me.

Bill DuBose (the head football coach at Monterey) respected me and said, "If you'll work them this hard in the off-season, you can have the football kids who are baseball players for the first hour."

That was the first time it had been done in Texas and most all places. And I worked the devil out of those kids and he never complained one bit. James Odom came in a few years after DuBose, and we kept the same arrangement.

GARY ASHBY '73:

At some point, somebody in Austin came up with a great idea that teams could only work out so long. I think it helped the later generations that they couldn't stay out there until Coach Moegle got hungry or whatever his motivation was to go home.

COACH MOEGLE:

When I first got here, there were only about five schools that played baseball very well. Deck Woldt up at Pampa, Blackie Blackburn at Abilene, Speedy Moffett at Snyder, Julian Pressly in Odessa were good baseball men. Ernie Johnson was another baseball man and he took over at Midland Lee a couple years after I got to Monterey. Other than that, they were just a bunch of football coaches doing cariocas and football drills and trying to get off the practice field in two hours.

Our prime competitors were Amarillo and Lubbock High, which had great kids back then. Tascosa was a powerhouse, and so were Pampa and Borger, because they'd had minor league baseball up there.

MIKE CRUTCHER '68, ASSISTANT COACH 1973–'78, 1982–'85:

He was way before his time when he got to West Texas, and that really helped him.

JOHN DUDLEY '62, ASSISTANT COACH 1968–'72:

I think Coach Moegle was passionate as a coach because he would accept nothing less than your best effort and success. When he first came to Monterey, I think he was one of the first baseball men to coach high school baseball in this part of the country. He set the standard for all other coaches, because in many cases somebody was just assigned the duty of coaching baseball.

When he came in, he took it to a new level. Other schools began to see what was happening with his teams and pressure was brought to bear to compete on the same level as Monterey. Other schools began to hire true baseball coaches to coach the baseball team. I think that goes back to the way he attacked it from the very beginning.

COACH MOEGLE:

There was a practice field on the south side of the school. 50th Street wasn't paved back then; it was caliche. We had to maintain the field ourselves. But Monterey had the most beautiful grass that you could possibly have on a school campus. In fact, Coach DuBose and my coaching staffs would walk through the west side of campus with our pocketknives and dig out any weeds. We had great, great grass.

There wasn't any budget for a baseball field, so it was built and maintained by me and my sophomores. I fell to tradition and had my sophomores do all the field development under my supervision. We'd have it all worked up before the varsity came out to practice. We eventually got batting cages.

When I first started, our games were played at Hodges Park at 40th Street and what is now University Avenue. We played there until Mr. Curtis at Lubbock ISD told me that a baseball field was going to be built east of Lowrey Field if I would draw the design.

I wanted the foul lines to run north and south like all your regular ballparks, but the piece of land they gave me ran to the southeast. Because of the wind, I set it up to be a hitter's ballpark, with the lines being 340 and 330 feet down the line and 390 in the center. That's a pretty good hitter's park, which I believed in as a hitter. But also it taught the kids how to pitch against the wind.

It was a flat piece of land with not much there. What we had to do to get it developed – the school system didn't have enough money back then to develop the whole field – was build it in conjunction with the city. We put the land in, they put the field in, we put the stands in, they installed lights and the city maintained it.

We built it in 1962 and started playing out there in 1963.

That was the working agreement we had for years and years until the middle 1980s when it came under the complete jurisdiction of the LISD. The city didn't have much interest in it in the spring months, so we did our best to maintain it ourselves. They did a pretty good job maintaining it in the summer, because it was used for a summer league field. Lowrey Field became mine, and we stayed there for a long, long time.

KELLER SMITH '63:

Don't think for a moment that he asked less of himself than he asked of us. This guy was out there all the time. He was the groundskeeper. Before practice started, he was out there raking the infield and sprinkling it down to make sure it was in proper condition for practice. When we left the dressing room at 6:30 at night, he was still there.

COACH MOEGLE:

I learned quickly that we had to spend a lot of time with the offensive part of the game early in the season because of the way the wind blew and how hard the ground was. There were a lot of benefits to being offensive-minded instead of defensive-minded. Once the grass started to green up and the ground got softer with the April rains, we spent more time playing defense. The wind would also change directions later and pitching would take over and we would have to play without mistakes. I spent a lot of time in April and May getting ready for the playoffs and demanding perfection. I didn't push really hard early in the year being perfect defensively because we spent so much time on offense. But later on we really tried to hone it down so we could play defense with anybody.

Once we got to the middle of district play, I started to demand perfection from them as fielders. Errors will kill you in that environment late in the season. The coaches in Houston and down on the coast have to play that kind of baseball year around – error-free, pitching-dominated, bunt, run, scratch and get what you can. We didn't have to do that out here early in the spring, as far as I was concerned. I was criticized a lot for being just a power-oriented offensive coach. But we focused on those skills later in the spring.

The wind in West Texas dominates the game of baseball. You have got to know where the wind is blowing, what direction, velocity and time of day. Weather out here has as much to do with field conditions as anything else. I had to learn that because I had never been in a dry, windy environment like this. It was a new world that I had to learn.

I had come through the disciplined approach of playing for one run and winning in extra innings and stuff like that. It didn't take me very long to realize that you'd better know which way the wind is blowing and to take full advantage of it. That's true because of defensive play and outfielders with balls in the gaps and take the extra base. It was the first thing I learned about West Texas.

KELLER SMITH '63:

If you look at the history of Monterey athletics, the role that Bobby Moegle played not only in baseball but in Monterey athletics cannot be understated. The school opened in 1955 and it never won a district championship in any sport until his first year, which was the baseball season of 1960. And in addition to winning district that year, they also won the bi-district. That team was not without talent, because that same team had won the state American Legion championship the summer prior to that season.

So, without question, they had talent on that team. But they were also generally the same guys who had not won district under a different coach the prior year. The reason for that is so obvious that it jumps off the page, and of course, the district championships from that point forward became common.

COACH MOEGLE:

I did all the coaching in the early days. I learned from Sal Maglie and Johnny Grodzicki that location was the key to a quality pitch.

And I learned how to throw a pitch in three different spots: low outside, low inside and up and in. A player had to learn how to pitch those three positions to be successful.

Our kids could throw the breaking ball well and locate the breaking ball well. That's the key to success in high school. That was our forte. I could take kids with average arms, and with all our drills we could be successful.

Our teams spent a lot of time swinging the bat – it wasn't anything unusual for them to take 200 to 300 cuts a day. I wouldn't let them out of the batting cage until the kid could hit consistently. Most of the time, I threw batting practice. The guy who throws batting practice knows the weakness of every hitter. So I'd throw, and I'd throw.

The last thing we did was run. I was a firm believer that the only consistent thing in baseball is running. In all the years I coached, I don't think we had a club that stole less than 100 bases. Our kids learned how to read a pitcher, and they learned to run. We built our program on pitching, swinging the bat and hitting the fast ball, and running.

KELLER SMITH '63:

The hitting was extremely emphasized. I've talked to many guys who played for other teams, and if they got 10 to 15 cuts per practice it was a big day. But we went on and on and on and as a result of that, our timing was excellent and our hand-eye coordination was as good as it could be with the skill level we had. In a typical practice that might last 3 to 3½ hours, we were going to be hitting for two of those hours.

There would be a lot of other things going on at the same time. He would be hitting groundballs to the infielders and flyballs to the outfielders, which was not only skill development but also conditioning. But the primary thing that was going on was the hitting. That's the reason we hit as well as we did because we got more training and opportunity than most did. He would take an average hitter like myself and turn them into a good high school hitter.

COACH MOEGLE:

Without a doubt, my overall strength was knowledge of the game of baseball. When I started, I was one of the few guys who could coach every position on the field. Very few people I ran into in the early days had a background of pitching, catching, and how to throw, field and run. I had studied that stuff so hard that I felt I could teach the proper technique or information to a kid, regardless of what his situation was, and I didn't have to fake it.

BURLE PETTIT, LUBBOCK SPORTSWRITER:

He looked like a baseball coach and he acted like a baseball coach.

JACK DALE, BROADCASTER:

He was a baseball coach. I think that was the difference that caused Monterey to be a baseball school and for Bobby Moegle to win so many ballgames there. Not only was he a baseball man, he was a disciplinarian. He communicated with those kids and had them believing that they were going to win. He started off winning. He not only built a team, he built a program. He really knew the game of baseball and had those kids doing things that other coaches in this part of the country weren't doing.

COACH MOEGLE:

We didn't have a JV or feeder program in those early years. The JV kids played on Tuesday or Wednesday and then came back to the varsity. We never kept more than 35 kids. Other schools had 100 or more kids, but I was by myself in those days. I didn't have an assistant until '63, and he was a football coach. He just came down in case I got in trouble.

The American Legion was a good program for Lubbock. Some of the players were right out of high school, some from college. Others had quite a lot of experience. I would put our sophomores and juniors up against them to play for the experience.

(Monterey basketball coach) Gerald Myers coached my Legion team in the summer of '64 when I was starting the baseball school.

KELLER SMITH '63:

To think about how (the program) started and grew and then how it moved on through the years is an interesting study. I'm certainly not saying I have the only slant on that. But I think that it started with winning, and that's not to say it didn't end with winning, also. The tradition bore fruit in the manner of victories. All the work and all the attention and all the dedication came forth with victories. If you go back and think about it, the 1960 team won bi-district, the 1961 went to the state finals, the 1962 team won bi-district, the 1963 team went to the state tournament and the 1964 team won bi-district.

If you refer to those first five teams as the "foundation years," think about how the foundation was set in place and how it got transmitted so that it did become a dynasty. I think once the victories became frequent and became expected, the tradition followed reasonably closely thereafter.

By the time I was a senior on the 1963 team, we had gone to the state playoffs three times – twice in school and once in American Legion. The winning was expected and had become a habit. Losing was not acceptable. Winning was what occurred on the field, and that was what we got from all the work and preparation we put in.

The leadership in '61 was immensely responsible for passing on the right qualities and attitudes to us, and that bore victories. By our senior year, it was entrenched in us that the senior – and in some cases junior – leadership were responsible for transmitting that directly and indirectly to the younger guys. That was part of our job. We got it and we passed it along. So as Gary Huey put it, by the time we graduated, the transmission of this to the younger guys put in their being an obligation.

I think that is what became the root of the tradition and the dynasty. We understood and the guys after us understood that the victories were the result, but our responsibility was to make sure

Coach Moegle - US Army

we produced that. The guys who came after us must have had that feeling much like we had, because the tradition was really taking on momentum and velocity. I think we may have had it easier in that regard than the guys who came after us, because they really bore a burden. I mean they had a serious obligation to continue this and not be the ones that in baseball parlance "dropped the ball."

COACH MOEGLE:

I made a call to Oklahoma State in 1963 to inquire about an open coaching position. I told them I was interested, but they had an alumnus they liked in Chet Bryan so they hired him. And three different times I was called about the Texas Tech job, but I would have to take a $12,000 to $15,000 cut in pay. They just didn't pay their baseball coaches back in those days. I also looked at the West Texas State job before they were West Texas A&M, because a fraternity brother of mine was the athletic director. But their facilities were bad, the weather was bad and their recruiting budget wasn't good, so I turned it down.

I never could better myself. Nowadays they pay so much money that a guy would go from high school to college in a minute. There just wasn't as much interest in college baseball in those days.

I felt like I could have maybe coached the same way in college. I don't know if it would have worked out that way. I don't know if my temperament and the work habits of the kids and all that would've worked. I think it would have, but that might be the only regret I ever had.

In 1962, Coach Moegle received his Master of Education degree from The University of Texas. His thesis, titled "A Survey of the Minor League Baseball Player," profiled the demographics and career choices of minor league players. The data was collected during the summer of 1959 while he was playing in Winston-Salem, North Carolina. He mailed surveys to 254 players on 16 Class A, B, C and D minor league teams. His response rate was a solid 63%. Among his formal recommendations at the conclusion of the thesis were:

Minor league baseball players should be reminded that the likelihood of becoming a major league baseball player is slim and he should prepare himself for another profession as he continues to play. High school boys ... should endeavor to secure a college degree in preparation for some other occupation than professional baseball.

Since most high school players participated in high school baseball, qualified coaches are needed to train the young players.

Because each player sets an example for the young people in a community, he should always conduct and maintain himself with the highest of character.

The recommendations were prescient given how more than 100 of his players would eventually play college baseball, how far ahead of his time he was as a coach, and how he demanded the highest of character in his future players.

> **JUNE 28, 1972, COACH MOEGLE INTERVIEW WITH DAVID MURRAH OF THE SOUTHWEST COLLECTION AT TEXAS TECH UNIVERSITY:**

DM: What do you do that other coaches don't do to be so successful?

CM: I really don't know, because I don't know what other coaches do. I've never been in a high school with a coach. I've always been my own, because I started out here. I've played for a lot of managers and stuff like this in professional ball who couldn't get it out of kids. When I first came to Monterey, I said the one thing I was going to do was work with a lot of kids and give them the opportunity to be a winner by the hard work they put in.

I inherited a real fine bunch of kids back in 1960. They had no limit to the amount of work they'd put in. They weren't just real gifted – there were two .300 hitters in the group. They had such desire and ability to work that we won. In 1961, I had a carry-over of all these kids, because of the year before. The '61 team was a real fine ball club. We were big and able to win. I think these two years with the kids staying with me and working as hard as I worked them contributed to our success in 1972.

Coach Moegle

CHAPTER 2

The Test and Baseball School

The baseball school was good to me because I got to know all the players, and I got to watch them at a young age. I could focus on the kids who were going to be outstanding and develop a personal relationship with them so they would look forward to playing for us in high school.

— *Coach Moegle*

COACH MOEGLE:

They (young kids) didn't understand the game and they didn't know the intricate details because they hadn't been exposed to it. And I didn't learn this stuff until I was 22 to 25 years old, so I felt like I could be way ahead if I could incorporate this into my youngsters when I first got them.

During one summer, I sat down and took all the information I had accumulated in the three years I was in the Cardinals organization, which included things from Paul Waner, the great Hall of Fame hitter; Sal Maglie, the old Giants pitcher; and Harry "The Hat" Walker, another great hitter. I took all the things I learned and made a written baseball test.

I think it had 319 questions. There wasn't going to be a concrete answer to those questions. It may be true or false, but it could go either way and they had to interpret what I had taught them or I could use it as a teaching tool. I'd grade it and give it back to them to see where their thoughts differed from mine. From the time I started until I'd been here three years and set up the baseball school, we were all on the same page in terms of what we knew.

Every kid knew what the left fielder was doing, what the shortstop was doing, how the pitcher was trying to turn the fastball over and how he threw the curveball. We all got center-focused with what I was trying to teach through that test.

I wanted the kids to be well-rounded in every aspect of the game, because it's a team sport played by individuals. Each individual is playing a position and doing his thing, but when you get down to it, there are a lot of things that overlap. A kid has to know when to back up this guy, or how to help in another situation, and teamwork is actually a big part of baseball, although we do it as individuals. I wanted us to all think alike and have a spontaneous reaction because this was the way it should be played.

I wanted the 2nd baseman to know exactly everything the shortstop did, because they were companions. I wanted the catcher to know everything the pitcher did, because they were companions.

BURLE PETTIT, LUBBOCK SPORTSWRITER:

Red Murff was an old major league player and later a scout for the Colt 45s. I sat with him in the pressbox one day, and he told me that he'd never seen a high school team make so few mental mistakes. He said, "Watch how they line up the cutoff man." This was something as a sportswriter that I wasn't aware of, but Red just sat there and pointed out the technical things Monterey did that high school kids just didn't do in those days. They didn't throw to the wrong base and they knew what to do if the ball was hit to them.

JACK DALE, BROADCASTER:

That (test) shows you the genius of Bobby Moegle and why he became the winningest high school baseball coach in history. I don't know that anybody else did things like that, but he did and look at his numbers.

KELLER SMITH '63:

I think there's no question that the test was a tutoring device on the game of baseball, which meant that you had better know what was going on with the game rather than just your one, little position. So the dynamics of what the 1st baseman was doing while the centerfielder was doing something else was something that you would understand and would make you a better player. He was evidencing to a bunch of 16- to 18-year-old kids that probably at the outset only looked at baseball as "a game." It was far more than a game and it was very complex, and if you didn't believe that, take a look at some of the questions on the test. As an adjunct to that, it was again a message to you about how little you knew and how much he knew, and not to forget it.

COACH MOEGLE:

It was my job to come in and teach – and this was something I always took pride in – and to get somebody to play above his ability.

JOHN DUDLEY '62, ASSISTANT COACH 1968-'72:

His written baseball test was extremely long with a multitude of questions. Coach Moegle just defied any player to pass it. During the course of the year, we would take that test. And even when I was a coach with him, I had a hard time with it because it was extremely difficult. I know that there are people who have taken copies of that test with them and still to this day have copies of it. The test created an aura of importance – that it was important to do the little things well.

KELLER SMITH '63:

We wouldn't get demoted to the second team nor would he run us extra for not performing as we should have on the test. We might have been in the upstairs gym in the preseason practicing, and we would go next door and take it there in the dressing room. We got it back and could take it home and study it. I still have mine. It was a test of our mental agility.

MARK GRIFFIN '72:

The test dealt with baseball rules, as I recall. It dealt with situations and how we were supposed to react in response to certain situations. As best I can recall, we sat down in the dressing room on the bench in front of the lockers filling it out and hoping like heck we got the answers right, because we thought we would pay if we didn't.

GARY ASHBY '73:

The written baseball test dealt with different situations and what we should be thinking about.

COACH MOEGLE:

I set up the baseball school in 1964 here in town. We took those kids from 7 to 8 years old and started them through it. It was a lot of repetition and it was passed down through younger brothers, plus I had kids come through the program who went out to coach in youth programs and they were teaching it.

So the things I started with in '60 and '61 were beginning to be passed down. It was simple and we didn't have to browbeat them to be intelligent because they were all going through it at some time.

Coach Moegle - 1968

My idea with the baseball school was that I was going to take a kid at 8 years of age and put him through the same learning process that I did with my high school kids when I got here in 1959. The baseball school was good to me because I got to know all the players, and I got to watch them at a young age. I could focus on the kids who were going to be outstanding and develop a personal relationship with them so they would look forward to playing for us in high school.

By the time we hit the late '60s and early '70s, we were a powerhouse in the state of Texas, strictly because of what the baseball school had done over the previous 8 years.

GARY ASHBY '73:

Everybody has a baseball camp now, but I don't know if there was another camp back then. So he pretty well got to see everybody at his camp. You wanted to put your best foot forward because you were trying to make the squad from the word "go," because of the tradition.

JIMMY SHANKLE '74:

At baseball school, he would give us a printout of the proper way to hit – the feet, the stance, the hands – and the way to throw. You had to do it right. He had it broken down with all the basics of baseball according to Coach Moegle. He had developed it over years of playing and coaching and it was the right way to do things.

JEFF HARP '78:

He was ahead of his time. The good thing about his camp was that we were taught fundamentals, so when it was time for baseball to start we practiced those fundamentals. Now, the select leagues take their money and they play a thousand games. But they don't get taught the little things that turn into big things.

JIMMY SHANKLE '74:

When I was 10 years old, I was one of the better players Coach Moegle had in his baseball camp. So after the first week he asked if I could "work" at his camp for the next couple weeks. I didn't have any transportation back and forth to the house, so that first day of camp that I "worked" (and got to play for free), Coach Moegle picked me up in what was probably an old maroon 1959 Ford with no back seat. That was where he put all the equipment – the bases, the bats, the balls and the whole bit.

He would drag the field with that car, and he'd let me drive the car and drag the field in between camps. He brought me home every day, and I lived over by Atkins Junior High, which was a pretty good distance from Monterey. On the way home, if we saw anybody in my neighborhood I would sit up and wave and make sure everybody knew I was in the car with Bobby Moegle.

COACH MOEGLE:

Shankle would sit up front in my car and he thought he was big time. (smiling) Heck, I did it for about four years. I took care of him. Of course, he was going to be a great player and I knew it.

He probably knew more about me as a person than any of the guys in his time or earlier. He was such a little bitty kid ... He was like a little son at 8 years old. I'd drive him around town and take him here and there. I really liked his mother and dad. His dad was an ol' tough truck driver and his mother was a schoolteacher. Just a good family.

JEFF HARP '78:

I started going to Coach Moegle's baseball school at about 10 years old, and when I got to high school I started helping with it. And I did it when I was in college – I think I helped him for 6 or 7 years. It was a legacy deal – that someone had told me something, so I wanted to share that thing with someone else. Jimmy Shankle taught at my first baseball camp. I think Marlin Hamilton might have been there, too. Shankle was always there, and I got to play with him a little in the summer with the Lubbock Hubbers. Jimmy kind of helped raise me in the baseball world because he came on as a graduate assistant when I played at Tech. And we got better when he was there. It's a neat deal.

I walked in the locker room one day and heard the tap on Coach Moegle's office window. I looked in there and he waved me in the office. I immediately began thinking if I'd done something wrong – if my hair was cut, if I'd gotten in trouble in school, if my grades were OK. He asked me to help him at his baseball school. Of course I said yes, and I had no idea what that entailed. After helping with baseball school that summer, I thought I might want to coach because I'd seen that I could help players get better.

JIMMY SHANKLE '74:

Monterey baseball was good because we had arguably good players, but we had a system and a coach that was far superior to anybody else's. There was a session in those baseball schools in which Coach Moegle would ask questions about the things he had taught earlier. If you got a question right, later on in the day you got lemonade and a cookie. He wanted to know who was listening and paying attention vs. who was there because their parents needed their kid babysat.

He wanted the kids who wanted to learn to play the game right. It was pretty neat. At the end of camp every year, he would ask you a couple questions regardless of your age. "What did we do to have fun?" and then "What did you learn?" It didn't matter if you were 7 years old or 17, we had to tell him something we learned. If you wanted to tell him about your swing, you would demonstrate it and explain it to him, one on one, which was intimidating for some kids. We went home and studied the stuff he gave us because we didn't want to fall on our face when we were called on in the gym.

GARY ASHBY '73:

He had a pretty good idea of who was going to be on his team and who wasn't. I was one of the kids who wasn't going to be on his team, because one year at his baseball camp he was giving hitting instruction and specifically pointed out something that I needed to work on. I was a little too big for my britches and so I said in front of everybody, "Well, I'm leading Dixie Little League in hitting." He told somebody later on that I would never play for him. Thankfully, I made it through the cut my sophomore year but I was one of only two kids who didn't get in the team picture.

MARK GRIFFIN '72:

Now we know that he was using the baseball school as a recruiting tool. Kids would come to camp and he would get a look at the best 10- to 12-year olds in town.

JIMMY SHANKLE '74:

He knew what he was doing. He had the players and knew how to push them and which guys to put on the field, and that started way back when they were 10- to 13-years old. It was like a farm system, but it was a legal farm system and it was a great benefit to the players and to Monterey baseball.

COACH MOEGLE:

I had so many kids who came to my baseball school who didn't live in my district. They had this feeling ,"If I went to that school and could get over there and get in the program that maybe I could play professional baseball or play in college or just play at a high level and go to the state tournament." This was kind of contagious.

RON REEVES '78:

The baseball school wasn't intentionally recruiting, but if Coach Moegle was honest about it, he was probably looking for players.

COACH MOEGLE:

I had all those kids from the time they were 7 or 8 until they got to high school. We got to know each other really well during the summer. And I'd make sure that if I could tell he was a good player, I'd get to know his parents. Our relationship together was pretty good starting off, and I think a lot of those kids that played for me when we got successful had started with me at such a young age we didn't have a generation gap.

Later on, I might've coached their dads. We had a pretty good relationship with all those kids because I'd known them so long. Now if we had somebody who was completely new, it may have been culture shock for him to come into our situation. But I'd say 95% of the kids who played for me had been in my baseball school and had already reached a maturity level on the field. In the classroom and socially, some may have been a little out of kilter, but when they got out on the field, my older kids made sure there wasn't any stuff going on and it was a self-policed deal.

JACK DALE, BROADCASTER:

Coaches try to build their farm teams down below the high school level in the grade schools and junior highs and so forth. Bobby was a master at doing that. Maybe that was the first time in the city of Lubbock that a system like that was set up.

NATHAN SWINDLE '81:

He was well acquainted with the players through his baseball school before they ever got to Monterey. He knew who they were. Every once in a while, somebody would come along who he wasn't familiar with, like Scott Reid who had moved to Lubbock in the 9th grade. He quickly recognized Scott's athletic ability.

I looked forward every year to participating in baseball school. We'd get a deal in the mail that he would send out to all the previous participants. One of the things in that mailing each year was a note about the first five people from each age group that got the registration in to him would get a free t-shirt. He lived over there close to us so as soon as that thing arrived in the mail, I had it filled out and rode my bike over to his house and hand delivered it. So, it was an opportunity for him to get to know us as well as for us to learn baseball skills. One of the reasons I participated was so he would know who I was.

JIM BOB DARNELL '66:

I never did attend any of Coach Moegle's baseball schools, because I don't think they were up and running when I was young enough to attend. But my little brother, who graduated from Monterey in 1970, attended some of the earliest versions of the school when he was 12 or 13.

CLINT BRYANT '92:

I went to his baseball school starting at about 7 years old. We saw the myth and the legend and when we finally got to high school we saw him every day.

COACH MOEGLE:

They just went through the same thought process at 15 to16 that we were doing at age 8 at my baseball school. They answered questions and we went through the drills. We worked on their hand-eye coordination and we just started them off as 8-year-old players and brought them along. Consequently, the ones that didn't have great success drifted off and did something else. The ones that came on through became very good players.

JUNE 28, 1972, COACH MOEGLE INTERVIEW WITH DAVID MURRAH OF THE SOUTHWEST COLLECTION AT TEXAS TECH UNIVERSITY:

DM: Where do the sophomore boys come from and how well trained are they when they come to you?

CM: Over the past five years I've had a baseball school, and nearly every kid who comes to me at the high school level will have been to my school at some point or another, whether it's 8, 9, 10, 11, 12, 13, 14 years old. They have a pretty good background. I get an awful lot of kids at 9 or 10 years old who come out to my baseball school and we spend time on fundamentals, and I talk to them. They get acquainted with me and I get acquainted with them.

Out on this ball club I had this past year, Mark Griffin and Donnie Moore were the only two kids who hadn't been through my baseball school. All the rest of them had been there. Moore and Griffin had transferred to Monterey so I wasn't familiar with those two kids. Every other kid I've had had been to my school, and most started when they were 8. The camps are held after the high school season ends, in the first three weeks of June.

DM: How does the baseball school work? Are they day-long sessions?

CM: No, we're half a day. We start at 9 and work to 12. I take 11- and 12-year olds in one group, 8, 9, 10 in another group, and then all the older kids, 13, 14 and 15 in another group. We just cover fundamentals and do the things that I feel like are best for the kids at this young age and try to develop certain habits that are good for them. This year it ran 15 to 20 boys per age group. When we got back from Austin this year, enrollment picked up real good!

DM: Do other coaches help you at the school?

CM: I have another high school coach, and I always have one player who's played for me. The kids like to look up to this person, because he's been through my program starting at 8 probably. This year it was Jimmy Shankle, a real fine young catcher I had in high school. He was All-District as a sophomore and will be a pro prospect someday. The kids all look up to Jimmy because he's a good ballplayer. I also had Moore out there some. I try to bring in kids who have gone through our program. It's a real good teaching experience.

DM: Why did you start the schools? Was it as an idea to advance the boy?

CM: Well, there are two reasons. One was, when I first came here, the kids had so many faults they couldn't all be corrected when they got to high school. There were so many kids with bad habits that it was extremely difficult to correct. The second thing was I didn't have anything to do in the summer. It gave me a way to do something I like to do plus I was helping the kids. It was good for me and the kids both.

Gerald Myers has his basketball school out here, and this has been an asset to the young kids to be able to go through it. Anything you can put them in in the summer that furthers their knowledge and ability helps. I think getting to them at an early age has corrected a lot of their faults and, of course, all kids are gonna have faults. They're not going to be perfect ballplayers. Getting to them at an early age has certainly helped them.

CHAPTER 3

Preparation and Off-Season

He felt like a lot of what oher programs worked on were things that weren't going to happen very often in a year. He wanted us to be working on the stuff that would happen a lot – lots of swings, lots of ground balls.

— *Tuey Rankin*

COACH MOEGLE:

You've got to be prepared. Preparation solves a lot of "lucky problems."

JIMMY SHANKLE '74:

We were never unprepared. He prepared us from the start of off-season all the way through the end of the season. His workouts were structured for all the right reasons. Running, conditioning, everything we did had a purpose.

COACH MOEGLE:

The first thing I would do at practice was start the kids off by getting loose with throwing. I was a strong believer that the only way to build arm strength is by throwing. They would throw far enough until we couldn't play catch and the ball would fall in front of them. If one kid's arm was much greater than the person's he was playing with, they would switch partners so they could continue to stretch their arms out. I wasn't a calisthenics guy. We did baseball skills.

After we loosened up over about 20 minutes, we would take infield with the entire group. During our infield practice, I would strive for perfection with them. I brought in the context of using two balls at one time, which I picked up from a guy in Lafayette, Indiana. We incorporated that in our infield drill to really speed it up and put a lot of life in our program.

Then after that, we would start our batting practice. Our batting practice would take an awful lot of time. I might let a kid hit anywhere from 10 to 100 balls, depending on how efficient he got. I really didn't worry about how deep I got into the day, as long as I had developed a level of perfection out of this kid to a spot that I was happy with him.

And while he was hitting, if I wasn't throwing batting practice I would be up there with him, but I would hit fungo to our infielders and they would be throwing across to 1st base. And we would have somebody hitting fungo to the outfielders. And consequently, our workout was repetitious, over and over and over. Everybody would rotate and come through the stations. This is the reason it took so long.

I demanded so much perfection out of these guys as hitters. When I played, they'd say "bunt two, hit five and get out." That didn't work for me. I was the type of player who had to have a bunch of repetitions because I wasn't a great, gifted athlete. I assumed that was exactly what I was inheriting – a lot of good athletes, but not any great athletes. So we had to put in lots of repetitions. There were a lot of guys who had a great swing but didn't hit the ball all the time. They'd hit the top or the bottom or the inside or the outside of it. We were trying to center-focus the ball every time we went up there, and that was the purpose of batting practice. Not to hit the ball far but to hit the ball on a line and hit it with purpose. That was the idea of the hand-eye coordination with us. I tried everything I could think of to improve that with each kid.

BURLE PETTIT, LUBBOCK SPORTSWRITER:

Bobby had a technical knowledge of baseball beyond all of the coaches in the district, or maybe in high school baseball anywhere. But you don't win on technical knowledge, you win on making sure players know how to play, want to play, and put out the energy to play. It's all about improvement. I'd watch a kid who was a sophomore for him and see the rough spots, but by the time he was a senior the rough spots weren't there.

COACH MOEGLE:

Defensively, we knew we'd make errors but I hoped that they were kept to a minimum. The way I tried to control errors was to put players in pressure situations. Maybe I would tell him he had to get 20 ground balls without a mistake and push him up to 18th or 19th ground ball and see if he would make a mistake under pressure. Then I would push him up to 35 or 40 ground balls without a mistake. I always tried to put a kid in a situation where he was in competition with that error and when the error was going to come. Routine plays were expected to be made. We repeated those so many times in our fundamental work that I didn't expect an error to be made on those. We sure didn't want an error to be made strictly because a kid didn't have confidence in himself.

TUEY RANKIN, ASSISTANT COACH 1997-'99:

He felt like a lot of what other programs worked on were things that weren't going to happen very often in a year. He wanted us to be working on the stuff that would happen a lot – lots of swings, lots of ground balls. He'd laugh about guys working on catching fly balls at the fence, for example. He would say, "How many times does that happen in a year?"

GARY HUGHES '65:

A coach has to improve the individual to improve the team. But those people have to fit in to the team and play together and not quit when they get behind. We never took the field when we thought we were going to lose that game. No matter how bad things looked at the time did we think we were going to lose. We did lose some games but we never had the attitude that we were going to lose.

GARY ASHBY '73:

He had a great attention to detail. We would actually work at making callouses in the off-season, so when we started real practices we wouldn't rub blisters when we were going to be working awfully hard and taking a bunch of cuts. I've never heard of anybody "making callouses" in the off-season. So the attention to detail, like the written test, was one of the reasons he was the most successful high school coach ever.

JIMMY SHANKLE '74:

"Making callouses" was a Monterey baseball phrase. We couldn't use batting gloves in those days. It didn't matter how cold it was. We took a lot of cuts and we had to grip the bat right. You had to hold the bat in your fingers and show the "V." We developed callouses in the same spots in our hands, and with the multiple of swings we took, those callouses and blisters developed. The callouses hardened and we took care of them, and it was a little painful, but he didn't care. We had to develop them. And that's how he knew we were holding the bat right.

JOHN DUDLEY '62, ASSISTANT COACH 1968-'72:

Back when I played, we used wooden bats – we didn't use metal bats until the '70s – and we didn't wear batting gloves. When we took batting practice, we were going to hit a bunch. Our hands had to be tough. We'd better have some callouses because if we didn't, we were going to have blisters. It would stand to reason that guys were preparing themselves for the upcoming season by getting callouses. I can remember having blisters show up, and that wasn't an excuse to take time off and let those things heal. We had to play through that and hope that things would callous over pretty quick.

MARK GRIFFIN '72:

He didn't allow us to wear batting gloves. There was a big tire that he had on a pole. Every day part of our program for practice was if you were on deck to hit, you would take so many swings into that tire. That would cause you to develop callouses and toughen the skin on your hands, but more importantly it strengthened your grip. He was a master teacher. People say he had really good talent, and he did, but I don't know if I've ever been around a better pitching coach or a better situational hitting coach than Bobby Moegle.

GARY ASHBY '73:

There was one year we hit basketballs off a tee. If you didn't swing through the basketball, it would just reverberate. There was one year that we worked on just slinging the bat. If you weren't swinging right, you wouldn't sling the bat very far. He had a tire on a pole and we'd go hit that tire, and again we were just working on strength and swinging through the tire, trying to spin that tire on the pole. I don't know whatever happened to that tire. We worked on hand-eye coordination and once they invented the pitching machine, they really started hitting a lot. He would throw to us in the early '70s, but he used the machine more and more over the years when he got to where he couldn't throw batting practice as much as he did when we were there. We'd get a lot of cuts of one form or fashion. We were always hitting something.

COACH MOEGLE:

Well, this sounds like a bunch of old rot, I guess, but you've got to have good fundamentals, you've got to have a good attitude and you've got to have good discipline over kids. I spend a whole lot of time on fundamentals in December, January and February before we even get outside. We're going through fundamentals – fundamentals and things that we want to do. These kids go through it so much and it's so repetitive for them that when the situation does arrive for them, they don't know that it's a situation, it's just another thing coming up for them.

GARY ASHBY '73:

We worked on fundamentals and things that nobody else would work on. We had wooden paddles that we wore to develop soft hands when fielding ground balls. That was before anybody else had those things. The attention to detail in the way we swung the bat, and the test that he gave us – that's all about a focus on fundamentals and discipline. The running and the bleachers and the "3 to the road" and the pickups … believe me, we ran more than the track team. And we worked harder than any team.

JIMMY SHANKLE '74:

He was well known because he coached fundamentally sound baseball. His best asset was that he was a better coach than everyone in West Texas. When we go to the Houston and Dallas teams it got closer, but he was a better coach than everyone else around here. I don't know if people realize this, but he was a great pitching coach. You look at his teams that won. Those teams had really good pitching with Gardner, Moore, Horn, Sorrells and Darnell.

He was so skilled. Every day before we played, all our guys would throw a little bullpen session in which they threw a few breaking balls and popped a few fastballs. He wanted to work them down just a little bit, so when the game time came the next day, they weren't full throttle and wild. My goodness it was successful. I caught those bullpens and listened to him talk to those guys about what they were doing. He was a masterful pitching coach. He was great with hitters, but we had great hitters from 1972 to '74. We excelled because of the great pitching.

GARY ASHBY '73:

It was every other year that he had a pitcher come along. Jack Darnell ... A couple years later Donnie Moore ... A couple years later Larry Horn ... A couple years later Scott Gardner. And that's about the way you need it – every other year. And then he developed some others beyond that. But believe me, he realized to win ballgames, you had to have pitching. He had good arms that he developed into great pitchers. But he had some mediocre guys that he developed into good pitchers. You can't win it all with one pitcher, although in '72 we probably came as close to doing that with Donnie Moore as any team. (laughing)

He always developed the second-line guys that weren't studs that could win those other games. You don't go 33-3 with just one pitcher. You develop the 2nd, the 3rd and the 4th guy. He was a great pitching coach and he knew that was where it started. He took the time to "hands on" develop those pitchers. But he was also the guy to "hands on" develop the hitters, too. We didn't have a large staff – it was just him and Coach (John) Dudley. I think you'd be hard-pressed to be a great coach if you didn't have a feel for pitching, and he had a gift for it.

RON REEVES '78:

He was one to take such a personal interest in different players at different times. I mean, he expected the same thing out of everybody in terms of work ethic. But if somebody was in a slump or something and he read an article about that, he would try to fix it.

He had players every year that he'd pull into the office. He would tell us about articles he wanted us to read. He did that with me all the time. I was never a consistent hitter and was always chasing stuff and being overaggressive. He tried and tried and tried to fix me, but I just wasn't that good of a hitter. He tried me in a George Brett stance for a while and all sorts of stuff.

TRAVIS WALDEN '81, ASSISTANT COACH 1989-'94:

The things I took from Coach Moegle ... I took the mechanical parts of the game, the strategies of the game, the motivating of players and handling of the parents. I was with the Rangers and Phillies organizations and then at A&M, and Coach Moegle's philosophy of how we hit in the early '80s was still what they were trying to teach to.

Mechanics like fielding a ground ball were things he always taught and let me know as a coach later on that I was prepared to teach fundamentals. When I coached with him, he would get a magazine and read and study up on it, or he would watch a pro game on TV. There wasn't a stone ever unturned that he didn't follow up to figure out why guys were doing it.

At one time, the slider became a prevalent pitch so he wanted to learn more about it. He had some of his guys who were pitching in college come in to teach him about the slider. He wasn't afraid to ask, and that's a pretty big thing to say about a guy who was one of the top coaches to ever put on a pair of shoes. He wasn't afraid to ask questions and to ask for help. But he would form his own opinion about how it was supposed to be done, and that was the way it was going be done once he had it right in his mind.

JIMMY SHANKLE '74:

I think Coach Moegle got that pitching coach ability from his time as a young player when he pitched a lot. Later as a pro player he was a great hitter and an outfielder. So he had both those aspects in his background. He learned pitching because he didn't just rely on what he already knew. He was always giving us articles from these magazines about pitching, hitting and baserunning.

HUNTER LANKFORD '87:

From the outside, it's hard to understand and from the inside it's hard to explain. Coach Moegle was constantly cutting out articles, printing out position instructions, reviewing strategy, technique, competition, psychology. What outsiders did not see were the little details he worked on in the background. Throughout my junior and senior years as starting catcher, I would often make my way up the stairs before practice and spend 10 to 15 minutes reviewing upcoming games, discussing who was pitching well in practice, who was hitting well, and what I thought about certain ideas or approaches he was thinking about for an upcoming game or series. He was always looking for an edge, looking for an angle, looking for weaknesses we could take advantage of against big opponents. New techniques in fielding or hitting ... Always advancing.

RON REEVES '78:

I only pitched one game on the JV in my sophomore year, and it was the only game that we lost. I really wasn't thinking I was going to be a pitcher, but from the very start he tried hard to make me one. He taught me a curveball and a slider. I loved the attention from him because I respected him a lot.

FRED OLIVER, MHS COACH 2000-'09:

He wasn't going to have a mediocre team. To reach his expectations, his teams had a great work ethic, and this was not a place for the weak at heart. His PE class was. And he directed many kids to the PE room.

KELLER SMITH '63:

Coach Moegle, being ahead of his time, had us training with weights in advance of the season. I put on almost 15 pounds between the end of football season my senior year and baseball.

JIM BOB DARNELL '66:

The thing I remember most about my sophomore year was that indoor workout stuff he sent us through. There was a room above the women's locker room, I guess. It seems like it was the size of a handball court. I don't think I ever saw much sweat in my life other than when we went up there. I felt like a lot of that was done as a way to weed out people. And it probably did. Of all the physical things I ever did in high school, that was the one thing I never will forget. It was hard.

KELLER SMITH '63:

If the weather wouldn't allow us to work outside, it didn't matter. He had a set of drills for indoor baseball, including hitting with tennis balls.

GARY ASHBY '73:

It didn't matter what the weather was, he would find a gym. We had a room upstairs and I don't know what it was supposed to be, but it wasn't supposed to be a workout room. He made it into one. We would get a lot of cuts in. We would hit wiffle balls off a machine or we would hit paper wads or rubber balls or whatever – we were hitting something.

JIMMY SHANKLE '74:

We played in all kinds of conditions. We didn't get to play in nice weather all the time. He didn't give us the excuse of weather.

MARK GRIFFIN '72:

I can recall playing in heat, rain and wind. Once again, I think it got back to toughness and mental conditioning. He was going to make sure we were prepared for any and all situations, whether it was a game situation or the weather that surrounded us. There was not going to be any excuse, nor was he going to be caught off guard.

JEFF HARP '78:

I preach to my teams now, and this came to me directly from Coach Moegle. You've got to be mentally tough to be a baseball player. People who don't understand the game DO NOT get that. If a guy strikes out with the bases loaded then goes out to his position in the field and doesn't get a ball hit to him all day hasn't helped the team and it's got to eat at him. If a guy hasn't made the error to cost his team a game, or given up the game-winning hit, or failed to get the big hit with the game on the line, he probably hasn't played the game for very long because it's going to happen to everybody.

GARY ASHBY '73:

The weather didn't have to be very nice for us to go outside. I can remember lots of times that we were still in the shadows of the buildings and we were practicing.

FRED OLIVER, MHS COACH 2000–'09:

I think the cohesiveness and the chemistry Coach Moegle developed was a result of his work ethic. Each player took ownership and pride in the program and what they did in it. He might only be the pinch-runner or the DH or a pinch-hitter, but the role was understood and he became a part of that program forever. The players worked hard and took ownership and it was harder to quit in a game. They were going to fight. The games were easy – the practices were hard, and it made chemistry for them.

BURLE PETTIT, LUBBOCK SPORTSWRITER:

Bobby's teams were well conditioned because that's what they had to be in order to play his style of baseball. Those guys ran more than track teams. You couldn't play for him if you weren't in top-notch condition. There's a strong belief among psychologists as well as coaches that physical discipline and mental discipline dovetail.

KELLER SMITH '63:

When we walked on the field against anybody, we were in better shape than the other guys. If we were better than them anyway, we would trounce them. If they were as good or better than us, many times we would win because we were in better condition than them.

GARY HUGHES '65:

He knew that to be in top form, and to be able to last in doubleheaders, conditioning was vital. So, he tossed pickups to me on the concrete floor. A pick-up is a conditioning drill in which we faced each other and he rolled a ball to the right and I ran and picked it up and flipped it back to him, then he flipped it to the left and I ran and picked it up and flipped it back to him. He had me do pickups until I was totally exhausted, just to prove to me that (Monterey basketball) Coach (Gerald) Myers had not gotten me in shape and that HE was going to get me in "baseball shape." We've laughed about that several times since then as he's told me his purpose. It seems funny now but it didn't at the time.

KELLER SMITH '63:

Most people thought we were the track team and not the baseball team, based on the amount of running we did.

JOHN DUDLEY '62, ASSISTANT COACH 1968-'72:

From the very beginning, Coach Moegle set a standard for physical conditioning.

KELLER SMITH '63:

If we weren't in shape – we were playing three ballgames a week and were practicing all the time – we wouldn't make it and we'd lose strength over the course of the year. Coach Moegle knew that, so our conditioning was for that purpose. It wasn't punishment, although certainly that was part of it. It was to stay in shape so we could stay in the long season, and of course, it worked.

JEFF HORN '96:

He prepared us for the season by putting us through rough workouts. At no one point was it so difficult that we couldn't handle it. It was an endurance test. If we could go through the practice and drills and the long scrimmages on Saturdays, it was a piece of cake to play a hard 7 innings against a good opponent.

KELLER SMITH '63:

The most common running was a 4-4-4 or a 6-6-6 on a bad day. That was on every Wednesday, unless our behavior or performance dictated more frequency. He would line us up in about three groups of four or five. We would run four 20s, four 50s and four 100s. The first group would run, and the next group would run right behind them, and the next. He would turn around and go back and whistle and that was the trigger to run. So we got a little bit of rest while he was getting from the finish line to the starting line, and then we'd run again. And that was on Wednesdays after practice and it was the last thing we did. We hated it and we dreaded it the whole time during practice. We used to joke to get through that.

COACH MOEGLE:

I would have my kids run quarter-mile sprints and competitive races to see who the toughest leader was and to see how the kids responded to the other kids. These were the guys who became leaders for me, and they did most of the policing and disciplining and controlling of the young kids. After it was passed down from the seniors to the sophomores and juniors, the next year I'd look for the new kid to come on the block and see what it meant to him. I think of Mike Crutcher ... probably of all the kids I coached, nobody was going to beat him. He wasn't the greatest talent in the world, but there was nobody that would beat him at anything he did. So, he became the team leader and he later coached for me for seven years. He was the type guy that I could turn something over to him and he would get it done. This is what I looked for in one or two individuals. I could go back 40 years and almost tell you each year who the main guy was and who everybody looked up to and who ran the thing from the player perspective.

TUEY RANKIN, ASSISTANT COACH 1997-'99:

I tell my own kids that the older ones should show the younger ones the right way to do things. It's the same in coaching – the older guys showed the younger guys the way. A lot of things never change.

MIKE CRUTCHER '68, ASSISTANT COACH 1973–'78, 1982–'85:

This is one of my proudest moments as a human being. We got beat in a three-game playoff to go to the state tournament in my junior year. I was the only junior starter. On the bus home from the game, he called me to the front of the bus and said, "Sit down right here. This is your deal now. What are you going to do with it?"

NATHAN SWINDLE '81:

In the fall we were out there on our own. He would write some things on the wall that he wanted us to work on. I clearly remember that list. It stayed up there the whole time I was there. One of the things on the list we were supposed to do was be able to run a six-minute mile by the end of the fall. We were truly on our own in the fall during football. We didn't have any supervision at all. The seniors and the kids who had been through it in prior years knew what we were supposed to be doing. The day I arrived, if anybody told me to do something because that was the way Coach Moegle wanted to do it, by golly I was going to do it that way.

COACH MOEGLE:

One of the criticisms I took as a coach had to do with how hard I was on kids. My overall objective was to take a kid who had good or average skill and develop him to a new level at which he could compete. Everything we did involved some sort of competition.

JEFF HORN '96:

He thought his baseball players got better by competing. He wanted his guys competing in football or basketball or competing in pixie sticks. If you were playing against somebody and you had the opportunity to win, he wanted you to do it.

COACH MOEGLE:

We would run against one another. We would take two balls and put them down on the ground out at a distance with the idea that three kids would run to get two balls, and the kid who didn't get a ball had to run again. We would run complete quarters – a lap around the track – me against you, to see who wanted to win the most. Then to teach teamwork, we would pick a relay team of four and would run against other teams of four.

We would learn to compete that way. We competed at every game we could play in the off-season. I played a lot of basketball with the kids, and the losers would do something extra and the winners would go in. We played handball and I'd play against them. The coaches would play against them and we would razz them and give them every opportunity to fight back. It was a learning experience for them to go through it. I always wanted our baseball games to be easy because they had competed so hard against each other. When they went against an opponent it wasn't that hard. I really felt that over the 40 years we did this, it was the strongest thing I ever did.

In our off-season work we were so competitive against one another that we never gave in. I remember that kids who couldn't run a lick would challenge that kid who could really run. He'd say, "I'll run you in the dirt – you're not going to beat me," just because of his attitude. It was something we built into those kids as competitors that I really cherished. I loved the competition part. I made a speech to the coaches association that the one thing I would hate to give up the most was the competitive preparation we did after practice or during the off-season.

NATHAN SWINDLE '81:

The other thing Coach Moegle did involved the parking lot to the east of the practice field behind the school. Instead of running the bleachers, on some days he would throw three baseballs out on the ground down by the parking lot and four guys would race for the balls. The guys who brought back a ball came in and the others had to run again. And there were no rules, so the last two guys going for that final baseball would produce some wrestling matches.

JIMMY WEBSTER '85:

I still use Coach Moegle's idea of daily competition. First, kids like it. Second, it makes it easy as a coach to see what you're dealing with – good or bad. I just think the more they compete, the more it moves things along. It expedites everything because the practices go better, the tryouts go quicker and better, the evaluations go quicker and better, and maybe I'm not a good enough coach so that helps me see what I'm dealing with.

I have never tried to be like him as a coach, because that's a quick route to failure, number one. But when you learn things that are successful, you want to emulate them. To me that's what good coaches do. We all steal from each other. I'll meet with anybody and listen for two hours and maybe only keep 30 minutes of it. There's a lot of things he did that are right. He saw the big picture of it and we try to use some of it because it's good and it's right.

NATHAN SWINDLE '81:

I seem to remember us running bleachers on Tuesdays and Thursdays. The bleachers were hard, but the killer deal was running the competition quarter mile after. He would put us in groups of four and the last place guy in the race would have to run again. I thought it was an ingenious way to design it, because we were always in it right up to the end. If he had just let the first-place guy go in, the rabbit in the group would take off and run away and everybody else might quit. We would give it some effort to avoid finishing last and running again. Nobody wanted to run again.

TUEY RANKIN, ASSISTANT COACH 1997–'99:

We still ran the competition quarters in the late '90s. I think that was done at Monterey from the '60s through the '90s.

JEFF HORN '96:

We had a unique group in that of our 10 guys who started, eight were seniors and six or seven of them had just finished a long football season. So in my senior year, I would say that our conditioning was less than years past, but knowing Coach Moegle he probably knew that we were going to make a long run and he wanted to keep us fresh. But our sophomore and junior years I remember running bleachers and competition quarters. He wanted to find out who had the strongest will.

BOB FANNIN '78:

I remember the bleacher running being right after football in the fall. He was trying to run off the "chicken-fry eaters." (smiling) He was talking about the "hangers on." Reality would hit when we would run those bleachers. This went on for several weeks in a row. I would come home from running bleachers and all I wanted was to drink some water. I wouldn't even want to eat for a while. Then I'd lay down on the couch and go to sleep. I would be so beat. I remember hearing my mom tell my dad, "I'm afraid he's going to kill one of them boys." (laughing)

JIMMY SHANKLE '74:

Every Saturday before the season started, we would scrimmage at Lowrey Field and we would start at 8 in the morning and went until it was dark. You brought a sack lunch if you wanted anything to eat. It turned in to a fun time for us because guys would swap sandwiches, or one guy's mom was good with dessert and he'd bring that. But don't get me wrong – it was hard. We would play 20 innings or whatever we had in terms of pitching. But that was his passion and it became a passion for several of us.

BOB FANNIN '78:

"Sack lunch Saturdays" ... We always went to Lowrey on Saturdays in February. People don't realize that we really packed our lunches. There was no lunch break. We would bring our lunch in the ballpark and we'd look up and Coach Crutcher would be over there eating our dang lunch. It was survival of the fittest. But we just played all day and never thought anything of it. It was fun, man.

JEFF HARP '78:

In my first Saturday practice, nobody told me to hide my lunch. So I had it sitting out there while we were scrimmaging. The next thing I know I looked over there and Mark Morgan and Tim Leslie were eating my lunch. I can still remember Morgan taking slow, exaggerated bites and saying, "Man, your mom makes great sandwiches." Of course, I was starving when I got home that night. I told my dad about those guys eating my lunch and he just laughed. The next week mom made two sack lunches. I sat their lunch out and kept mine hidden. (laughing) They came over and got their lunch before practice and I still had something to eat later on.

NATHAN SWINDLE '81:

We had all-day practices on Saturdays in February. We would bring our lunch and practice and scrimmage all day. We did ours out at Lowrey, which was nice because it was a change of scene and a change of pace from the practice field at school. We felt like we were getting closer to the season when we were out there.

JEFF HORN '96:

We would scrimmage for countless hours, and we would play different positions and learn what each position did. If we didn't know what to do on the field, we weren't going to play. That was very evident.

TUEY RANKIN, ASSISTANT COACH 1997-'99:

We would work some bunt coverages and cutoffs and relays on one of those long days out at Lowrey Field, and we wouldn't come back to that stuff until we got to the playoffs.

MIKE CRUTCHER '68, ASSISTANT COACH 1973-'78, 1982-'85:

On those long Saturdays in February, we would work on situations like bunts and the 1st and 3rd double steal, and then scrimmage all day. We wouldn't spend too much time on the situations, and then again maybe before the playoffs we'd go through it again. There was just an expectation that you'd better get it right. If we didn't get it right, we'd get verbally abused and might not play. That's just the way it was.

Chapter 4

Philosophy and Gameday

When I was coaching the JV, I was going to keep 14 kids one year. He told me, "We don't carry 14, we carry 13." If there were two who were close, he said I'd better make a good decision. He said we didn't have that many uniforms, and we didn't want to have to deal with that many parents. He said, "That's 26 parents."

— *Travis Walden '81*

> **JUNE 28, 1972, COACH MOEGLE INTERVIEW WITH DAVID MURRAH OF THE SOUTHWEST COLLECTION AT TEXAS TECH UNIVERSITY:**

DM: Tell me about the local Little League program. Is that an advantage to high school ball?

CM: The Little League program has a lot of advantages. It starts kids off in an organized, systemized type program. The Little League has a big disadvantage in that they put so much emphasis on winning, on the competitive part. You know, it would be just as well for those little ol' kids to go out there and play and have a lot of fun rather than have all the pressures.

I have had a lot of kids at the baseball school who have never had the experience of winning and never had any confidence in themselves. By working with them on this side, it has helped them with their ability. I think Little League puts too much emphasis on winning, but I don't know. The American way of life puts emphasis on winning, that's the way we work. Maybe this is the reason the kids start out this young. I think that the pressure on a 12-year-old to win in a Little League program is a little too much.

DM: Do you think athletes are born or are they trained?

CM: I think definitely kids are born athletes. I think they have a natural ability that has to be uncovered. A kid may have certain abilities except hand-eye coordination. He might be able to see the ball but not the ability to do anything with it. If he can't coordinate the hand and the eyes together, he'd probably never be a good athlete. He'd never be able to have any success. Overall the thing is they are born with it; you just have to progress it along the best you can. I don't think you can take a kid out there who has no ability whatsoever and make a player out of him.

DM: What are some of the things that will remain consistent in the '60s and '70s and into the '80s?

CM: Fundamentals are the first thing. And the routine that you go through, the overall effort you put into your work and all this type stuff remains the same. Nothing changes in baseball. In football and other things, it's a lot different. In baseball, the hand-eye coordination skill is still there and that's what you work for.

DM: How do you put together the quality of teams capable of going to state, given the caliber of boys you get to choose from, and what is the number that try out?

CM: We probably have a few more out than most schools in Lubbock do. On the sophomore level, we have between 40 and 60 kids try out. I try to keep 12 or 13 of the best ones. On the varsity level I have about 23 or 24 kids working and probably 17 will make the squad. As far as looking for people, you only have so many kids coming in that can play. And you try to take them and develop them to a peak of just real fine texture and making him as good as he can possibly be with his talent. I don't look for anything in particular, except in my pitchers. I like to have a kid who can throw real hard. I can teach him the curve ball. If I get these two things going together for him, then we don't have much problem there. But I don't know how to put them together. I just take the kids who are available and give them something to work toward. They seem to always respond for me.

DM: So you have to make some cuts especially in the sophomore group?

CM: Oh, yeah. Out of the 40 to 60 kids who try out on the sophomore basis, I keep 13 or 14. When they're seniors, you hope to have about 5 of them playing – starting. Most of the other kids will cut themselves or get involved in other things. You have some problems, but you get them all worked out, with about 5 seniors playing. This year, I had 4 seniors with 3 playing. Next year, we'll have a little bit more. We've got 6 juniors out on the squad.

DM: Did you purposely arrive at this formula of 4 or 5 or 6 seniors, or if you have 9 good seniors, would you play them all?

CM: Well, I've been at this for 13 years and I've never had 9 good seniors. I don't know about any formula, but over a period of time, it seems like the most seniors I've ever had that stayed in the program was 5. Sometimes you have less, but next year I'll have 6 who played regular this year.

I'm going to speak to a Little League group Friday night and that's going to be one thing I'm going to tell them. I've talked to about 140 12-year-old kids to make them realize that when they are 17 or 18 years old, only about 4 or 5 of them will still be playing. It's a very discouraging thing for a kid, but that's the way it works out.

DM: What's the principal reason for the drastic drop in players – going from 40 or 50 sophomores down to 5 seniors?

CM: It's lack of ability with other kids coming in. This is what we're confronted with. You have 12 kids that have pretty good ability on the sophomore level, and then when they get to be juniors, a few of them fall out because their ability remains the same. The other good kids progress a little bit, but then you have a new group of sophomores coming in. Of that group you have 5 or 6 who have good ability again. This just naturally pushes the ones on the bottom of the ladder off and you keep your 4 or 5 good ones. It's process of elimination really.

DM: Did you have a philosophy about playing out of state?

CM: We never played out of state, but we were invited to play in Florida and in California. When we won the state championship in 1972 when I had Donnie Moore, we got a lot of national recognition for being a great program. Then we came back and won in 1974. So, I had a lot places like Miami that picked up on us and wanted us to come out there and play those top-notch schools in Florida and California.

They'd house you, feed you, put you up, travel you and everything. I always told Eck Curtis and Pete Ragus that I only had to go 120 miles to get all the competition I wanted. So I'd go down to Midland, play Midland Lee, Abilene, Abilene Cooper and they were as good as anyone you could play in the country. We didn't have to push as hard to play that schedule because we were familiar with it. So I never went out, although I was invited several times to go.

All the competition I needed was just south of here. Odessa and Permian back then, Lee and Midland High, Abilene Cooper could all play. We didn't even go to Dallas or Round Rock or San Antonio to play like they do now. I didn't want to. I was too much a family man. I wanted to be home. I hated the 3-hour ball games. They'd drive me crazy. I wanted to get that thing over in 2 hours and go home."

COACH MOEGLE:

To keep them focused for long periods of time wasn't as hard as you might think because I never had a big squad. I never had a lot of kids. Probably the largest group of kids I ever kept was around 35. Now they try to brag about having 125 kids in the program. I wouldn't have ever learned their names because all I was interested in was the top kids that could play. My objective was to find the five or six best seniors I could. Then I wanted 5 or 6 best seniors sitting and waiting, and the rest were sophomores. And each one of them learned what their role was. He was going to go through the fun part of competing and learning and following the leadership of those seniors. By keeping a small number, we passed it on to one another and it was a feeling of being elite to be part of it. But I would tell them just because they were one of the 13 or so sophomores, they might not be here when they were seniors. It began when I started here, and it was accepted until I left. And they knew they had to earn the uniform every year.

TRAVIS WALDEN '81, ASSISTANT COACH 1989-'94:

When I was coaching the JV, I was going to keep 14 kids one year. He told me, "We don't carry 14, we carry 13." If there were two who were close, he said I'd better make a good decision. He said we didn't have that many uniforms and we didn't want to have to deal with that many parents. He said, "That's 26 parents – 13 sets of parents." He didn't keep many. We didn't have more than 30 to 35 kids in the entire program.

COACH MOEGLE:

If a kid is in the program and he either isn't 100% on my side or he's very selfish, he draws away from the tail-end kids who will follow him. I thought that the lowest guy on the club was just as important as the top guy. And if the top guy couldn't perform at the level he was supposed to, then the other guy would get a chance and usually come through.

TRAVIS WALDEN '81, ASSISTANT COACH 1989-'94:

For the people who didn't fit in his mold, that didn't bother him. There were plenty who wanted to, and he'd rather have the people who were passionate about it. Our state championship team in 1981 only had 13 guys, and we really only had 11 players because he brought up a couple guys to run bases. He used to tell us, "It only takes 9, so if you don't want to be in it, hit the highway."

JIMMY SHANKLE '74:

Coach Moegle's hitting philosophy ... He broke it down and started with the feet shoulder width apart, flexing the knees, and then on up to the shoulders and the hands. He taught a slight downswing – he hated uppercutters – because that meant the ball would carry to the outfield in the West Texas wind. He would make an average ballplayer swing down a little more.

In '74, we had Rocky Alburtis who could hit a ball farther than any human I've ever seen. My goodness it was unbelievable. Rocky was 6'4" and weighed about 200. I was 6'1" and weighed 180. Larry Horn was 6'2" and weighed about 225. Rocky hit 3rd, I hit 4th and Larry hit 5th and we hit 30 home runs in '74. He would let us do a lot more than he let a Richard Holt, who played 2nd base. He wanted him to hit line drives and hard ground balls.

But because we were a little bigger and stronger, he adapted his style to us and turned us loose to hit a lot of home runs and doubles and score a lot of runs. Together with the pitching we got from Larry Horn and Scott Gardner in '74, we were totally different than '72. In that year we only hit a few home runs, so we hit more ground balls and line drives and Dwayne Clanton and Tommy McIntyre who could really run didn't hit the ball in the air.

Mark Griffin had a great swing – he didn't have big power but he was a doubles guy. The bread and butter swing at Monterey was to rotate the hips, which was something everyone didn't teach at that time, and to swing down. He hated guys who couldn't hit the ball out of the ballpark but still hit fly balls.

We had a team concept offensively – swing down and hit hard ground balls. If a kid was a little more talented and could get the ball in the outfield and hit the ball out of the park, he was fine with that. But we still had to stay within the team concept. He didn't put everybody in a box and say "You're 6'1" and 185 and while you might hit 12 home runs, you're going to hit line drives and hard ground balls."

He told me "If you hit it on the ground, you're doing them a favor. Hit the ball in the gaps and hit the ball out of the ballpark." He didn't tell that to the other guys because that wasn't their game. So he tailor-made his program to his talent. In years when he didn't have as much talent, they played small ball and bunted and hit-and-ran. We didn't do that because we didn't have to.

JEFF HORN '96:

He would never make the moment seem bigger or smaller than it was. He was an even keel guy. I say that ... he was very intense, don't get me wrong. We were trying to win a state championship on February 4th just as we were on June 6th. We were always pushing toward that. So when it came down to that game, I think everybody was pulling in the same direction. I would not say that he said or did anything specific. That was his strong suit – he had prepared us already, and he didn't really have to say anything once we got there.

COACH MOEGLE:

I had a funny philosophy about preparation for games. I did all my game preparation during the off-season. It got us prepared to play all the way through May. I never formulated a game plan for a specific game. My plan was always the same. We were going to pitch the same way. We were going to approach game situations in a way that put things in a high percentage in our favor.

I never wanted to get into a situation where we were going to be very specific and then the situation never materialize. I liked to get into a situation where we saw what the problem was, and we adjusted to it as we went through it. As a game progressed and it was going to be a tight one, then we knew we had to go to the bunting game or the small ball game. If a game was going to be a slugfest, then we had to get up there, slug and start running and gambling and taking exceptional chances.

So, our preparation in the off-season was that we were going to play the game a certain way, then the game situation dictated how we would approach it. I gave the kids an off-season game plan – they didn't know I gave it to them. But I went through an off-season game plan for everything we would face in the season. And I did that for years.

TUEY RANKIN, ASSISTANT COACH 1997-'99:

He would never talk to the kids after a game – it was always the day after. Now he might tell the kids they wouldn't need their gloves the next day if they'd played bad and he was going to run them, but that was about it. I asked him about it one day, and he said, "They tune you out. They'll listen to you the next day. After the games, they are ready to get out of there." Stuff like that made him a good coach.

JIMMY SHANKLE '74:

When we had bad weather, we didn't go home. We had a skull session. He'd get on the board and write out how we were going to play our defense, or how we were going to work on our baserunning. And we'd go over the signs and we'd take tests over all the aspects of the game. Every year we took those tests.

His coaching philosophy was so far above others, because we had to know the system, and the system worked and let great players like Donnie Moore, Larry Horn, Scott Gardner, Rocky Alburtis and me have that freedom to hit and play. But we still had to play within that system. We went over the situations of the game time and time again. We were in better shape and we knew the game better and the games were the fun time. We would go to perform and show our wares and play as a team and beat people because we were Monterey High School and that meant something to us.

COACH MOEGLE:

I very seldom ever called a pitch in all the years I coached, because I taught my catchers so hard and my pitchers so hard to be on the same wavelength. When the catcher put a "2" down for a curveball, the pitcher knew that was the appropriate pitch, unless he wanted to change it. We were so much on the same page. The only rule I ever gave my catchers as far as conferring with me about a pitch was for them to go with their gut reaction in a tough spot. They might look over at me in a tough situation and I might just shake my head and say, "I don't have any better idea than you do. I've taught you. Use your gut and go after it." It was a team thing, winning and losing together.

JIMMY SHANKLE '74:

We had some unbelievable talent in Donnie Moore, Larry Horn, Jack Darnell and Scott Gardner, who was a sophomore when I was a senior. They were tremendous pitchers, and he treated them a little different than the guy who threw 75 miles an hour and had to throw a curve ball every time. He gave them a little more leeway and a little more tailored instruction. He didn't show favoritism, but he would fine-tune that better pitcher and make those other guys better because they wanted to excel, too.

COACH MOEGLE:

I expected my pitchers to go out and be dominant. Whether he threw 78 miles per hour or 88, he still took his ability to the mound and dominated. It worked. A lot of times I didn't have a great kid, but he thought he was great. I've even had kids and parents tell me that it was an honor to be in the program and that they looked forward to the opportunity to start and be a contributor. That's the way I wanted them all to feel.

JEFF HORN '96:

He knew when it was time to pull a pitcher and when it was time to leave him out there and teach him a lesson. He just had an incredible feel for that aspect of the game.

TUEY RANKIN, ASSISTANT COACH 1997-'99:

Sometimes it's not what you know, but what you can get your players to understand. He never changed his signals. I asked him about that once. He said, "I'm more concerned with our players knowing our signals." He wanted to make sure our guys knew the signals and knew how to execute. I think things like that are what made him successful.

KELLER SMITH '63:

At the beginning of each inning, we sprinted to our position. And at the end of the inning, we sprinted from our position back to the dugout. And that was a rule that was never violated, and by the way it was never mentioned. It was just part of it. If he was sitting here today, he would say that when we pulled up in the bus in the parking lot before the game was to start, our position was to be ahead four runs at that time. And if you think about that, it fits extremely well.

By my senior year, everybody knew about our program. And when we came on the scene, we had the best uniforms, the best equipment, the best coach, the best transportation, we had the best preparation, we had the best record and the best tradition, and when we got off the bus the score was 4-0 in our favor. If we got off the bus thinking we were ahead 4-0, we believed we were better than the other guys.

As a result, we didn't care about them. We were there to take care of business and take them down and go to Furr's Cafeteria and have a big meal. If we had a great game and we were doing well, sometimes we would get to Furr's and have the "all you can eat" routine, and believe me, we could do some serious damage there (smiling).

TRAVIS WALDEN '81, ASSISTANT COACH 1989-'94:

I know one thing that bothered everyone who ever watched a Monterey team play was how they would line up out by the home plate circle to watch the opposing pitcher warm up. Everybody always thought they were trying to intimidate them, and that used to fire people up.

In '94, which was a year we went to Austin, we were playing at Permian. Our guys were lined up watching the pitcher warm up and the next thing you know that pitcher fired one over the top of our guys' heads. It almost hit Coach Moegle. That would've been the worst thing that ever happened if he hit Coach Moegle before the game ever started. (smiling) Coach Moegle picked the ball up, handed it to (Permian) Coach Highley and said, "You need to control your pitcher."

I think our guys standing up there watching the other pitcher warm up was an intimidation deal, but in Coach's mind he just wanted the hitters to see the pitcher's stuff. But to everybody else who saw it, they thought the Plainsmen were trying to intimidate people. I can remember in the '70s they looked like a football team. They were so big, and Coach Moegle would have them decked out in the best uniforms and the best gear. They'd get off the bus and everybody thought they were down 2 or 3 runs, just based on the way Monterey would go about their business.

COACH MOEGLE:

Wearing a uniform and wearing it right was very important to me. It was instilled in me as a professional player in spring training. I ran my program just like professional baseball and this was the way we dressed. We played a lot of teams that would come out when it was really hot with no shirts on. Now there was one thing I did that was different than anybody else out here, and it was when it was hot I would let the kids wear shorts in practice. It was easier to get more out of the kids in the heat if they wore shorts.

I would say I never went on the field without being fully dressed and I don't think my players ever went on the field without being fully dressed. And I know one thing – we never had a kid on the field with his hat on backwards like they do now. That just galls me to no end. (chuckles) But that's just me being old-timey.

KELLER SMITH '63:

Every position player on the team was ready for every pitch. We were in a baseball position at all times, as we were taught to be. We also were in the game mentally. There were a number of techniques that we used in that regard, but I'll give an example of one. Our shortstop gave signals to all the outfielders as to what the pitch was going to be. It gave the outfielders a little better jump on the ball because we knew the pitch that was going to be thrown. There was no daydreaming in the outfield.

JEFF HORN '96:

He was the best in-game coach. He would use the whole bench in playoff games with all the pinch-running and pinch-hitting. With the high school re-entry rule, he was really smart and knew how to take advantage of that.

TRAVIS WALDEN '81, ASSISTANT COACH 1989-'94:

In terms of game strategy, he knew how to run a game. I've been around coaches who were great teachers of the game, but when it came game time they wouldn't make the right decision. When I coached for him, I'd be over at 1st base and he'd send a runner home and I would think, "What is he doing?!" And the runner would be safe. Or he would put on some kind of play and I didn't think it would work and we'd score two or three runs. We'd get to the dugout and I'd look at him and he'd just shake his head. I think he wasn't afraid to take chances and challenge the opponents, and he wasn't afraid to put pressure on them.

COACH MOEGLE:

We approached every game the same way, in that we were going to go out and set the tempo and be aggressive. We may get thrown out a couple times trying to steal a base early, but we were going to set the tempo ourselves. I was not going to let our opponent dictate the tempo of the game. We'd have a team meeting before we played people and I'd go over what to expect. But once we got in the ballgame, we could kind of adjust to anything we ran into.

TRAVIS WALDEN '81, ASSISTANT COACH 1989-'94:

We were getting ready to go to Austin in 1981 and face a guy named Compton from Nacogdoches. Coach Moegle had called a friend and gotten a scouting report on him so he set up the pitching machine to throw the most wicked breaking pitch I'd ever seen. I don't think anybody even fouled it off in practice. (smiling)

So coach told us we couldn't win and that we'd never beat Compton. He had us so psyched up that when we got down there and Compton threw his first breaking ball, we didn't think it was the devastating breaking ball we had practiced against. We got some runs off him and stole a bunch of bases and won 11-4. In practice, he taught us how to steal bases and the keys to look for with pitchers. He gave us all the reads and the more a baserunner learns about reads and develops the technique and timing, the better they get.

He wasn't afraid to put on the steal, either. He was one those riverboat gamblers and he would run and run. And if he ever found a weakness, he would grind it. Going in, we didn't know the catcher was that bad. Scott Reid probably stole a base early in the game, and after that he just poured it on them.

COACH MOEGLE:

To be a good baseball player, you've got to be well rounded. You've got to be able to run, hit, throw, field and play with intelligence. That's the way I taught it. The first thing I always said that a player had to be able to do was run. You didn't have to be fast, but you had to understand how to run. This is the only thing that is consistent in the game of baseball is your ability to run. If a kid can run a 4.2 to 1st base, then he was going to run that from now on, most likely.

I made a speech at a convention one time that we had stolen 100 bases in every year that I had coached. It wasn't because I was a good runner, but because I had studied the art of base stealing and reading pitchers' moves, pitch counts and things that contribute to running the bases. Knowing how to take the extra base, when to take the extra base, why to take the extra base and put the pressure on the defense.

Using their ability to run was the most consistent part of the game. We spent a lot of time learning how to run bases. I don't care if it was a big fat kid, if the situation demanded that he run, we were going to run. In 1981, we were playing Nacogdoches in the state tournament and they had a big kid on the mound that they said couldn't be beat because he had a great slider. We stole nine bases on him and set a Texas state tournament record, strictly because we knew how to run. People were amazed that we could do it. We didn't do anything special – we just spent a lot of time on it. It was the most consistent part of the game and the easiest part of the game to conquer.

In the 1971 state semifinal victory over Corpus Christi Carroll the Plainsmen stole six bases, which was one short of the state tournament record at the time.

JIMMY WEBSTER '85:

I think his aggressiveness in the really big games showed a lot of trust and a lot of courage to force people's hands. Think about it, when we were in practice in intrasquads, we got free stolen bases. To encourage us to steal, we got to steal and if we got thrown out we went back and did it again. That's what he did to encourage people to want to steal bases. And now as a coach, I think about it slowing the whole day down because a kid goes, he gets thrown out, he goes back to 1st base, everybody stands around and waits, the pitcher throws over three times, and then he goes again. It takes forever, but it's genius because the pitcher, the catcher and the baserunner all got work.

CHAPTER 5

Hearts and Minds

When I first came to Monterey, I said the one thing I was going to do was work with a lot of kids and give them the opportunity to be a winner by the hard work that they put in.

— Coach Moegle

COACH MOEGLE:

For me to coach kids, I needed to have them think they were going to play at their very best. They didn't know how good they were, but they were just going to play to the best of their ability. I had high expectations for every kid who ever played for me. I look back on my career and I think about the dedication and the hard work that started in the early '60s and how that was passed on, having kids go to college on scholarship and going into professional baseball. The expectations were passed down to the kids later on.

JOHN DUDLEY '62, ASSISTANT COACH 1968–'72:

I think the reason the majority of Coach Moegle's players performed at such a high level, goes back to the fact that he set the bar extremely high. One of the things I've learned over the years is that if you set the standard at a certain place, the majority of the people who will play for you will try to reach that standard. If you set the bar low, that's as high as they're going to go.

He set the bar extremely high for us as players. In doing so, he brought out the best in us because deep down inside, we all want to be successful. We learned that to be successful we had to reach so high. Sometimes there were a few who were unwilling, and those people would fall to the wayside and what was left over were those who truly wanted to be there and to achieve, and that's the nucleus of the team.

BRAD WALKER '85:

As I reflect on the impact of my time in Monterey baseball, there are a couple of things that stand out. The first is that we really did have something special – he built an amazing and special experience for each one of his teams. That is the only time in my life I'll be in so deep with a group of guys.

On a personal level, he was exactly what I needed. The coaching cliches that I had heard all my life but was not actually seeing at home had caused a great deal of confusion and frustration. Being part of the Monterey baseball program, the cliches were on steroids. We didn't just work hard or give "110 percent." We ate, drank and slept baseball and we worked out until we threw up. There was no program that put in more effort to winning baseball games and returning to the state tournament, and nobody was more confident when we took the field.

COACH MOEGLE:

I didn't put up with any foolishness – I didn't treat 'em bad, but I didn't treat 'em good, because we're out there trying to win. We're not in recreational sports; we're trying to win to the best of our ability. I put it all together with fundamentals, good discipline, a lot of hard work and it seemed to come out good for us.

JOHN DUDLEY '62, ASSISTANT COACH 1968-'72:

Coach Moegle is a great coach. When he was coaching football, he approached it the same way he did baseball. You were going to perform at a high level and you were going to win. When he was coaching offense, he was demanding and it was going to be done in a specific way. When he went to defense, it was the same way. He approached everything from the standpoint of doing it the best he could and by expecting his players to do the same.

FRED OLIVER, MHS COACH 2000-'09:

He coached in four decades – 40 years at Monterey, which is unbelievable. His coaching style and demeanor set the tone for his players and his team. He demanded consistency and respect and to play the game the right way. It's a simple game when it comes down to it. But yet it was a no-nonsense style for Coach Moegle, and the kids understood that and knew what to expect.

JIMMY SHANKLE '74:

You know that saying "One man with a passion is worth 100 with an interest." That comes to light when you think of Coach Moegle as a baseball coach and an educator of young men. Passion means you go the extra mile ... Whatever it takes ... All those sayings. He had a passion and he made sure we had a passion. The workouts were hard and they were long. They were meaningful and they had a purpose.

He had a schedule and he stuck by it. If we didn't do things right, we had to run 3 to the road and back. If we didn't do something right, we stayed extra. Coach Moegle not only had a passion for baseball, he had a passion for molding and shaping young men in his way. He wasn't an easy guy. He wasn't going to pat you on the back and tell you, "Boy, you're really doing a great job and I appreciate you." When he didn't run you, you knew he appreciated you. When he didn't get after you, you knew you were doing right. That was his way of showing it.

JOHN DUDLEY '62, ASSISTANT COACH 1968-'72:

Coach Moegle did not pass out praise casually. You had to do something special to earn that praise. But it's also indicative of the fact that his expectations for players were so high that he wasn't just going to brag on you for doing something mediocre. You had to reach that high level that he wanted. But I think that praise was there when it was needed.

It also motivated you as a player. I wanted him to have reason to say something nice about me. I wanted him to praise me. A lot of times he would get on us so hard in practice that we would think he'd never say something good about us again. Then, when he finally did say something nice – he was very, very good about picking the right time to do it, which made it all that more special and made us work harder.

BURLE PETTIT, LUBBOCK SPORTSWRITER:

He was intimidating, but intimidation wasn't Bobby's purpose. His purpose was convincing and selling his kids that they had to put out their best effort. There was a consequence to not doing things to the very best of their abilities. There was a consequence for not reaching that level. I believe the kids were fearfully respectful.

GARY ASHBY '73:

It was just the way things were. He was the boss. I used to think I hated him when I was there. But I don't think I hated him – I think I feared him. That was the reason I ran through the wall. I guess everybody had their own reason, but we were all willing to do it for him. Be it for fear or respect or just from the tradition that the years before had set, his players always ran through the wall for him. The kids who wouldn't just weren't around. They didn't survive.

MARK GRIFFIN '72:

He might be very hard on kids, but all he wanted out of them was what he knew they could do. Sometimes his expectation was higher than what that player thought he could do. He saw them differently than they saw themselves. I didn't have the "pleasure" of being with him for three years. I was just with him for the spring semester. He treated me very well. He was accommodating, and he was very patient with me. But I hear stories from the guys who were with him for three years and it was rough.

KELLER SMITH '63:

Adulation and praise were not part of the reward system. The issues of not performing and not doing our job ... that's where the action was. If there was any commentary or interplay between the players and Coach Moegle it had an emphasis on the negative as opposed to the positive. Don't take that wrong, because one might say, "then all you ever heard was what you did wrong."

That's not the case. There was a lot of interplay from Coach Moegle, but it was teaching and instruction about how to do it. Then if we didn't perform, we got the negative side of it. But praise was few and far between. Of course, those who played for him and worked for him were expected to do the same. We understood and appreciated that and we performed. We didn't require a bunch of praise.

GARY ASHBY '73:

I don't remember a great deal of praise. (smiling) I'm sure I'm forgetting all that praise he gave me. Maybe I just remember the times I screwed up and was told about it. I don't remember a lot of praise. Maybe it'll come to me. (smiling)

BURLE PETTIT, LUBBOCK SPORTSWRITER:

I know they kept striving to please Bobby. I believe they didn't feel like they deserved praise for something they'd been trained to do.

JEFF HORN '96:

The greatest motivation was in pleasing him. Just beating a team wasn't good enough for him if we didn't play up to our potential. He was always trying to instill a killer instinct in his teams, not just do enough to get by but to bury the competition, if at all possible.

TRAVIS WALDEN '81, ASSISTANT COACH 1989-'94:

He had a lot of different things and some of it was like fatherly instincts. He knew what to do with each kid, and that was the thing I took from Coach Moegle more than probably anything. He would finish the day off and let us know why he got on to us. But he also let us know if we didn't fix it he'd be right back on us tomorrow, because we knew what was wrong and we'd better fix it because he'd given us the information on how to do it.

JIMMY WEBSTER '85:

One day I was catching in the outfield at school, some flat ground pitching work. I was catching with my back about 20 yards from the field house wall. I remember he walked behind me and said, "You are the worst catcher I've ever had." I thought he was going to stand back there and watch some pitches, but I turned around a couple pitches later and he was gone. That was it. It was just a parting shot.

LARRY HAYS, LCU & TTU COACH '71-2008:

From where I was, getting to see and hear what he'd say, I really appreciated somebody who really, really cared about the kids but hid it. Mark Morgan said, "He told me I was the worst player he'd ever had." And then one of Mark's teammates who had played for Coach Moegle said, "He told me the same thing!" He just knew what buttons to push. But he had enough to him that he really didn't care, and that helped him. I'm saying two different things, but he's so complex. I can say he's a caring guy, and at the same time he didn't care. How do you tie that together? Well, he was smart.

GARY HUGHES '65:

We knew how he felt because of his body language. When he was coaching 3rd base and we would look bad on a pitch, he would turn his back on us. It was a pretty clear message that we weren't looking good and it was enough to fire us up for the next pitch. And woe is you if we did it again.

JEFF HORN '96:

I didn't care who we were playing. Nobody will tell you they wanted to lose. Of course they didn't want to lose to Midland Lee or Permian or Coronado ... Of course they didn't want to lose. They didn't want to make a mistake and have Coach Moegle get on them. He knew that by creating that mentality, he was creating a team that would be good enough to compete.

I can remember looking at some "strike threes" that I thought were bad calls, but he didn't see it that way. He saw a kid who didn't swing the bat. I would say that watching strike three was at the top of the no-nos for Coach Moegle. I can remember him putting his hands in his back pockets or just shooing at us from the 3rd base coaches box and telling us we were terrible. He would tell us, "I can't even put you in the lineup. All you're going to do is strike out."

MIKE CRUTCHER '68, ASSISTANT COACH 1973-'78, 1982-'85:

When I got there as a player in the mid-'60s, everything in that program was tough. He tried to make it as tough as he could on everybody. NOBODY went in that coaches' office like they did later on. I mean NEVER.

And what's strange now is that here at Wylie East we have tremendous facilities with beautiful indoor workout areas, a huge weight room, everything – beautiful stuff. Our coaching office is a big, open room with the JV football coaches on one side and the varsity football coaches on the other side. Sometimes the kids walk through and they'll stop and talk to the coaches. Boy, I don't go for that. The other coaches ask me why I don't like it. If you ask those kids, I think a lot of them want to talk to me.

It's like me and Coach Moegle when I was playing. I wanted to talk to him, and he wanted us to want to talk to him. It was kind of a game, and I still do that with kids now. I want my kids to take a bullet for me, and they'll do that if you give them just enough sugar. They get a little and they want more and more of it.

JIMMY WEBSTER '85:

When he would slap us on the back on the way up the stairs with a little compliment or something, it was like water in the desert. It would give us another day and a little hope that he believed in us. So everybody didn't go down the drain that day together. The next day somebody had a little bounce in their step and was still moving. It was very interesting, his ways of keeping things moving forward with just a quick body language or something.

TRAVIS WALDEN '81, ASSISTANT COACH 1989-'94:

Guys just thought he was hard-nosed all the time, but they forget the times when we'd be walking up the stairs after practice and he would pat them on the back and say, "You had a good day." There were days when we were mad as heck at him, but by the time we walked out the door headed home at night we were disappointed that we'd let him down or let the team down. He had a way of having a human touch.

From the outside looking in you'd hear people say, "That's the meanest man around. I'd never want my son to play for him." But once you've been inside the walls with him and you're playing and figuring out what's going on, 10 years later you're raising your kids and you start feeling those same kinds of instincts he tried to teach us. That's what it's all about. As tough as he was – there was a heart in there. He knew what he was doing. I think the difference in coaches is that some want to be so hard-nosed, but they forget about the human side. Those days walking up the stairs meant so much if we got that sign of approval.

JIM BOB DARNELL '66:

Coach Moegle never told us that we were good players. I still remember the last game I played against Pampa. My senior year I got hit on the elbow by a pitcher from Tascosa. I hit right-handed (and threw left-handed) so it wasn't a good thing. I had quit football thinking it would end my baseball career, but it was baseball that ended my baseball career. He took me out of that final game against Pampa near the end of the game. One of the guys who was sitting on the bench came over to me and said, "You won't believe what Coach Moegle just said about you." He was going on and on about what a great player I had been.

JEFF HARP '78:

My senior year we were playing over at Coronado at their old field behind the school. Derek Hatfield was on the mound. It was game two of the doubleheader. They had a runner on 2nd base with 2 outs. Derek uncorked a pitch and it was nowhere close. I stood up and turned and somehow got a lucky bounce off the backstop. I caught it barehanded and turned and threw the guy out at 3rd. I ran to the dugout and Coach Moegle said, "That's one of the best plays I've ever seen."

I thought, "Is he talking to me?" But I remember feeling like the best catcher on the planet. I was thinking that Johnny Bench better move over because I was coming. (laughing)

BRAD WALKER '85:

It should be noted that one of the things that made Bobby Moegle a great coach was his ability to treat a player like me differently. Yes, he was gruff, insensitive, brutally honest, etc., and that was the culture of the program. But within that, there were compliments that built you up and made you feel invincible.

I pitched an early-season game against Midland Lee and I was on fire. I had a 2-hit shutout through 6 innings. I found out later that Coach Moegle told the dugout, "You sophomores watch ol' Brad here, he's showing you how to pitch." The compliment didn't last long – I ran out of gas in the 7th and lost a 3-0 lead for a 4-3 loss. He left me in to take it. The next day at practice he told me he felt sorry for me. Coach Crutcher told me I had learned "not to try and be a hero." It was classic Coach Moegle.

JIM BOB DARNELL '66:

For whatever reason in my sophomore year, Coach Moegle decided to start me at 1st base against Borger, which was the first game of district in 1964. They had a pitcher named Joe Robinson. He was a lot better pitcher than Bob Arnold at El Paso, and I thought Arnold was really good. In that game, we were tied with them 1-1 in the 7th inning with the bases loaded and 1 out.

I was hitting 8th in the lineup and Coach Moegle called me down to him and said, "You are going to squeeze bunt. Which pitch do you want?" I don't know why but I said, "2nd pitch." I guess I thought the pitcher was going to stick it in my ear on the first pitch. Anyway, I got the bunt down and we won the game and I thought I was the best player in the history of the game.

JIMMY WEBSTER '85:

We went to Amarillo to play Caprock my senior year. We got off the bus and it was pretty much "show and go," (meaning we didn't take batting practice or have a long warmup). My granddad lived in Amarillo and he was there when we got off the bus. He stopped me and we talked for a second. When I got to the dugout, Coach Moegle asked me if that was my granddad. I told him it was, and he asked if he lived in Amarillo. I told him he did and Coach Moegle nodded.

In the game, Mike Eckles pitched a great game and we beat them. I probably went 0 for 3 and didn't do anything special. About five days later, I got a letter from my granddad and with it was the game article from the Amarillo newspaper. They had interviewed Coach Moegle about the game and in the article he talked about how great I did, knowing that it would get back to me. He had said something about what a great target I'd given Eckles all game, because I hadn't done anything exceptional. (laughing) But he knew exactly what he was doing. That's a guy who understands people.

DUSTY BUCK '99:

One of the more special moments happened to me my senior year. I battled arm injuries all year and things didn't go like I had always dreamed they would, both in terms of personal performance and as a team. We were still in the playoff hunt and we were playing Coronado late in the year. I came in with the bases loaded and 2 outs in the 7th. I struck out the hitter and Coach Moegle met me at the foul line and simply said, "Good job young man."

I can't explain how much those four words meant to me. Coming from him – a man that I looked up to tremendously and loved – it was such a special moment. He was proud of me and I knew it. It was a sincere and raw moment to cap off all the years I had poured my soul into the program. Twenty years later, it still sticks with me.

CLINT BRYANT '92:

In my senior year, I had study hall after lunch. I would go to his office and it was usually me, him and Coach Walden. One day we were in there in his office and the phone rang. He answered it and I could hear his side of the conversation. "Oh yeah, I know that Bryant kid ... uh-huh ... uh-huh ... Why don't you call back when he's hitting his weight. I appreciate the call." Then he hung up.

I asked him, "Who was that?" He said, "It was Ole Miss. They were asking about you." I never heard from Ole Miss again. (laughing) So sometimes I hated that honesty part.

JEFF HARP '78:

One day before a game in infield we were doing "one and cover." I threw one into center field. He stopped and told me, "I've got five college coaches calling me because I've told them you can play and you're making throws like that." After that I put every throw on the bag.

TRAVIS WALDEN '81, ASSISTANT COACH 1989-'94:

One thing people forget is that on the field he would be tough and would get after us and boy, we didn't want to be in his doghouse on any particular day. When that practice was over and we walked upstairs to the locker room, there wasn't a day that went by if he had gotten on a guy that he wouldn't tell him why. He'd come up to us and tell us he had higher expectations about this or that.

There are certain coaches who can get on players and have them respond while others get on players and they turn away. Coach Moegle could get on a player, and he would have them eating out of his hand because he would get those guys thinking that he believed in them.

JEFF HARP '78:

I had a broken wrist my sophomore year, so Coach Moegle had me catch in for him as he hit fungo. He was mad at the team for a bad practice so he ran us, and I was part of the running, cast and all. I hadn't done much in six weeks so I thought I was going to die. I was bent over and sucking air and he walked by and patted me on the butt and said, "Winners don't have their heads down." I stood up and continued sucking for air, but I knew he'd noticed me.

TRAVIS WALDEN '81, ASSISTANT COACH 1989-'94:

Every day he watched everybody hit and he would evaluate everybody, good or bad. If we had a bad day, we'd be walking up the stairs to the locker room and he'd let us know that we'd better have a good day tomorrow. There wasn't any sugar coating. When we walked off the field, if he hadn't said anything negative, we knew we had a good day. If he did say something negative to us, we had to respect the fact that he was watching.

As players, we used to laugh and ask, "How does he know?" He would be over there working with the infield on the other side of the field when we'd be pitching on the practice mound. He wouldn't say anything at the time but later he would say, "You didn't throw very good today." He saw everything and we always wondered how. We couldn't get away with anything.

MARK GRIFFIN '72:

I've seen military men who didn't have the way with "the troops" that Coach Moegle did with his players. I think his time in the military had to have played a role, because we're all influenced by our surroundings and by our environments and by our experiences, and he was no different.

I think he did bring a lot of that military aspect to it, but it wasn't just for the sake of doing it. It served a purpose, and that was the diligence and work ethic and mental toughness that was going to be required. And he took that personally. A defeat was like him having to wave that white flag of surrender and his "troops" began to understand that very quickly. (laughing)

COACH MOEGLE:

The story about running back to the hotel from the ballpark in Amarillo in the mid-'60s is a true story. Sometimes it's taken in different directions and I don't tell it exactly the way the kids tell it. Back in those days we played just north of Dick Bivins Stadium in a makeshift ballpark just to the west of the professional stadium. We were playing Amarillo High and we were not a great club because our best pitcher that year, Jim Bob Darnell, had come down with a sore arm and we didn't have much depth.

We lost a close game to Amarillo High and we really played poorly. It was just not indicative of how we had played in my years as a coach. It was a complete relapse of where I thought we should have been. Rather than get on the bus ... (chuckling) we didn't get on the bus. We picked up the gear and ran back to the hotel.

MIKE CRUTCHER '68, ASSISTANT COACH 1973-'78, 1982-'85:

My sophomore year was Coach Moegle's first team to not win district and make it to the playoffs. We were playing Amarillo High up in Amarillo at a field that used to be next to the old Gold Sox Stadium, just north of Dick Bivins. It had an old tin fence and they played JV football there in the fall and in the spring threw a baseball field out there.

We got beat and that cost us the district championship. I was the only sophomore on the team and had to carry that big bag of wooden bats everywhere. We were getting on the bus after the game and Coach Moegle said, "Oh no, you're not going to get on the bus. We're going to run back to Lubbock." I thought to myself, "It's 125 miles to Lubbock," but I also thought he might be mean enough to do it. I had those bats and we lined up and ran down the street back to the hotel.

JIM BOB DARNELL '66:

It really bothered me that we didn't win district when I was a senior. We lost to Lubbock High twice that year. The first time we played them I had gotten a blister on my finger pitching against Amarillo High. Never ever had I gotten a blister after the season started. I couldn't pitch for about two weeks. The second game I think we lost 2-0 or 3-0. Lubbock High had some really good players.

MIKE CRUTCHER '68, ASSISTANT COACH 1973-'78, 1982-'85:

My senior year, we won district and so did Lamesa. We weren't in the same district with them because they were in a smaller classification. But we both had a week off, so we scheduled a game with them at Lamesa. We were the big school and thought we were pretty good, and they had a good left-hander who WORE US OUT.

I was the cleanup hitter and I don't remember the exact situation, but it was something like bases loaded in the last inning and they were up by a run. I was batting and I hit one a mile, but it was foul. Coach Moegle was on me yelling, "That's all you can do is hit a foul ball!" On the next pitch I struck out. It was hot and we had those old wool flannel uniforms and our bus driver was ol' Stogie Austin. Coach Moegle wouldn't let us put the windows down or run any air or anything. It was a sweat box back to Lubbock.

JIMMY SHANKLE '74:

Pressure ... After the game and the next day if we didn't do well ... THAT would be pressure.

TRAVIS WALDEN '81, ASSISTANT COACH 1989-'94:

As far as motivating players, I think the best motivator he had was the work ethic. There wasn't anybody who ever walked on the field that we thought had outworked us. When we stepped on the field, we were ready to go. And if we weren't ready to go, we'd know it the next day at practice.

GARY ASHBY '73:

We lost a scrimmage – not a real game. We're out there in the outfield afterward and we couldn't even see him because it was so dark. All we could hear was him whistle. We'd take off running. He'd run to the other end and we'd hear him whistle and we'd run back to the other end. So we learned at an early age that losing wouldn't be tolerated. He ran us to death. We didn't lose a JV game – we'd lost a scrimmage. But we were taught that we wouldn't lose.

CLINT BRYANT '92:

We got beat by Amarillo at Lowrey Field one time. We "didn't show up" and were losing bad. Coach Moegle was coaching 3rd base and just stopped looking at us when we were hitting. He would face left field. After the game, he told us to go to the foul pole and he ran us. He said we wouldn't leave until our parents and girlfriends left the stands, so we were out there running and yelling at them to leave. It's funny now, but we actually turned it around because we went on an 8- or 9-game winning streak and went to the region semifinals.

TRAVIS WALDEN '81, ASSISTANT COACH 1989-'94:

When I was coaching (with Moegle), we played Amarillo High here and got beat 10-0 in 5 innings. After the game, he told the boys to go shake hands and that he'd see them on the foul line. He told them to get a partner and to get 45 pickups and if they didn't want to run, to hit the highway. There were two of them that walked, and one of them was probably the best pitcher on the team. But it may have been the best thing to happen to that team because they were waiting for him to step up and take charge, but he didn't.

From that point on, we went on a winning streak with better effort and attitude. I remember them running out there and their intensity was getting better. We played the next day in Amarillo and Coach Jones, who had played for Coach Moegle, told us he thought he woke a sleeping giant because we were a different team. I told him we'd lost our best pitcher and he said it didn't matter because of the way they had changed.

Coach Moegle didn't turn his back on a problem – he addressed it and got after it. One man walking away was another man's opportunity. There was always somebody waiting and he had good enough players. When a coach wins 20 games a year for so many years, he had built a program. It's not like if one guy walked away that piece of the puzzle was gone. He had somebody to fit into that piece of the puzzle and he could keep it going. The program wasn't built around one guy.

COACH MOEGLE:

The story is told about me losing to Amarillo one time and we didn't play well and that I took the kids and did pickups and ran foul lines after the game. It was really just a "come to Jesus meeting" that we were having out there. I did have two of my better kids quit – a center fielder and a pitcher. That was a choice they made. They didn't want to be part of what we were doing. I gave them an option of running with us and absorbing the loss or checking it in right there. Those two kids checked it in, but it didn't bother us because we had two kids respond and get to a higher level.

I had a philosophy that if we played somebody and they were of less talent than us – and we didn't play at our maximum – we didn't bring our glove to practice the next day. They had taken a day off the day they were supposed to play, and they would give me that day back. It was just something I always did. I never accepted mediocrity on the part of a kid. If he would perform at a high level, then I expected us to win or be very good. I tried to instill this through competition or really hard work in the off-season. Once we got started with games, it was built in the kids. And after I got the program built, it was just passed down; it wasn't as hard as when I first started.

JIMMY SHANKLE '74:

He made you a better person because you had to follow the rules. Don't get me wrong. It was hard. A lot of guys didn't like it and a lot of guys didn't like him when they were 16- to 18-years old.

JOHN DUDLEY '62, ASSISTANT COACH 1968-'72:

I think that with Coach Moegle in dealing with players, with parents, with umpires and everybody involved – his focus in the beginning was that the team will find a way to be successful. Whatever decisions he had to make were based on what would be best for that team. I know there were some tough decisions. When I coached with him, there were some personnel decisions he had to make where he had a friendship with a particular parent, yet the decision he made regarding the player and his family was directed toward the betterment of the team and not the individual.

COACH MOEGLE:

We had several rules and there were several times that I would give a kid a choice. I was going to punish them if they violated team rules. If it was severe, I would just run them off. I wouldn't put up with it. But I would give the kids a choice to either go through my punishment, or they could get out. I hate to say this, but I had several of them just say they weren't going to do the punishment because they weren't guilty, but I knew they were.

That was fine with me, because I would find somebody else to take their place. That often bothered me because I had known some of those guys since they were little bitty. In fact, I had known some of their parents extremely well. It was a tough decision for them to have to leave our program or for me to have to run them off. I never let anyone know it bothered me. I just took it as part of the process.

Sure, there were times that kids didn't perform like I wanted them to, and I would really be hurt by it, but I would not let them know. We were just going to have a running session, and I was going to run them until I was satisfied that they were committed to the team and it wouldnt happen again.

JEFF HARP '78:

People think he was a slave driver. He was hard, but most of us would do anything for him. That's the kind of relationship I try to create with my players because if the trust is there, they'll do anything for me.

JIMMY WEBSTER '85:

The paradox of him was that people on the outside thought he was just a guy who yelled at us all the time and if we didn't do what he said, he would run us. When I look at the newspaper articles from our senior year ... we lost up in Plainview for our second loss in district play but had already clinched district and were headed to the playoffs. He said we'd had an emotional letdown but he wasn't bothered by that. He was mostly bothered by the defensive letdown, but said we'd be fine.

As I look back on it, that was pretty intelligent. He knew that was our last game and we'd won 8 or 10 in a row and had won district. He didn't say much to us that night. We just ate dinner at Furr's, got on the bus and headed home. Then we were in the state tournament a few weeks later.

GARY HUGHES '65:

A lot of the players said he wasn't as tough on the players his daughters' age as he was with us. I think the reason for that was in the days I was playing, he was single and we would stay out at practice until the sun went down. It wasn't unusual to stay on the practice field from 3 until 7. I think in the later years they might've lucked out because he wanted to get home and see Carolyn and his girls. They may have lucked out, although I can't imagine he was too much softer because he had success throughout his coaching career. The rumor was that he was getting softer, but I didn't buy that!

GARY ASHBY '73:

Those guys in the '60s – they had it rougher than any of us in the '70s – but believe me, we had it rougher than anyone in the '80s. And probably the guys in the '80s had it rougher than anyone in the '90s. Coach Moegle mellowed a little over the years. In the '60s, he wasn't married and he didn't have anything else to do. I don't think there were any UIL rules, so they'd be out there until dark.

We were fortunate that he was married, but it was still extremely grueling with long hours and all of that. And then he had the daughters and I think when they got a little older he thought, "Maybe I should treat these kids a little better than I've treated them over the last 20 or 30 years." But I don't guess he ever killed a one of us. (smiling)

BOB FANNIN '78:

I think what we saw in '76, '77, and '78 was a little bit of a softer side, because his girls were getting a little older and he was seeing things through their eyes as a parent.

MIKE CRUTCHER '68, ASSISTANT COACH 1973-'78, 1982-'85:

Coach Moegle will tell you this, I think. As he got older, he started to mellow. We would talk about it and I would ask him, "What makes you mellow?" And it was the girls. They were in high school or in junior high and you want the boys to appreciate the fact that you've got daughters. I would wear him out about this.

If I saw Coach Moegle today I would kiss him. I love the guy. I think he really liked me and respected me, so when I would say, "If you weren't so soft, you'd wear these kids out like you did when I played." You talk about "pushing buttons!" (laughing) I would push his button a little, and he'd say, "You're right."

I remember one time (in '85) we beat Tascosa at Lowrey Field but didn't play well. I was in his ear telling him we didn't have any guts anymore, and I told him we should run them until all their girlfriends left and the ballpark was empty. And we ran until they all left.

TRAVIS WALDEN '81, ASSISTANT COACH 1989-'94:

I don't think you can come in these days and coach to the level he did. He'll tell you himself how he coached in the '60s and got a little softer in the '70s and a little less in the '80s. He would tell me that and I would laugh and tell him I would've hated to be with those teams in the '60s.

GARY ASHBY '73:

One reason Coach Moegle was such a great coach was that he didn't worry about parents, and he didn't really worry about what the kids thought. He just knew the way he was going to win. He evolved and mellowed, and had to really, because he couldn't start out today and be "Coach Moegle."

TUEY RANKIN, ASSISTANT COACH 1997-'99:

He got softer near the end with his conditioning. He was just as ruthless as ever with the things he would say to kids. It was funny, because he probably couldn't do this had he not won state and been to the state tournament as many times as he had. He was asked about the team in an interview on the TV news one night and he said, "You've got to understand – we're dealing with a different level kid now than we're used to. It's a lot harder to get there because we've got a different level kid at Monterey now." (laughing)

COACH MOEGLE:

Each youngster had individual qualities that had to be developed. Some were real fighters. Some kids didn't know how to fight. Some kids that didn't know how to fight had great skill. Some kids that really fought didn't have great skill, but they would bully you. My job was to incorporate all of that. It was my responsibility to see the potential of each individual and push him to a new level. Or maybe I had to tone him down to a lower level, so his emotions didn't run rampant. That was an art that a lot of great coaches have – to take an individual and push his buttons and not miss very often. That's a real skill in coaching – to get the most out of a kid. Maybe some needed to be promoted or demoted to get him going. It's really hard to take a mediocre attitude on a mediocre kid and make a good player out of him.

MIKE CRUTCHER '68, ASSISTANT COACH 1973-'78, 1982-'85:

Coach Moegle really knew how to get kids going. He could get under your skin. He didn't have to do that to me much because I was kind of a self-driven kid, but boy there were people that he wore out. And it didn't matter what the setting was. I remember being in the office a couple times and a kid had made a mistake in the infield and he just undressed the kid. It was brutal. He would get fired for it today for embarrassing the kid or something politically incorrect (laughing). But he knew when to push the buttons. He was a master at that.

JEFF HORN '96:

If you did something well, you were supposed to do that. If you did something bad, he needed to remind you about how you didn't need to do that anymore. If you struck out, not only did you strike out, but you were going to hear about it. Some people would hear about it for the next few innings, or the next four days, or the next three games … "I can't even put you in to bat because you're just going to strike out again."

NATHAN SWINDLE '81:

One time in the locker room after practice we were getting dressed and he looked at me and said, "You don't compete like your sister." How do you respond to that? (smiling) My sister had been there four years prior on the tennis team. I didn't want to hear that, period, and at that time I sure didn't know how to answer it.

JEFF HORN '96:

He put our backs against the wall a lot from the day we stepped foot in the program, just to see what we were made of. Not only did he want to see who could play, but to see who he wanted on his team.

COACH MOEGLE:

I've had a lot of kids with great potential, but they didn't have the makeup to be great. And I've had a lot of kids that were great players and they would fight to the end. I often ask, "If I was hanging off a cliff, who would I want to hold the other end of the rope?" There were a lot of kids I wouldn't want on the other end of the rope because they would let go.

TRAVIS WALDEN '81, ASSISTANT COACH 1989-'94:

He knew what each kid could handle. The ones that could handle it, he would really get on them. And the ones he didn't think could handle it, he wouldn't get on them as much. I know there were a couple times he probably thought a little more of some guys in terms of their toughness, and he got on them and they couldn't handle it. It may have affected their play.

But on the other side, he got on guys and handled them a certain way and it made them better and got what they were supposed to get out of their ability. He handled individuals a little differently. I wouldn't say he ever backed off anybody, but I know there were a couple guys on each team that would get a little more than the others. They were generally seniors and guys he had more expectations for as far as being leaders and carrying the team. He wanted juniors to understand his expectations and seniors had better step up and get the job done.

COACH MOEGLE:

My best players were probably a little bit hyper and a little bit more competitive. They would all maybe have a similar skill level, but the real competitor would end up the best. I think my really great pitchers never let up and never conceded a pitch.

My great hitters wanted to be at the plate and wanted the challenge of a 3-2 pitch from the best pitcher. I'd say that overall if you had to judge a kid, you wanted the one that was more competitive. The better competitor was more confident. I think of Donnie Moore and those kids who wouldn't concede anything to you.

MARK GRIFFIN '72:

One of the aspects that I think made him the coach he is was his reputation. What I mean is that people knew good things would happen when you were in his program. There was a confidence. You might not have liked the way he treated you day to day, but you knew good and well you were going to be prepared to play, and you were going to have some of the very best players around you and they would know what to do and what their roles were. That gave you an inner confidence because he had always been a winner.

So you had that expectation and I think it was one of the greatest things he brought to the program. If you were going to play on that team, he was going to get you ready to win. That's not to say there might not be a high price to pay for that, but the reward was going to far outweigh what you had to go through to get there. The guys I played with described being in a relationship with him as "running through the gates of hell." (laughing) It was hellacious.

But the heavenly reward you got at the end was more than worth it. I just think there was an expectation and a quiet confidence that you were going to be successful. He had always been that way. He was going to find a way to make that team successful.

TRAVIS WALDEN '81, ASSISTANT COACH 1989-'94:

I think players who failed to live up to Coach Moegle's expectations gave up on themselves somewhere along the line and didn't give it everything they could have. I know him well enough to know that he would put guys on the bench, but he wasn't putting them there to leave them. He was putting them there so they would fight harder when he put them back in the game. I think certain people took it personally, but in his mind, players had to go out and earn it every day. Guys that didn't buy in and have the toughness to fight through it would get replaced.

TUEY RANKIN, ASSISTANT COACH 1997-'99:

I really believe this. There were some players who couldn't play with Coach Moegle's coaching style. There were other guys, though, that if he hadn't coached like that, they wouldn't have been the player they were. So, it worked both ways.

COACH MOEGLE:

I treated every kid a little differently according to his makeup. The tougher he was, the harder I pushed him. If a kid was kind of meek or insecure, I didn't push him. I wouldn't browbeat or take him down a lot because he would just fold up. I had to be careful. I treated nearly every one of them differently, because of their personality or background or whatever it was.

LARRY HAYS, LCU & TTU COACH '71-2008:

He could handle the tough guys and the easy guys.

JEFF HORN '96:

I think he knew he could get the team to come together and band against him. He knew that it would be good for the team if he created stress and uneasiness. A lot of it was directed between the team and himself.

RON REEVES '78:

We were practicing over at Hodges Park one Saturday. I don't know what was wrong with our field, but it was one of those days where we were taking infield and we were all messing up. He sat us all down and went right down the line and ripped us, all in our individual way. He did all his usual lines, "You can't do this, you can't do that, you can't help us, and where am I gonna play you?"

He was going all the way down the line through Breudigam, me, you name it. And when he got to Dana Rieger, he stopped. Dana loved baseball and played hard when it was game time. Coach Moegle could've found a whole lot of things to say to him because he was undisciplined off the field. But he got to him that day and said, "Dana, you're the only one I don't have anything bad to say about," and just went right to the next guy. We were all sitting there thinking, "Whaaaat?!?!" But he had that innate sense ... I think he knew it would rip Dana's heart out if he got on him. But the rest of us ... he would just piss me off. We didn't have a bunch of bullpen guys back then. There were just two or three of us who pitched and that was it. We never got pulled out of a game. He would come out there and get me pissed off at him (laughing). He tells the story all the time about rattling my chain and making me mad so I would pitch better.

COACH MOEGLE:

This was something I learned in professional baseball while watching my manager Al Unser work with our players and how he handled each individual. I could take a rough, tough kid with good ability who was used to a little bit of harshness and push him to another level. I would say most of the kids I coached could be pushed to a level they didn't think they could reach.

But there were also certain kids who were very, very important to the program that we couldn't push to that next level. We had to leave them where they were and try to bring them out as best they could. Some would get on to the next level and be very competitive. I could take a kid and line him up and run open quarters or run the stands or do my off-season drills and I could almost tell the ones I could push or the ones that would kind of back off when I pushed them.

There were certain kids in certain game situations – Ron Reeves was one of them. I could go out to the mound when he was pitching and rattle his chain a little. He'd get so mad at me and he'd take it out on the next hitter. I could name off a bunch of those kids that I could almost infuriate to get them to respond at another level. A lot them would react like, "I'll show him!" I could walk off and almost laugh because I had gotten him to that point. But there were others who would make a mistake and if I got on him he might make two more mistakes before he could get normal again. So there was a balancing act that had to be done. I think all coaches have this in some respect.

TRAVIS WALDEN '81, ASSISTANT COACH 1989–'94:

I feel like he motivated each individual in a certain way. He knew who to push and who he could challenge. I've heard the story about the time he went out to the mound to get on Ron Reeves in the region finals against Midland Lee. Ron was walking people and pitching behind in the count. When he got there Ron barked back at him and told him, "I'm not out here throwing balls on purpose!" It fired Ron up and he shut Lee down the rest of the way and they went on to the state finals.

RON REEVES '78:

I walked a bunch of people one time and finally got out of the inning. Coach Moegle had been on me from the dugout to throw strikes and this and that. I was walking to the dugout and was happy to be out of the inning and he was standing there at the top of the dugout wanting our eyes to meet. I knew he was over there glaring at me but I wasn't going to look at him. I walked over to the other end of the dugout by the bleachers and sat down on the back of the bench. I knew he was still standing there looking at me.

I finally looked up and he said, "What are you throwing balls for!? Why are you walking people?!" I threw my glove down and yelled, "I'm walking them on purpose!!" It just came out. I didn't know why I was throwing balls. The dugout just stopped – no noise. I didn't know what was about to happen – if he was going to throw me off the team or what. He just stood there and looked at me and his expression never changed. Then he cracked the smallest little smile and turned and walked to the 3rd base coaching box. He had rattled my chain. (laughing)

BOB FANNIN '78:

Coach Moegle expected so much out of Ron Reeves. He knew he could give it to Ron, and Ron could take it. Reeves would go out there and pitch, and like a lot of guys, if you were going to score on him you'd better get him in the first inning. I was playing 1st and Reeves walked a guy and here came Coach Moegle to the mound. I got over there to the mound as Coach Moegle was getting there and Coach said, "What's wrong with strikes?!" Reeves fired back, "I like to throw balls!" (smiling) He was the only guy that could get away with that. Coach Moegle said, "Well, OK then" and walked off. Ron bowed up and struck out about 15 in that game. (laughing) But Reeves could take it and it made him better. We knew if he got on Reeves, the rest of us were fair game.

JIMMY WEBSTER '85:

Coach Moegle was so smart. He let Coach Crutcher deal with me. He would say something every once in a while, but he let Coach Crutcher handle me, which was brilliant. He knew how invested I was. He knew he didn't have to worry about that part of it. I remember only two or three times that he really raised his voice to me over technique or hitting or baserunning.

He didn't do it to me, because I think he knew I might crumble. Or he knew that I was peddling as fast as I could with what I had at the time to keep my head above water. He might've also known that if he raised his voice to Gus, Welch or Eckles, that he was raising his voice to me, too. In my mind, if Doug Welch had just got his butt chewed out, I'd better watch my step.

MIKE CRUTCHER '68, ASSISTANT COACH 1973-'78, 1982-'85:

We were playing at Plainview and they had a left-hander who was a really good athlete. When he wasn't pitching, he was playing center field. He could throw it through a wall. It was a close game and I was on 2nd base and he was playing in center. We hit a routine fly ball to center field and Coach Moegle was yelling, "Tag up!" I was thinking I needed to go halfway, but I know now that he wanted me to tag and bluff like I was going.

But that day I thought he meant to tag and go. So I took off to 3rd and I think the ball passed by my head as I was about three feet past 2nd. I was out by about 50 feet! At that time Plainview had the old-fashioned dugouts. Coach Moegle grabbed me by the shirt and he pushed me up against the wall and said, "I told you, we go halfway!" I said, "But Coach Moegle, you told me to tag up." That was the only time I ever said anything like that ... Anything! Back then it was just, "Yes sir."

We didn't disrespect Coach Moegle, but I know that he liked it when a kid would push back a little and show some fight. Right now, on our coaching staff, I'm by far the guy who gets after people the most. And I'd much rather have a kid bow his neck at me when I'm getting on him rather than tuck his tail and give up. I can't stand that. In today's society there's a bunch of that.

GARY ASHBY '73:

We only lost 3 games in 1971 and one was the state championship game. Our second loss was to Lubbock High.

This is how competitive Coach Moegle is. He saw that there was a problem. I was a sophomore and not even suiting up for the games. We were probably 15-2. Most coaches would just be tickled to death to be 15-2, but he wasn't. So, the next day at practice he said, "We are going to scrimmage today, and whoever does well in the scrimmage will start tomorrow against Coronado. Even YOU, Ashby." Me being me, I said, "Well, you remember that." Now I might not have been quite that forceful, but I said it.

I got a couple hits in the intrasquad and Coach Dudley and Coach

Moegle kept me out after practice and said, "All right, you're starting against Coronado tomorrow." So I went from the foul ball shagger one day to starting the next day. And the reason I was #17 in high school, college and in pro ball, was because the senior he took the jersey from wore 17. He gave me the senior's jersey and the senior never suited up again.

When we went to the state tournament, the senior didn't go. That's how Coach Moegle was. I started and did fine the next day and started all the way through the state championship game. That'll show you how competitive Coach Moegle was and how much he wanted to win. I'm sure he realized this team could do great things and maybe just needed a tweak here or a tweak there. He did that over the years with other guys. Coach Moegle had the ability to make decisions and stick to them but was not afraid to make a change – to the delight of some and to the chagrin of others.

LARRY HAYS, LCU & TTU COACH '71-2008:

There were certain things his players understood. There was no doubt about the way he would react. They knew they'd have to run and would be throwing up and all that. He was so dependable and consistent with who he was. When Shanon played for him he said if he messed up, he would head right to him in the dugout rather than trying to run away from him. He had seen what happened to those guys who ran away from him to the other end of the dugout.

TRAVIS WALDEN '81, ASSISTANT COACH 1989-'94:

If Coach Moegle ever had an issue with something, it wouldn't be addressed later. It would be addressed right there on the spot. I remember a couple guys got into a fight in the dugout over a girl. And I kid you not, he separated them and put them both on the bench. After the game he took them in the outfield and ran them and ran them and ran them. When he had a beef with something, it was going to be handled right then, his way or the highway.

JIMMY SHANKLE '74:

It was his way or the highway. But his way was the right way. The beauty of that is he didn't just come on the scene when we got there. Now back in the '60s, I'm sure as hard as they worked ... he was a single guy and they worked harder than we did in the '70s. I can't imagine it, but apparently they did. He had nothing else to do because he didn't have a wife and kids to go home to. We had to be on time, and we had to do those things. It just gets back to being a disciplined person. And if we were disciplined in that part of life, then later on in life it was going to help us.

KELLER SMITH '63:

One should not make the mistake of thinking that there was a lot of love and affection being exchanged between player and coach. Clearly, there was not from coach to player, and that was pretty much the way it was from player to coach. He was an easy guy to stay upset with and to resent at times, but never disrespect. The sensitivity side of it was more on the raw emotion than it was on the gracious side. I'll tell you, there were many ballgames ... many ballgames that we won to spite him. We were going to show him that we were tough. Of course, at the time we didn't realize he had all that figured out. It was one of the chief ways he motivated us.

GARY HUGHES '65:

I was warming up the day before the game and he came to the bullpen. I told him my elbow was hurting. He quickly got after me and told me I was gutless and that I was afraid to pitch the next day. Being as competitive as I was, that got all over me. I was determined to pitch the next day, no matter how my elbow felt. Amazingly, the next day I had no elbow problems and was feeling great. I remember thinking that he had willed the elbow problem away. Whether it was psychological or not, it was gone the next day, so I give him credit for some miracle work there.

TRAVIS WALDEN '81, ASSISTANT COACH 1989-'94:

We can all remember days when we didn't feel good and he didn't cut us any slack. I remember one day a guy hurt his ankle playing frisbee in the park and the next day he came in and was trying to hide it so Coach Moegle didn't know he was hurt. Coach found out about it and the first time the kid got on 1st base he got the steal sign. He was limping down to 2nd and got thrown out. He got to the dugout and Coach Moegle asked him, "What are you doing?" He said, "Coach, I hurt my ankle." Coach Moegle asked him how he'd hurt it and the kid said he'd hurt his ankle playing frisbee the day before. Coach Moegle told him "You're letting the team down. Get out there and play."

KELLER SMITH '63:

Coach Moegle had a saying that he used, "You're just not tough enough." He would apply that 1,000 times to 1,000 guys. Being "tough" was driven into us. It was expected and we either developed it or we were probably going to have to find somewhere else to play baseball.

JOHN DUDLEY '62, ASSISTANT COACH 1968-'72:

When he came in here, he took a blanket approach and said this is the way it's going to be. But he had to do that in order to get his message across and to get the standard set for everybody. I do believe that over the years one of the things that happened with him is he tailored his approach to fit different personalities. That happened in the early years, as well.

Sometimes we as players thought he was always on us, but he was trying to get the best out of us. As we look back on it we can see that there were times he dealt with one of us a little differently than others. I think this is the sign of a good coach – that he learned there were certain things to be done with certain players in order to bring the best out of them.

JEFF HORN '96:

Coach Moegle's way always worked because he knew where the line was. He knew to handle some kids differently than others. He was just a masterful tactician when it came to the mental part of motivating a kid to play.

MARK GRIFFIN '72:

He had a real knack for being able to have that insight as to what kids would respond to. There were some non-negotiables. He treated everybody the same in some respects. But when it really came down to performance, he knew how hard to ride and he knew when to back off. Some he could ride harder than others, and some he had to put his arm around. He didn't do that a lot.

Many times we felt like he treated us all the same – like dogs. But he knew he had some special "puppies" he could take special care of to get the maximum out of. He knew how far to go and when to back off, and that was one of his effective traits. One of his tricks was to badmouth you a little bit, just to see how we would respond. He wouldn't do that to everybody. There were some he never would ever say a tough word to because he knew they couldn't handle it. But for those who could handle it, it would raise their level of performance. He knew who he could say those things to and who he needed to leave alone. It's not that he mollycoddled anybody but sometimes he'd just leave us alone. He was a master psychologist in that regard.

JEFF HORN '96:

He tailored his approach differently. He handled Mark Martinez differently than others. There were other guys he rode really hard. My dad had played for him and I think he expected a lot out of me. I can see that now but at the time I wondered why I seemed to catch his wrath daily. I think all of us look back and are glad that he expected a bunch from us. If he hadn't expected anything out of me, I might not have turned out OK. He had a unique way of determining psychologically how to treat one player to the next to maximize their potential.

BURLE PETTIT, LUBBOCK SPORTSWRITER:

The discipline that worked on one kid wasn't a one-size-fits-all. He did what it took to motivate each kid. Sometimes it was rather harsh, and sometimes it was – I don't think Bobby ever got "tender"

... "tender" being a relative term – but he knew how to handle each kid psychologically.

JEFF HORN '96:

Mark Martinez was just a phenomenal high school pitcher. At about age 12, he developed a very good curveball. We had played against him in youth baseball, and when he got to Monterey as a sophomore he started contributing right off the bat. Mark was a bit of a loose cannon. He was very intense and learned how to channel that.

By the time he was a senior, he was as close to unhittable as any high school pitcher I've seen. He would strike out 15 batters a game regularly. And he did it with a good fastball, but a big league breaking ball – the bottom would just drop out of it. Any time we could get any type of lead with him on the mound, we felt very confident that we could win the game. One other thing about Mark – we talk about how hard Coach Moegle was on players. But Coach Moegle knew he had to handle Mark with a lot of care. I give Coach Moegle credit, because he handled Mark the right way and brought him along so he could be dominant as a senior.

KELLER SMITH '63:

Anyone who thinks that Bobby Moegle became the most winning baseball coach in the United States because he had more talent than anyone else would be asleep at the wheel. That was not the case at all. He had talent, and he knew how to find talent and develop it. But the main thing that he did beyond anyone I've ever been around was to get the most that was available out of a guy.

GARY HUGHES '65:

Coach Moegle always threw down a personal challenge to everyone who played for him, and I think that's what made his players give the very best we had. In many of the 40 years he coached, he didn't have the talent other programs had assembled, but he got the best from the players on his teams.

GARY ASHBY '73:

One thing a coach better have is some players. If a jockey is riding a mule and everyone else had a horse, he's probably not going to win. So Coach Moegle had some good players, but he got more out of those players than probably any coach. I mean, if it was in there, he would get it out of you. If it wasn't in there, he would run you off (laughing). He had good players and developed good players. He also had good players and made them great players.

COACH MOEGLE:

Mental preparation is almost as important as the physical preparation. Kids at 15, 16, 17 thought I was playing mind games with them, but I would just inflate a situation one way or the other. If an opposing player was outstanding, I would tell my team that we hadn't seen this type kid before and that he's so much better than we are that we would have to get to a higher level.

If he had a great breaking ball, we would set up the pitching machine to throw it at an exceptional level. If we were playing someone that wasn't very good, I would tell them that we ought to beat them by 10 runs and that if we didn't beat them by 10 we would have a bad day. I just tried to be truthful with them. A lot of times I stretched the truth to make the opponent better, or to make us seem a lot better. But mental preparation for the kids was very important to me.

When we walked in, we felt confident about what we were going to do. I always wanted to get off the bus and have people see a bunch of kids walk in with some swagger and a little cockiness. We wanted everybody to look up to us. If we played somebody exceptional, we respected their ability, but we never wanted to walk in and feel outmanned. So, I guess I played mind games, but they always had a purpose.

GARY HUGHES '65:

We took the field on occasion thinking we were 10 runs behind because he had told us that we were going to get blown off the field.

It seemed like we took the field every game with that attitude, and that mental exercise he would put us through would get us to play at the top of our abilities.

TUEY RANKIN, ASSISTANT COACH 1997-'99:

At the time I was there, I coached with Coach Moegle and Coach Morton (the Monterey football coach). Coach Morton's style was so positive about what we were going to do. If we were going to go play Southlake Carroll or Desoto, we were going to beat them. He believed that we could win the state championship at Monterey. Everything was very, very positive and optimistic as far as where we were as a team, when sometimes we weren't very good. He came out with this deal in 2003 after we had been beaten in the third round of the playoffs in 2002 by Euless Trinity. Trinity was very good and ended up losing at the very end of the state championship game to Lufkin.

He came up with a scenario that we were just a few points away from competing for a state championship. But that was one reason why he was good because he had to let the Monterey community know we were good enough to compete at that level. It was more than just beating Coronado – it was about beating Desoto and Midland Lee and Permian.

But Coach Moegle was different. Early in my first year of coaching with him (in '97), the team was coming off the state championship and we weren't playing well at the time. I said something about the state tournament and he laughed and said, "With this group?!" And later we were going to play Mansfield in the playoffs and as we were loading the bus somebody said, "Good luck Coach Moegle!" He said, "We're going to need a whole lot more than luck." (laughing) And in the final practice before we played Mansfield, Coach Moegle was telling the team about how good Mansfield was.

He said, "I'm telling you boys, Mansfield can really play. They are a cut above us. And we're going to have to really hump up to play with them. Personally, I don't think we can do it ... The bus leaves tomorrow at 1:30." There was the challenge. Coach Morton never would've said anything like that. (laughing)

TRAVIS WALDEN '81, ASSISTANT COACH 1989-'94:

He did use the team concept when he was motivating us. I remember one day it was snowing up in Tulia and headed our way, and we went outside to practice and it was freezing cold. He told us, "Coronado is painting their locker room today and we're outside getting better." So he used different methods for bringing everybody together as a team, and that's the one thing I think he did the best. We always knew who was in charge and we always knew when we stepped on the field we'd be prepared mentally and physically. There were different ways to do it, but he knew how to motivate each guy.

COACH MOEGLE:

As far as the commitment from kids, about the only thing I ever requested from a kid was that he or a parent call me regarding attendance. If he didn't come to practice, he'd become a back-burner kid for me and I'd find somebody else to take his place. It was just to show him how valuable I felt like every kid was to our program. If they had a serious problem, I could understand a phone call to tell me.

I would say in 40 years I probably had three opportunities for a kid to miss practice. Now I've had some miss school and show up to practice, but I very seldom had a kid miss practice. After I got it started in the early '60s, the word got out that they would be there, sick or otherwise. So, I had their commitment and I didn't really have to work hard regarding attendance because it had been passed down that they would have to earn their way back if they missed. It took care of itself after the early '60s.

JOHN DUDLEY '62, ASSISTANT COACH 1968-'72:

Coach Moegle laid it out and said this is what we're going to do. And we fell in line and did it or we didn't play. In my senior year, I thought I was sick one day and missed school with a little cold. When I got to practice the next day, I found out somebody else had my job. I'll guarantee you I did not miss another day the rest of the year. I was going to be there and not take a chance on losing my job.

That's the way it was with him.

We were going to be there, and we were going to work hard, and there was going to be a positive result at the end – that we would win. We got to the point that we expected to win – not that we hoped to win, but that we expected to win. We expected to be at a certain level in the playoffs every year. It wasn't that we hoped to get there. We knew we were going to get there because the expectation was there.

BURLE PETTIT, LUBBOCK SPORTSWRITER:

Bobby expected his players to put out in the classroom the way they did on the baseball field. He demanded it. He never let them believe that they were baseball players and not students.

COACH MOEGLE:

The reason I always checked on the kids and their grades and attendance in class was because that was the reason they were there. They didn't come to play baseball and athletics, they came to go to school and I wanted to make sure they all did. I know if the kid attended class and did what the teacher told him, school was more enjoyable.

JOHN DUDLEY '62, ASSISTANT COACH 1968-'72:

Even before "No Pass No Play" we had rules about eligibility. Coach Moegle was always pushing us about grades. Then when I was coaching with him, he was also pushing kids about their grades. I know he spent time visiting with teachers about certain kids to assure that they were doing what they were supposed to do in the classroom.

GARY HUGHES '65:

He seemed to always know where there was a problem in one of the classrooms, and we had to face him if there was.

JEFF HORN '96:

If you weren't making your grades or you were cutting up in school, not only were you not going to play, you might be kicked off the team. He wasn't going to put up with that. Personally, I can remember getting an academic honor and Coach Moegle took notice of that and told me "Good job."

CLINT BRYANT '92:

I ran into him at the airport one time when I was playing at Tech and he told me how proud he was of me. I had received an academic honor, and I think he was prouder of that than he was of my baseball accomplishments.

JOHN DUDLEY '62, ASSISTANT COACH 1968-'72:

If we didn't meet his standards academically and athletically, then we didn't play. Somebody was going to have that job. If we didn't meet the criteria he had outlined, it was "My way or the highway." And that is certainly what happened to some of those guys.

BOB FANNIN '78:

In my senior year, I had a D at midterm in an English class. Coach Moegle got the midterm report, and we all know the walk up the stairs and that we were going to have to see him as we walked through the locker room door. Coach Crutcher was sitting in there with him, and he always knew something was up and he would be looking for us. He knew I had this D and of course I had six more weeks to get the grade up. But I knew what was coming.

Coach Moegle saw me and said, "Don't even bring your glove – just your tennis shoes." Coach Crutcher giggled at me. I dressed and put on my shoes and headed down there to practice and went over to see him. He said, "You know you have a D in class." I said, "Yes sir, I'm going to bring it up." He said, "Oh, I know you're going to bring it up. Just go ahead and start running, and you run the whole practice." So I ran around the school, from Indiana over to

Gary, and from 50th over to 47th. I ran the whole practice – probably for three hours.

When practice ended, they went upstairs to the locker room and I kept running. Ron Reeves told me he reminded Coach Moegle that I was still outside running around the school, and Coach Moegle told him, "Why would you care? He's making a D in class so that tells you what he thinks about this team." So Ron came outside and caught me running across the front of the school and said, "Coach Moegle said to just keep running."

Later, Coach Moegle pulled out of the parking lot and went home and he drove right past me while I was running. Ron came by a few minutes later and said, "He's gone. Go ahead and stop. But in the morning about 5 o'clock, you should come back up here and put your stuff on and start running again, so he'll think you've been out here all night running." (laughing) I brought the grade up and finished in good shape.

GARY ASHBY '73:

The Monterey locker room is still the same as it was in 1960. We'd go up these stairs and turn and go up some more stairs and there was a door. Coach Moegle's door was right inside the locker room door, and there was a big window after that. So I would sort of gather myself and open that door and try to get by that window and just pray that I wouldn't get called into the office because it wasn't going to be anything good if he did.

It wasn't going to be "How's your day?" or "How's your girlfriend?" It wasn't going to be anything like that. I'd just try to get by there and hope he was looking off or on the phone. If you could get by that window without being called in, you had half the day whipped, until infield started. Once infield started that was another deal.

FRED OLIVER, MHS COACH 2000-'09:

His players would tell me about coming up the stairs to the dressing room. The dressing room is at the top of some stairs, and to the left of the door to the dressing room is the coach's office. It has glass windows. I was told that the kids would come up the steps and peek inside the door to see if he was in his office behind his desk.

If he was in his office, the kids would get on their hands and knees and crawl through the door and crawl past the office windows and into the dressing room to get ready for practice without him seeing them. They didn't want him to call them into the office and talk about something that day or about how they'd been playing. It was unique. Now if he wasn't in there, they'd just walk on by. But they'd peek just to see if he was in that office.

GARY ASHBY '73:

Every now and then, Coach Moegle would have a player that would actually feel comfortable going into his office and sitting down and talking. That was a rare occasion. But occasionally there would be a guy like Jimmy Shankle, who had a little bit of rapport with Coach Moegle. He would open the door and go in the office and sit down and visit. It's an unusual event, maybe once every five years a kid like that would come along. I wasn't one of those kids, and most weren't.

JOHN DUDLEY '62, ASSISTANT COACH 1968-'72:

I think through the years, kids would hear stories about what it would be like, but they didn't realize how tough it was once they experienced it. I think for young people – especially those sophomores – it was tough to get through that. Once they got acclimated to it, it was no longer a big problem and it was expected. It was geared toward getting us mentally and physically prepared to compete on a high level.

If a kid goes through a lot of physical conditioning, certainly he was going to be in better shape as a result of that, but it was also going to impact him mentally. We knew if we had gone through all this and didn't win, what was it going to be like the next day?

There was a motivating factor there, as well. It caused us to want to reach back and give everything we had. We didn't like it when we were doing it and we would just as soon not do it, but we would see the benefit when it was said and done. We used to work long hours back then, and a lot of times it would be dark when we would line up to run. We were tired at the time and we'd get 2/3 of the way through all those sprints and we were really tired. There was a row of bushes down there on the north end of the practice field by the field house. We were always daring each other – because it was so dark and maybe he couldn't see everybody – to see if somebody had the courage to hide in the bushes and not make a return sprint back to him. But nobody ever had the courage to do that, so we went ahead and ran all the sprints.

NATHAN SWINDLE '81:

We didn't hear the "Coach Moegle legends" from him. They were passed down from the upperclassmen. I got into a minor infraction one day at school. I was talking during class and the teacher said I needed to come in after school. That scared me to death because I had heard we should never miss practice for any reason, and certainly not for classroom discipline.

That got my attention enough that I went to the teacher and told him I couldn't come in after school. He told that I was going to come in after school. I asked him if I could do something different and he asked what I meant. I asked him if I could go get licks instead of coming in after school. He said yes, so I went down to the office and got licks from Mr. Zorn. I was more afraid of Coach Moegle than I was of getting licks. (laughing)

MARK GRIFFIN '72:

He knew exactly what his players were doing. If they didn't perform in the classroom, that young man was going to pay a dear price. I think he took it as an affront to the teacher. If that boy wasn't turning his work in, it was a poor reflection on him as a coach and he would take that personally. He would see to it that his young men were as successful as they could be. He wasn't expecting everyone to make straight A's, but he was expecting everyone to make their best efforts to prepare for exams, just as his expectation was on that field.

GARY ASHBY '73:

The discipline goes without saying. We weren't a problem in the classroom and we certainly weren't a problem out on the field. It's hard to put your finger on what makes somebody better than everybody else. Maybe if it's a pitcher it's because he throws harder than everybody else. But with a coach, I don't know. It's just the fact that early on in his career, people bought into it and a tradition developed from that, the fundamentals and the discipline everybody adhered to. I really think developing the tradition had as much to do with it as anything. That and having a good pitcher every other year didn't hurt anything either.

GARY HUGHES '65:

He was able to identify the different personalities and realize what it took for each one. I guess some people thought that he was too aggressive verbally over the years with certain players. But I never heard any bad language from him, nor did I ever hear OF any bad language from him. In my case, my dad had died when I was young and I think he realized I needed to be pushed hard because I had probably been real independent. And that was a true statement. He realized I needed some pretty strong discipline and I think he was able to make that analysis on each player by using their backgrounds and what he knew about them and their personalities. I think that's what made him very effective.

BURLE PETTIT, LUBBOCK SPORTSWRITER:

Bobby's kids accepted discipline that wasn't intended to make them better baseball players. I realize that all these years later. It was to make them better at what they did by realizing there was a consequence for not paying attention, or not trying and not giving it your best – and there was a consequence for not practicing everything they'd learned. Those were things that would be important in their professional lives.

The kids learned to focus on the goal and not to make mistakes. Bobby was a strict disciplinarian. I think the reason that he and Bobby Knight's strict discipline is the reason that those players at

Indiana and Texas Tech and Monterey High School have been successful. They learned that. A kid told me one time, "When the scars all heal, you realize what you learned." Bobby was a disciplinarian, but he was fair. He had no favorites. (smiling) Yes he did, if a kid was hitting .400 or winning 16 or 17 games, he was the favorite because he was doing what he had been taught to do.

LARRY HAYS, LCU & TTU COACH '71-2008:

The thing about Coach Moegle was that he could adjust. It was the same thing I saw in Coach Knight. I had read all of Coach Knight's stuff, and then when I went to watch him practice, I thought, "I missed all of that." Ninety percent of the time he was one of the most positive coaches you would ever want to be around. But that other 10% you don't want to see. Coach Moegle was more consistent with how he dealt with people and his opinions. But he would change in a heartbeat if he saw something and thought it was a better way to do something.

FRED OLIVER, MHS COACH 2000-'09:

I think Coach Moegle had a lot of God-given things, but he also studied the game and knew the game. He played in the minor leagues and he carried those things with him into coaching. But I think maybe because of the military, he understood the discipline and work ethic that was involved. I think his drive for excellence and not being mediocre and lazy – and by doing the little things right – resulted in him being successful. He had those qualities, and I think he was meant to be a coach and a leader. He fit that mold and the kids that bought into his system and could withstand the rigorous practices were going to be winners.

BURLE PETTIT, LUBBOCK SPORTSWRITER:

He coached not for the parents, not for the administrators, and not even for the fans. Bobby coached for the players. He coached for the good of the team. There are some parallels between Bobby Knight and Bobby Moegle. Now, I'm going to draw a very strict line here because Bobby Moegle is a guy of great civility. I watched him coach for years and never heard a profane word come out of his mouth.

I think he proved that you can make a point and make it very heavy and use words that are already available and acceptable to whatever momma is watching. But where they dovetail, Knight and Moegle, is in their players after they leave them. The strict discipline works, if the players are convinced the good of the team and the good of the individual is at stake.

TUEY RANKIN, ASSISTANT COACH 1997-'99:

We had a kid who wasn't really mentally tough, but a pretty good athlete. He was playing right field in a game and he made an error out there. Coach Moegle got someone off the bench in the middle of the inning and sent him in. It was the "jog of shame" coming back to the 3rd base dugout, with all the fans there.

Later on, in the state tournament, he got a bunt down in a key spot or something like that and it really helped us win the game. It came up later in our conversation and Coach Moegle said to me, "I guess that paid off." I loved working with Coach Moegle, but that was something I couldn't believe – that he pulled someone in the middle of the inning. But he had his reasons. There was purpose in what he did. He was the best at psychology of any coach I ever worked with.

BURLE PETTIT, LUBBOCK SPORTSWRITER:

I think Donny Anderson once told me that Vince Lombardi "treats us all the same – like dogs." (laughing) And yet for every player who played for Lombardi, or Bobby Knight, or Bobby Moegle, the discipline was meaningful and perceivable. I think that's maybe the secret.

GARY HUGHES '65:

Many of us grew up with very little coaching so by the time we got to Monterey he had to undo everything that we had ever learned. But I think his genius for winning was in the mental preparation he put us through. He would show his disappointment if we didn't follow his instructions. Not only would he show his disappointment in terms of his attitude and body language, but he would also discipline us with running and he would make our lives miserable to get our attention. That kind of discipline worked well for me, certainly, but also all my teammates. Young guys 16- to-18-years-old don't think they need discipline at the time, but when we reflect later, we recognize that we needed it.

COACH MOEGLE:

I had to get into their mindset and see where they were, and know something about their parents, too. Were their parents going to back me when I pushed them or were they going to turn on me? I had to understand that. There were a lot of psychological things that were going on that people didn't realize in manipulating the kids.

GARY ASHBY '73:

I'll give our parents from that generation credit. They turned us over to Coach Moegle and they felt like he knew what was best. They didn't try to outthink him, they just let him go. If you lived to see the "other end" of it, it was a worthwhile venture. A lot didn't.

MARK GRIFFIN '72:

The parent involvement was very, very limited. I think people were probably intimidated by Coach Moegle, not that he wasn't approachable or acceptable, but he was in charge. I think parents in that time understood that. There was a high regard for him. They might not agree with everything exactly as he did it, but the results spoke for themselves. There was never ever any doubt from the first day he was at Monterey to the day he left as to who was in charge of the program. There were lots and lots of good players who just didn't complete the process. And those were decisions they had to make. But those who stayed were rewarded.

JEFF HARP '78:

At the beginning of my senior year, he called me over and told me, "We need a catcher." He asked me if I had ever caught and I told him, "No sir." He told me to go with Coach Crutcher. Coach Crutcher had a mitt and the gear and I put it on and he gave me about a 5-minute lesson in blocking baseballs and then he worked me over. Then he spent a few more minutes on catching pop-ups, and he started shooting them up the silo and I caught them all. All of sudden he whistled across the field at Coach Moegle and got his attention and gave him the thumbs up. After that I was the catcher.

My dad was upset because I'd been a pretty good 2nd baseman. It was kind of a surreal moment later on in non-district when I hit a home run to win a game down at Midland Lee. After the game I was talking to mom and dad and Coach Moegle walked by and patted me on the back and said, "Big hit." I said thank you and he took about three more steps and turned around and looked at my dad and said, "... and Jeff CAN catch." And he walked off. I was blown away.

Mine were the kind of parents that said, "If YOU have an issue with Coach Moegle then YOU go handle it." They knew that I wanted to play baseball and I wanted to win. I think they respected him so much. They knew how successful he'd been. Dad didn't necessarily agree with me moving to catcher. But they respected him so much and he was up front about everything.

JEFF HORN '96:

I think today's kids could benefit from his style of coaching if parents didn't get in the way so much. There's a lot of people who have coached in similar ways as Coach Moegle – maybe Coach Knight, maybe Coach Krzyzewski, and some other guys of their generation. I think that society has changed and they want their kids to be told that they're great and that they can do no wrong. I personally believe that's just not the way you build a stronger person or team. I think Coach Moegle's ideals would still work today, although I'm not totally sure some of that stuff would be allowed to occur.

RON REEVES '78:

When I was 15 years old ... From getting to know Jimmy (Shankle) and another guy named Dennis Blair at baseball camp, they bought me beer. Shankle and I have talked about that a lot of times since then in terms of how much trouble we would've had if Coach Moegle found out he was buying me beer.

I ended up getting kicked out of school near the end of my 9th grade year at Hutchinson (Junior High) for drinking. There was going to be a big party on Friday night and somebody's big brother had gone to get a bunch of alcohol for the party. At lunch we all went to a house and were getting the stuff and paying for it, and a few of the kids stayed there and started drinking and didn't go back to school. That tipped people off and the party fell apart that afternoon. We heard rumors all weekend that a couple girls got sick and got in trouble and gave up everybody's name who was involved.

On Monday morning at school, one at a time people got called out of class to come to the office. I didn't get called until Tuesday morning – I was one of the last ones. Roy Grimes was our principal and he was bringing people in and asking, "Were you there, and did you drink?" If we said "no," he'd let us go. Some people told the truth and some people lied. I sat there in class thinking, "What am I going to do ... what am I going to do?" And it wasn't like I was an honorable guy at the time – I wasn't against lying. My mom was the PTA president and I was president of the student body.

But when I got face to face with Mr. Grimes and he asked me, I couldn't lie to him. He started crying and said, "This hurts me so bad, but I've got to expel you." It just so happened that this was the last couple weeks of school when football spring training was going on at Monterey. After school every day at Hutch I'd go over to Monterey to practice. Well, I had to go tell the coaches that I had been kicked out of school for drinking and that I wouldn't be able to be there for the last week of spring training.

This is one of my most memorable Coach Moegle stories. I told Coach Odom and the other coaches that were in the office at the time what had happened. They were mad and Coach Odom told me that they didn't tolerate any drinking and that as far as he was concerned, I was off the team at that point. He told me he would watch how I acted over the summer and that they would make a decision about me in the fall. I was glad that I had a chance to get things right.

As I walked out of the football dressing room there in the field house, I went through that metal door to the parking lot – my mom was parked outside the door where the coaches used to park – Coach Moegle was walking in. He knew what was going on, and he gave me a shirt tug and had me pinned against the wall and said, "I hear you got yourself in a little trouble, big boy."

I had just made a commitment to accept Christ on like April 1st at a First Baptist Church youth event. I didn't know he went to church there, but he did. I just went to a big pizza dinner night and had no intention of doing that, but me and Scott Isbell both accepted Christ into our hearts that night. And I did change, but I still thought I could drink and stuff like that. Coach Moegle said, "I heard you made a commitment to the Lord. You better get your priorities in order before you get over here." Then he just walked away from me. I got in the car and my mom was mad at Coach Moegle because she had seen him get on me. She should've been mad at me because I was the dumb-butt who had messed up.

BURLE PETTIT, LUBBOCK SPORTSWRITER:

I don't know how today's kids would respond to Moegle-type coaching. I'm very concerned about a generation in which everybody gets a trophy or rewards are given to keep from embarrassing a kid. I would want to stand off 30 or 40 feet to hear Bobby's view of that approach to teaching and rewarding kids. I wouldn't want to be close enough to be deafened, but I can only imagine what his approach would be.

Wall Street Journal had an article on this. In the workplace, corporations are having problems trying to bring kids out of that mindset. One youngster just out of college told his boss he "wasn't there to work, he was there to be fulfilled." I can only imagine Moegle saying, "I've got your fulfillment right here." (smiling) So I don't know. I wish there was another generation of Bobby Moegles coming along, but we've run out of them.

GARY ASHBY '73:

He mellowed a little in the '80s and '90s. The way he went about things in the '60s and '70s – especially the guys who played before he got married – wouldn't work today. There are just too many other things kids can do. We had kids quit in the early '70s just because they couldn't handle it physically or mentally. But nowadays kids have too many other options, and I don't think that we as parents have raised our kids to be mentally tough enough to handle the way Coach Moegle went about things.

A coach couldn't start out today doing what Coach Moegle did – parents would not tolerate it. He had the reputation and the tradition and the history behind him once society softened and parents became probably too involved. That sounds bad – but some parents tried to run everything instead of letting coaches coach and parents parent. He had the program going when society softened to the point that kids weren't as mentally and physically tough.

JIMMY SHANKLE '74:

He disciplined us and worked us so hard to get that physical toughness and mental toughness we needed to be a great player and a great team. He did all that and instilled it in us and it made it easier for our dads, who didn't have to be the "bad guy." Coach Moegle was the "bad guy," and at times we all needed it. In my particular situation, I got it from Coach Moegle and I got it at my house. I got double-dipped so I definitely knew where my place was.

BURLE PETTIT, LUBBOCK SPORTSWRITER:

Administrators overreact to parents like I think they never have before. You'll hear this from all of us my age – the worst thing that would happen when you got a bustin' at school was that you were going to get another bustin' at home. Now, momma shows up at the school with six lawyers, and administrators can't help but respond to that. I know that if Bobby was still there, he'd be coaching like he always did, no matter what momma was saying.

MARK GRIFFIN '72:

There was no doubt who was in charge. He wasn't there to nurture us and love on us. He was there to teach us how to be men and how to play the game of baseball. He was, in my opinion, very successful at that. The days of parent interaction and influence didn't exist at that point in time.

I can remember him telling me this story. One time a parent came up to him and he had cut his kid, or the kid had chosen not to continue in the program. He was visiting with Coach Moegle about that and maybe questioned some of his techniques. Coach Moegle's response was, "If you don't like it, go get your own team." So it was pretty obvious who was in charge and he had his own ideas of what his expectations were. We could either meet them or go do something else.

GARY ASHBY '73:

The parents wouldn't put up with it these days, the administration wouldn't put up with it and the kids wouldn't put up with it, but back then you could. For several reasons, the parents were either part of the Depression or their parents were part of the Depression. My dad, McIntyre's dad and several others worked hard to make a living. They didn't have time to wonder if Coach Moegle was being hard on their boys or not. Plus, they were probably a little harder than our generation was in terms of work ethic and things like that. Our generation has a few things going for us that my dad's generation didn't, in that we desired to be at the ballpark and be involved.

TRAVIS WALDEN '81, ASSISTANT COACH 1989-'94:

For it to be done his way nowadays would be very difficult. A coach would have to be very established. People would have to buy in to it. With the way we are now, if things don't go the right direction quickly, they're going to start pointing fingers and moving their kids to another school. There isn't that commitment or willingness to stick to it.

TUEY RANKIN, ASSISTANT COACH 1997-'99:

I played for Ernie Johnson at Midland Lee. Both Coach Moegle and Coach Johnson were big on fundamentals. That was a huge thing. Both were old school, and that's not a secret. When I played for Ernie, we had to cut our hair and have it above the ears and short in the back. Kids still had to do the same thing at Monterey when I coached with Coach Moegle. Both Coach Johnson and Coach Moegle weren't into building self-esteem. Both were going to shoot you straight and not sugarcoat anything. I don't think you can coach like that today. There are too many moms and dads that would be calling. I'm not saying kids are better or worse than they used to be. We sound really old when we say "back then." It's just different now.

BURLE PETTIT, LUBBOCK SPORTSWRITER:

I was standing there waiting to talk to Bobby after practice, and a dad went over to him and said about his son, "Sometimes he responds better to compliments and praise." Bobby looked at him and said, "I'll baby a .300 hitter but I'm not babying a .190 hitter," and walked off. I don't believe I saw that dad at practice ever again.

FRED OLIVER, MHS COACH 2000-'09:

A story that sticks with me is one that all coaches have – a parent steps in and wants to have a meeting about a lack of playing time. A mother came to Coach Moegle and asked for a conference. His reply was, "Ma'am, the only conference I have is with that pitcher on the mound." So, the mother didn't get a conference, but the pitcher did.

MARK GRIFFIN '72:

I think it is human nature that if our parents try to be tough on us it's effective for a while, but then it kind of loses some of its value. When we hear it from a third person – it could be the first thing that our dad had said – we would hear it differently and have a different appreciation for it. In that respect, I think he probably played a role in assisting mothers and fathers of boys on his team.

JOHN DUDLEY '62, ASSISTANT COACH 1968-'72:

If a dad were to try to push his son as hard as Coach Moegle pushed us as players, the son is not going to respond to dad like he would to Coach Moegle. But what Coach Moegle was able to achieve was to get that son to perform at a level that the dad wanted to see. He was the guy who could do that job, and if any resentment was borne by anybody, it would be by Coach Moegle.

JIM BOB DARNELL '66:

Being a parent of a kid who played for him was frustrating. One of the times I got really mad at him as a parent was when Jared was a junior at Monterey. Jared's grandparents on my wife's side lived outside of Washington, D.C. The first time they ever saw him play was in a game over at Coronado. I don't remember what inning it was, but the 3rd baseman made a bad throw to Jared at 2nd and the umpire ruled that Jared hadn't touched the bag.

Jared stopped and didn't throw the ball to 1st base, and Coach Moegle took him out of the game. That was the only game his grandparents ever saw him play. I don't know if Coach Moegle knew his grandparents were at the game or not, but after the game I was livid. He said, "He made a mental mistake." I said, "Yep, we made a lot of mental mistakes but you never took us out for that."

KELLER SMITH '63:

There was never any question who was in charge. Discipline was a major part of his coaching makeup. It was one of the big arrows in his quiver.

COACH MOEGLE:

I was reprimanded once by my principal. He told me that I could never be an administrator because I didn't have enough gray in the middle. It was my second year at Monterey, and I cut a kid who wanted to go skiing and not play baseball. He was the son of a school board member. I was reprimanded by the principal, but he understood why I did it and that got me started.

GARY ASHBY '73:

He didn't keep people just to keep them. He didn't keep them because their dad was on the school board or because their dad had a lot of money and could pitch in and buy this or that. If he thought somebody could fit a role or develop into something that could help the program, he would keep them.

LARRY HAYS, LCU & TTU COACH '71-2008:

The thing he did better than every coach around was he kept the parents out of it. You just look at the poor coaches today and they can't do it. But if he was still coaching, they'd still be out of it. That's the thing he would do. That is an important thing for kids to see – that mom and dad can't help me and I've got to do it myself. He might hate the dad, but if the kid was good enough, he would play. And he might love the dad and not play the kid.

JIM BOB DARNELL '66:

He taught us to play the game the right way. He had certain rules and he didn't bend those rules. I remember some guys wanted to go skiing one time. (Shaking his head) I was like, "I can't do it."

He was hard to play for … I don't think I ever talked to my parents about this, but I know they moved us into the Monterey district so we could go to school there. But in a way they probably wanted us to be playing for Coach Moegle because of what they'd heard about him. I tell people all the time that the three people who had the biggest influence on my life are my dad, Coach Moegle and Bill Dean. Bill Dean should get a lot of credit for Coach Moegle's success because he steered a lot of players his way. When we were 10, 11, 12 years old, we don't think about that stuff. But when I look back on it, I realize that Bill Dean and Bill Boyd loved baseball and enjoyed teaching kids how to play the game. The ages of 12 to 15 aren't the easiest times of our life, and I look back on that and I'm glad that I came into contact with all three of those men.

JOHN DUDLEY '62, ASSISTANT COACH 1968-'72:

It seems like in this day and age, as a coach we have to explain exactly why we're doing things and lay it all out so everybody understands the justification for things. When Coach Moegle first started and I was playing for him, there were no questions asked, and we did it because we wanted to be a part of that program.

TRAVIS WALDEN '81, ASSISTANT COACH 1989-'94:

There wasn't a more talented part of Texas in terms of baseball, and some of those players were getting cut. I see a lot of coaches who are afraid to motivate for whatever reason. He wasn't afraid of anything or anybody and he was going to attack the situation and do what was right for the team.

GARY HUGHES '65:

He was quick to cut you from the team, and I know that was a source of irritation to many parents over the years. But I think the fact that he expected you to make an effort and to perform and to live up to a certain standard shouldn't have been a surprise. He just wouldn't accept anything less than your best.

NATHAN SWINDLE '81:

He thought through all that stuff – haircuts, the bleachers, all that stuff. To him that was a way of weeding people out. I heard him say it several times – if it wasn't important enough for a kid to get a haircut, I don't want him out here. It was all pretty calculated and cut and dried, for sure.

HUNTER LANKFORD '87:

All of the victories, championships, accolades and even the few losses are easy to reflect on and are naturally etched in my memory of playing for Coach Moegle at Monterey. What's important about being a part of a successful program, and most certainly what is most important about being one of Coach Moegle's players, is the responsibility we had for becoming one of the "Moegle men," remaining one of the "Moegle men," and leading as one of the "Moegle men." Making the varsity as a sophomore, much less at all, was a very high honor. Going through tryouts and making the team under Coach Moegle was hard and to this day there are guys who are bitter about not making the team or getting kicked off.

You would not make the team without the skills, and you would get kicked off the team for not adhering to his rules and principles. Whether it be your haircut or attitude, quickly you realized the responsibility of what it meant to wear that uniform.

The expectation was about effort and hard work, not winning. Such as life, hard work, maximum effort and around-the-clock accountability for good decisions are what Coach Moegle expected. Certainly it is hard for some to understand how it is encouraging to hear, "You can't run. You can't throw. You can't hit. Where are you gonna play?"

But for the few of us who had the benefit of being on the receiving end of that eloquently delivered criticism, it fueled us. It motivated us. We felt responsible for working harder and earning our positions. And as our seniority took hold as upperclassmen, we felt the responsibility of knowing that the program was ours and we needed to lead by example and pass it to the up and comers.

JIMMY SHANKLE '74:

He would cull out the guys that didn't really, really, really want to be there. If a guy was talented but didn't want to work, it wasn't for him. But if a kid was less talented but worked hard, he could be a player at Monterey by his junior or senior year. If he was talented and he worked hard, he could be a great player. The conditioning was all a part of becoming a man and learning the discipline it took to be a part of Monterey baseball.

GARY ASHBY '73:

I remember one basketball player who came out after basketball season. He was a good ballplayer and would have probably started in center field. He came to practice the first day and Coach Moegle told him he'd need to get a haircut. He said, "Yessir, I'll get a haircut." He came back the next day and Coach told him, "No, I told you to get a HAIRCUT." In other words, it wasn't short enough. The kid said he wasn't going to cut any more off and Coach told him he wasn't going to play baseball. There's your starting center fielder going out the door. There wasn't any bend in it.

JACK DALE, BROADCASTER:

Coach Moegle could cause players to go far, far above anything that they probably even thought they could achieve. Because of the leadership of Coach Moegle, he could bring them to those heights. Not just single seasons but for 40 years with almost a different set of kids every year. You know there were some great challenges with some of those kids, and some of those challenges he was able to work through. Some were unreachable and went to try another sport.

JIMMY SHANKLE '74:

"To the road and back" during practice meant that when somebody made a bad throw, everybody dropped their gloves and ran to the road and back. So if the 3rd baseman had a bad day and air-mailed two or three of them, the peer pressure was applied. We practiced with more pressure than we had to play under, because he made practices harder than our games, which were a whole lot easier than the practices.

TRAVIS WALDEN '81, ASSISTANT COACH 1989-'94:

With as much pressure as he put on us every day, we just learned to get through it. There wasn't one specific thing he was going to say that would knock us down. We got to where we hardened and got through it.

JOHN DUDLEY '62, ASSISTANT COACH 1968-'72:

For the most part, Coach Moegle tried to bring out the best in us by putting as much pressure on us as he could. At the time as players, you wondered why he was doing that to us. What we didn't realize was he was trying to put us in a pressure situation in practice, and if we could handle that we could handle what we would face in a ballgame. Looking back on it now, it's easy to see the method to his madness. He was extremely successful with this.

GARY HUGHES '65:

On certain days when we took infield, if there were mistakes made, everyone would run. It would cause all of us to be completely supportive and rooting for every position because we did not want any mistakes made. It put some pressure on some people but that also prepared us for those tough game conditions when we were in the playoffs. We were a lot more likely to make that play after having been in those pressure situations from our teammates in practice when a mistake meant we would run.

GARY ASHBY '73:

Jimmy Shankle was throwing up from running one day and Coach Moegle told him, "Don't worry Shankle, you'll pass out before you die." So I guess that was sort of what we lived by every day. We knew we would pass out before we died. (smiling)

JEFF HARP '78:

Coach Moegle was running us one day. Kelly Smith was a sophomore and he was wheezing and bent over and hurting. Coach told him, "Don't worry, Kelly. You'll pass out before you die." (laughing)

JIMMY SHANKLE '74:

"To the road and back" – Anybody who ever played for Coach Moegle knows that phrase well. It was from the practice field through what is now the tennis courts to the parking lot and back. We had to do that "up and back" three times at the end of practice once or twice a week. And we had an assigned time. If we were having a bad infield, or if we weren't doing the right thing as we were hitting, or if we came out with a lousy attitude, we went to the road and back however many times until it got fixed.

"To the road and back" was near and dear to us, and we didn't want those during practice because we knew we were also going to do it after practice. He would give us a time to beat, and the time was less and less as the season went along because we were expected to be in better shape.

Tommy McIntyre could come back from being hurt, and we'd do three to the road and backs on the first day and he'd beat everybody by 100 yards. It always burned me up that no matter how good of shape we were in, he could come out after being in a cast for two months and beat everybody by 100 yards. That's how great of an athlete he was.

GARY ASHBY '73:

We'd drop our gloves and run to the parking lot and back. Somebody would throw one away and we'd drop our gloves and go again. I played 1st base and was closer to the road than the left fielder and 3rd baseman who would run even further.

JEFF HARP '78:

I'll talk to my parents on the phone after a practice (after I started coaching) and they'll ask me how it went. I'll tell them, "I had to pull a 'Coach Moegle' on them." My dad will then ask, "How much did you run them?" I'll tell them, "A lot."

MARK GRIFFIN '72:

"To the road and back." That was Coach Moegle's attention grabber. If there was a need to get our undivided attention, he would send us to the road and back. We practiced on campus at that time and he would send us east to the parking lot, which was around 200 to 300 yards there and back. That was his way of getting our attention and sending direct messages.

Subtlety was not part of his makeup, so we knew exactly what was expected of us, and if we didn't perform to a certain level, it wasn't going to be pretty. Having come from Lubbock High over to Monterey, the first couple weeks, I wondered if I was on the baseball team or the track team. It seemed like we ran a whole lot.

But that was his way of mentally and physically conditioning us for the games.

Quite frankly, I think the practices were more challenging than the games. The games became fun to us because of the way he made us practice so hard, and the conditioning was part of it. "To the road and back" will always carry a special memory to me because of why it happened and, unfortunately, the number of times it had to happen. (laughing)

KELLER SMITH '63:

"To the road and back" was another way we ran. When there were continual bad performances during practices, he would stop practice and send everyone to the road and back. It was a good distance down there and back.

So let's just say we were not performing up to par, and he was hitting infield practice and we made a bunch of errors. He would say, "The next error and you guys are going to the road and back." We would run down there and back and of course our tongues were hanging out. Then somebody makes another error and here we go again. It was a self-perpetuating cycle. The more you ran, the more tired you got, and the more errors you would make. (laughing)

The other thing we would do was called "10 around." It meant 10 times around the bases. We'd start at home plate and be expected to run full speed around the bases. It was specific punishment for losing a ballgame we shouldn't have lost. If we pulled a stunt like that, we knew the week on the practice field would mean "10 around." That was a tongue-dragger, for sure.

RON REEVES '78:

I definitely remember running bleachers and quarters and three "to the road and backs." I remember running a bunch and being in shape. I remember searching for the lost baseballs after practice. I think Dana Rieger finally figured out to have a couple balls ratholed somewhere so we wouldn't have to run if we came up short. I'll bet every group did that sort of thing.

NATHAN SWINDLE '81:

We hid balls and would keep spares around, because at the end of practice he would count the balls and if we didn't have 35 balls in the bucket we would have to run. We would keep spare balls in our bag in case we couldn't find one.

JEFF HORN '96:

If we were taking infield and things weren't going as they should, in his later years he wouldn't even have to really say "to the road and back." He would just take his fungo and point toward the road and we would take off. In the '90s, he had gone from being so demonstrative with his voice to just the looks he would give us. I think that we caught some of the worst looks and not the vocal side. He definitely could look at us and make us melt.

NATHAN SWINDLE '81:

I think we've all heard that he mellowed over time. By the time I got there, it wasn't so much dressing us down if we screwed up. We didn't want to screw up, and if we did it only took a look or a couple words because we didn't want to disappoint him.

MARK GRIFFIN '72:

Our attention to detail was vastly improved after those running sessions. It was an effective technique to get us in shape, but I think it was more about the mental toughness he was trying to impart to us.

TRAVIS WALDEN '81, ASSISTANT COACH 1989–'94:

I respected that he showed up every day with enough intensity to get after us when we didn't do it right. There was never a day where he gave us slack. Every day we were aware of that and went out with some work ethic and toughness, and I really believe that's why he has the record he has.

COACH MOEGLE:

We always felt that we were at the top of the list, and when we took the field, they (the other team) had to look up at us. I felt like if we ever got down to where we were voicing an opinion or taunting or teasing that we had lowered ourselves to another level. I just wouldn't allow the kids to do that and we would try to be the example-setter. We didn't throw bats and helmets and all that kind of stuff that became popular later in my career. I tried to teach the kids that heckling from the opponents meant that we were doing something well. We just tried to do our thing consistently from a high level and let everyone else play up to our standards.

TRAVIS WALDEN '81, ASSISTANT COACH 1989-'94:

It was us against the world, because everybody wanted to beat Monterey. He had established a tradition before I'd gotten there that everybody was after us and everybody wanted to beat us and that we were up against everybody.

JEFF HORN '96:

Anytime Monterey was playing baseball, people were going to show up on the opposing team wanting to beat us, because we were the best around and had been the best for a long time. That was something that the new groups every year had to get used to – bringing that level of intensity to the park because Monterey baseball was kind of like the Yankees, and everybody wanted a shot at the champs.

JIMMY SHANKLE '74:

We wanted to go out and win baseball games and play the best we could. And we did it in a class way because we had a class coach that didn't allow all the arguing with umpires, throwing helmets and not running out balls. We played the game as it was supposed to be played and kept our mouths shut and got after it.

JACK DALE, BROADCASTER:

Coach Moegle had his rules and he expected those rules to be obeyed. I've heard some of his players talk about one of those rules being that they wouldn't be mouthy or taunt the other ball club. Coach Moegle, being the gentleman that he is, wouldn't stand for that. He would make sure his players knew his stance on things like that, and I'm sure some of his players found out that wasn't a rule to be broken.

MARK GRIFFIN '72:

We didn't heckle. He wanted us there to play and not talk. We just didn't do it. That was unspoken, and anybody who did paid a dear price. His teams were going to get out there and play the game the right way and be respectful of the game and be respectful of the opponent. That's not to say we didn't want to win and be successful. We would do whatever we could within the bounds of the game to be successful. We weren't going to be sarcastic or rude. That wasn't part of his makeup and he took it personally.

GARY HUGHES '65:

He did not like us talking or mouthing off to the other team. He wanted us to show what we could do on the field. One time we had been mouthing off with the Permian players. I guess if we were going to mouth off, we'd better win the games, and we lost both games of the doubleheader. On Monday, Coach Moegle strolled through the dressing room and told us we could leave our gloves in the locker room that day. We just looked at each other and knew what that meant. We spent the afternoon running – running bases, 4-4-4s and whatever else he told us to do.

TRAVIS WALDEN '81, ASSISTANT COACH 1989-'94:

When I was coaching with him, we were at the Midland Tournament, and we had an umpire who you could say wasn't the most honest umpire. I got thrown out in about the 2nd inning, and in about the 5th inning Coach Moegle grabbed his own collar and the umpire saw it and said, "Are you calling me a choker?" Coach said, "No, I'm just fixing my collar." The guy tossed Coach Moegle and he got all over him. I think his reputation preceded him to every ballpark he ever went to, and every umpire walked out there knowing that he'd better bring his "A game" just like every player did. He brought out the best in everybody, and he made high school baseball in West Texas what it is.

JOHN DUDLEY '62, ASSISTANT COACH 1968-'72:

I think Coach Moegle always understood what he could say and what he couldn't say to umpires. I think at times he felt like there were certain umpires he could intimidate. Knowing that an umpire isn't going to chance a call, he would plant some seeds knowing that he might get a call later. He would take care of the umpires and we as players needed to focus on playing the game.

MARK GRIFFIN '72:

He said that there would be five calls by the umpire that might make or break the game. He would say, "I want all five of them. Do you understand?" (laughing)

TRAVIS WALDEN '81, ASSISTANT COACH 1989-'94:

There would be times when he didn't think he had to work the umpires, or times when he felt like he needed to. It might've been the first pitch of the game and he would bark something out of the dugout and let the umpires know he was ready to go.

His relationship with umpires was hilarious. In the time I was there as a player and coach, if a guy wanted to become an umpire, he had to be able to handle the wrath of Coach Moegle.

BURLE PETTIT, LUBBOCK SPORTSWRITER:

I believe that Bobby had a feeling that if you let a kid believe that the umpire was the one beating him, it took the responsibility off the kid. I believe that kept Bobby from getting on an umpire until he really wasn't doing his job right. Bobby expected the same kind of perfection out of the umpires that he did from the players.

JIMMY SHANKLE '74:

We didn't argue with the umpires – that was his deal. And he did a great job of it. He had won so much by the 1970s that he was a very intimidating guy for umpires. Umpires didn't want him in their face, and he didn't have to do it very often. We got the close calls at Monterey because of who our coach was.

KELLER SMITH '63:

He was easy to get along with as long as the umpire did the job properly. If he didn't do his job properly, he was going to hear from Coach Moegle. I think most of the umpires probably knew what to expect, and I think if anything they tended to stay on their toes and take care of their business. His attitude toward the players in that regard was simple. The umpires didn't have anything to do with the outcome of the game. If we got a bad umpire, we had to beat him like we were supposed to beat the other team. The umpire was no excuse.

From the players' perspective, we were never allowed any commentary, opinion or body language toward the umpire. If a player wanted to get some serious running the next week, just cross that line. If there was going to be any umpire commentary it was going to come from Coach Moegle and not us.

Certainly some of the umpires were excellent and did it because they loved it, and others were just terrible. We figured out the terrible ones and we knew what to expect. Unquestionably, there were the homers. We'd go to Borger or Midland or someplace and would run into a guy that would do his dead-level best to see that we went home a loser and that the home team won.

BURLE PETTIT, LUBBOCK SPORTSWRITER:

He said what he thought. Its isn't good of a sportswriter to say this, but there were sometimes that I didn't put something he said in the paper, simply because of how it was going to sound. But Bobby was always interesting to talk to because he had an insight that gave me a little meat for a story. And he wasn't one to sit around and worry about whether I got a good story or not. His willingness and openness made him very good copy.

Losers are losers for a reason. They aren't much fun to be around. On the rare occasion they (Monterey) lost a ballgame, I never heard him make excuses.

MARK GRIFFIN '72:

He didn't make excuses and, quite frankly, he really wasn't receptive if we were going to make excuses.

JUNE 28, 1972, COACH MOEGLE INTERVIEW WITH DAVID MURRAH OF THE SOUTHWEST COLLECTION AT TEXAS TECH UNIVERSITY:

DM: I've heard that kids today aren't like the ones 10 years ago. Do you agree? Do you have to treat kids different today than when you were a teenager?

CM: We do have different values, and we have a lot easier life over in our part of Lubbock. But kids are still the same. You throw something out there real good that they want, and they'll go to work for it. I don't care whether it's in scholastics or athletics or something in the business field, I believe that if a kid really wants something, and he really wants to pay the price, our kids are just as good (as those in previous years) right now.

They might want to grow their hair a little longer, they want a little more freedom or they want to voice themselves a little bit, but when it comes down to a competitive streak, this is where I think the kids nowadays are just as good. Plus kids are a lot smarter than they were 10 years ago. They have access to more freedom, and they pick up things real fast. If there is a change in kids, it's very slight.

DM: What discipline rules do you have?

CM: This is going to sound kind of funny, but I let the kids set up their own rules. I oversee it. But as far as the time we're gonna get in, the things we're gonna do, what our overall goals are, I let the kids set these. This way, I think they stay within the realm of, the period, or the era that we're in. I don't ever ask them to do anything that I wasn't able to do myself.

The one thing that I think has helped me is I try to be consistent. The things we did in the '60s are the things we do in the '70s. And if I'm here in the '80s, we'll still try to do it the same way. I try to be consistent with the kid. Always put the kid first, as my first goal is to help him. And to teach him something about values and morals and the competitive spirit. Kids are just as good today as they ever were.

CHAPTER 6

Success and Tradition

To be the winningest coach in the United States is phenomenal. It's a number beyond recognition.

For people who don't understand what goes into 1,100 wins – yes, it's longevity. But over a 40-year period, they had to do things right and win all those ballgames. He averaged 20-plus wins a season for all those years. That number is unbelievable.

— *Fred Oliver*

KELLER SMITH '63:

Winning is no more natural than losing. Winners win and losers lose. Winning can become a habit and losing can become a habit. In the Bobby Moegle method, there was no habitual losing. Winning was it. That's what the goal was, and that's what the target was, that's what the object was, and that's what we did. Look at his impact on the baseball program at Monterey – those statistics speak for themselves.

What a lot of people have forgotten and don't give him the credit for, is that he lifted all the athletic programs at Monterey. With him came Gerald Myers as coach of the basketball program, and soon after, James Odom became the football coach. Would Gerald Myers have had a successful basketball coaching career at Monterey without Bobby Moegle? You bet he would have. But he likely would not have done as well, if winning had not already become part of the fabric of the high school. I can assure you that was the case in the football program, which had suffered with real mediocrity for the most part, until his arrival.

This is something a lot of people do not recognize. When James was hired as head football coach, he asked Coach Moegle to join him on the varsity, and Coach Moegle remained his assistant coach for 20 years. In those 20 years, they won 68% of their games, and in the 20 years he didn't coach, they won 48% of their games. Part of that can certainly be attributed to Coach Odom, who was a great guy and a great coach, but coincidences just don't occur with that type of frequency. I mean, look at the baseball victories, the elevation of the basketball program and look at the football performance and what's the one constant? Bobby Moegle.

JOHN DUDLEY '62, ASSISTANT COACH 1968-'72:

Winning was extremely important from the standpoint of not bringing him anything personally, but more so that he wanted his team to enjoy the success. For the team to enjoy success it was going to require sacrifice from those players, and they were going to have to put in a lot of time and effort. And he was going to push and pull and bend and shape to get all those guys going in the same direction and get them to the point that they would perform at a high level. And when it's all said and done, we forget about the pain and suffering to get there, and we enjoy the success and the spoils of victory.

COACH MOEGLE:

The first state tournament I went to was in 1961. We had a good team and beat Lufkin, and they were the #1 team in the nation at the time.

It was an experience I will always remember. I don't think you could ever get 18 better kids as close knit as they were. They had gone through that first year in 1960 with me as juniors and seniors.

I had inherited one great pitcher – Donnie Bumpass. When I first came here I saw him pitch an American Legion game. He threw 36 straight strikes. He never threw a ball. He had that kind of control. I mean they were genuine pitches. Donnie actually had to learn to waste a strike. We played up in Palo Duro one time and the game only went an hour and 14 minutes. He'd just shut you down – throw strike after strike. He was competitive with anybody we played.

DONNIE BUMPASS '61:

My best game at Monterey was a pitching victory over Lufkin in the 1961 state championship semifinal. Lufkin was likely a better team that year.

KELLER SMITH '63:

I had a great seat for the state tournament games in 1961 because I was on the bench the whole time. I got to watch some terrific baseball and saw guys with hunger and other guys with fear. I had eyes as big as saucers to go to Austin and play in front of such huge crowds.

COACH MOEGLE:

We were shy of a #2 pitcher, so I had to use an infielder the next night when we played Baytown. I had a lot of problems because I didn't understand high school rules. I had come out of that pro ball stuff.

We had a pop-up behind 3rd and that ball got up in the wind. My 3rd baseman was Bumpass. He went back to field that ball and it started drifting for the stands. It was the first time we had ever played in a place that had extra stands that were covered. That wind came across there and blew that ball back behind the shortstop. Baytown got 3 runs and were up 3-1 with 2 on and 2 outs in the bottom of the 4th inning. We were sitting there in Clark Field and it started raining, and it rained and it rained, and then we heard an announcement: "This game has been called and we will resume with the same battery, the same situation tomorrow."

I had never heard of a game that was going to be continued after 3½ innings. He said it was either over or it was complete. We were starting the game with the same pitcher and the same count. The director of the UIL was Rhea Williams. I later found out that no one, I mean NO ONE, confronted Rhea Williams on ANYTHING. Boy, I challenged him up in those stands. I got chest to chest with him. Lord a mercy was I reprimanded! I mean I had set an example that was unapproachable back in those days.

We went ahead and started the game the next day with the same count on the hitter, same pitcher, same batter, same baserunners and everything. I never did understand that about high school stuff.

KELLER SMITH '63:

One of the strangest things I remember was that the state championship game was proceeding along, and we were behind 3-1. I believe the UIL had a rule that if a game was rained out after 4½ innings, it was a complete game. If it was rained out before 4½ innings, the game would be restarted the next day. I was told by James Ellis, who was pitching that night, that Coach Moegle instructed him to stall and drag it out as much as possible because it was sprinkling and he knew the rain was coming. He of course wanted the opportunity to start over again, knowing that we were behind at the time.

However, once it rained out, the UIL decided to suspend the game and resume from that point the next day, rather than restart it. We went ahead and lost the game 3-1 and will forever believe that if we had started over, we would've won the game.

DONNIE BUMPASS '61:

The 1961 state championship game that lost 3-1 was the toughest loss we had at Monterey. We were the better team. Coach Moegle deserved that victory.

JOHN DUDLEY '62, ASSISTANT COACH 1968-'72:

The 1961 ball club was good. I was a junior and didn't get to play very much because we had a very strong senior class. James Ellis, Ronald Bandy, Donnie Bumpass and Johnny Mack King – those were some really outstanding players. It was a hard-nosed ball club. That 1961 state championship game was suspended because of weather, and at the time I believe Coach Moegle was thinking that the game would be restarted.

So, it was disappointing to lose, but at the same time to finally get there and play in the state championship game was really great. I think when that game was over, everybody was down and disappointed because we believed we had a better ball club than Baytown did, particularly after getting through Lufkin to get to that point. Obviously, those feelings of disappointment disappear over time and we realized what an accomplishment it was to get there in the first place.

KELLER SMITH '63:

The guys that led the 1961 team were extraordinary as a group and as individuals. They really exerted influence on the young guys and carried with them a measure of character that became the common denominator and the expectation for those to follow. There was a huge feeling of accomplishment, simply that we had gone to state and had won the first game and had come very close to winning a state championship. Obviously, we would have preferred to come back to town and have a tickertape parade and so forth. But I don't think there was a negative attitude about the loss. There certainly wasn't in the community.

COACH MOEGLE:

In '63, I took another real fine group of kids to Austin — we were 34-4 when we went down there. I felt like we really had a chance of winning because we had been to the Legion tournaments the year before. We got down there and had a real bad night the first night and got beat by Bellaire 3-1. But we were in the process of learning how to go to the state tournament.

JIM BOB DARNELL '66:

When we played at Borger and Pampa we would share the bus up there with Lubbock High. Ol' Stogie Austin was our bus driver. We would sit on one side of the bus and Lubbock High would sit on the other side of the bus. We never talked to them and they never talked to us. (Laughing) It was strange. When we would play the Amarillo schools, it was the same way. The bus driver would drop one team off at one school then go to the other school and drop the other team.

Later in college, I had a few friends who had gone to Lubbock High. We always joked about that. We never talked to them on those trips because they were the enemy. Today, kids don't do that. But then, we didn't have any association with the other high schools.

GARY HUGHES '65:

When we saw the success, we realized later that had he not been as hard on us and as demanding as he was to get the best from us, we would not have won the championships and had the opportunity to be in the key games that we were.

JIM BOB DARNELL '66

(Regarding the final game of the '65 season – a 1-0 loss to El Paso Austin in 15 innings in El Paso. MHS had won the first game of the series in Lubbock on a Monday, then lost in El Paso on Wednesday to set the stage for the finale on Thursday.)

After the first game in El Paso, Robert Junell's father took us out to dinner. He was president of a bank in Lubbock and was also associated with a bank in El Paso. He took us to dinner at the bank. That's all I remember from the first game down there, other than the umpires being "less than partial."

The second game in El Paso (the final game of the series) is obviously the one we all talk about. I didn't remember exactly which inning I was tossed until I recently saw a newspaper article from the game. It was the 11th inning and obviously the score was 0-0. They had a runner on 1st and laid down a bunt. I fielded the bunt and tagged the runner as he was running down the 1st base line, but the umpire called him safe. He said something like, "Why did you look back at the runner – the guy running to 1st base?" I had looked at the runner going to 2nd base after I tagged him, but I don't recall looking at the runner going to 1st after I tagged him. Anyway, I don't know what I said – I never ever used profanity toward him or any umpire in any game I played in.

The next thing I knew, he said, "#8 is ejected from the game." (#8 was Robert Junell.) And that's what set Coach Moegle off, because Robert was standing out in right field about 150 feet away from the umpire. Gene Graham, our 2nd baseman, is the one who said whatever it was the umpire assumed Robert said. We all thought he threw Robert out because he had 2 hits in the game.

The thing I remember the most about the game is not that play, other than the fact that Mike (Parker) dropped the fly ball in the 15th inning, and we've never ever let him forget about that (smiling). Unfortunately, Mike made a comment after the game back at the hotel – something to the effect of, "Well, there's always next year." I don't know how well you know Robert Junell, but he's pretty intense. He went ballistic because he was a senior and he wasn't going to be back next year. He was ready to kill Mike at that point in time.

Gary Hughes and Tommy Toombs ... I can't even talk about it to this day ... both pitched two of the best games I've ever seen pitched, because they basically had to throw the ball right down the middle of the plate to get a strike called. We knew before we ever went out there that it might happen, because Coach Moegle had played there earlier in his time at Monterey. He warned us about that. And I don't want to take anything away from Bob Arnold. Just to do what he did was pretty amazing. But we had a really good team that year.

(In the final two games on consecutive days, El Paso Austin left-hander Bob Arnold pitched 22 shutout innings, allowing only 6 hits and whiffing an astounding 46.)

My dad never missed a game, but he decided not to go to those two games, because he said, "We'll just go to Austin." (long pause) He made for sure that never happened with my little brother. It was heart-wrenching.

It was ironic ... When my son, Jared, was a junior (in 1998), they had to play a playoff game in El Paso. When they won I was so relieved. He had heard all those stories.

One of the funniest stories, or at least it was to me, was when Jared was probably about 10 or 11 years old. Mike Parker, our center fielder, had a daughter who came to Tech to play golf. I played golf out at Hillcrest then and Mike and his brother-in-law were there. I introduced Mike to Jared and Jared said, "Is he the one who dropped the fly ball?" Of course, Jared had heard the story a jillion times. I said, "Yep, he's the one." I always felt bad about that, because Mike is a great guy. He would give anything to change that moment, and he was a great player. I don't remember him ever dropping a fly ball other than that one.

COACH MOEGLE:

My next appearance was in 1970 and we got beat in the semifinals 2-0 by Aldine High School out of Houston. The state tournament was always an adverse situation, especially when we had to go against the Houston schools. They were so big and they had the weather, year-round programs and feeder systems. They had so much more to offer than we did and to know that we could compete with those people year in and year out was really gratifying.

In 1971, we got beat in the state finals by Bellaire, 5-4. They had a left-handed hitter double down the 3rd base line late in the game to drive in 2 runs and beat us.

GARY ASHBY '73:

In the state championship game in 1971, we faced Houston Bellaire and Coach Ray Knoblauch. He was the south Texas version of Coach Moegle and had made multiple trips to the state tournament and had won state championships. But what I really remember about that game as a 16-year-old sophomore was missing a pop-up. The infield fly rule assured that the batter was out, but when I missed the pop-up the baserunners advanced from 1st and 2nd to 2nd and 3rd. The next guy singled and so instead of one guy scoring, two guys scored. We eventually lost the game by 1 run.

I remember the sheer disappointment of getting there and not getting it done. When you're that age, you don't realize that it's such an accomplishment to get there. You want to get it done and we didn't get it done. He had other teams that had been there and not gotten it done, so we felt disappointment for not only ourselves but also for Coach Moegle and Coach Dudley because of how hard we worked. At the hotel after the game I remember telling Coach Dudley, "Don't worry, Coach, we are going to win it next year."

In the 1972 state championship game, which was a rematch with Bellaire and Coach Knoblauch, I didn't miss a pop-up this time, and Donnie Moore pitched "lights out" in relief and we won 2-1.

COACH MOEGLE:

In 1972, we won our first state championship. This was the beginning. It took five different trips to get over the hump and win a state championship. Mark Griffin hit a triple off Jim Gideon to win it 2-1, with Donnie Moore being one of the dominant pitchers in the state of Texas. That was the beginning of us learning how to win down there.

MARK GRIFFIN '72:

We were standing in the dugout right before the state championship game about to go out and play Bellaire, and for the life of me I don't understand why Coach Moegle said this, but he said something to the effect of, "I don't think you guys have a chance so just go do the best you can." All that did was make everybody mad. In retrospect, it was a genius psychological ploy on his part. It made everybody go out and play harder because we knew we had a chance to win that game.

GARY ASHBY '73:

I think the difference between us winning in '72 and not winning in '71 was Mark Griffin's triple. Had he lined out to the center fielder and not hit the triple, I might be one of the Buffalo Bills who could get there but couldn't win it. But Griffin did hit the triple and Donnie Moore did shut them down at the end of the game. Mark Scott threw five pitches in the championship and was taken out, then Glen Yarbrough came in and kept it close until Donnie took over, because Donnie couldn't throw every inning. (smiling) We had a little bit of luck that year ... We didn't have a sophomore first baseman miss a pop-up that year (laughing), so we had a little bit of luck.

MARK GRIFFIN '72:

It was the top of the 7th and as best I can remember, Tommy McIntyre got on and Jimmy Killion bunted him over to 2nd, and it was my turn to hit with 2 outs. They started a left-handed pitcher and then brought in Jim Gideon, who was their ace. He was a senior and was going to be a high draft choice and would later be a great pitcher at The University of Texas. Jim had come in relief in the 5th inning and struck me out on fastballs. I guess Jim outsmarted himself because he hung a curveball to me on the first pitch. Why he threw me a curveball I don't know, because I would have kept throwing me fastballs. I was fortunate to line it to the gap at right-center to score Tommy and I ended up with a triple.

It was pretty exciting. We were ahead 2-1. Donnie came out in the bottom of the 7th, and they got a hit, bunted him over, then a walk and an infield hit. The bases were loaded and there was 1 out, and he's got a 3-2 count on Gideon. Donnie struck him out and then faced Duncan Shanklin. He was an outstanding player, but Donnie struck him out to end it. If he had walked him, or gave up a hit, we would have either tied or lost the ballgame. So it was pretty exciting.

We had an interesting episode that probably kept us from being able to do a lot of the fun things we wanted to do following the championship game. During that exciting 7th inning, Bobby Evans and Larry Horn were playing catch down the foul line. Larry was a big, strong sophomore, and he was probably getting loose to come in to play 3rd base or even pitch. They were both trying to watch the game and warm up, and Bobby turned to watch a pitch. Larry didn't see him turn his head and threw and hit him right in the nose with the ball.

So our first stop right after the championship game was at Brackenridge Hospital to drop Bobby off so the doctor could stop the bleeding and set his nose. That delayed the celebration a little bit, but as I recall we went back to the hotel and some people had pizza and we went and ate somewhere. Nobody was man enough to get Coach Moegle and throw him in the pool or do anything else to him, because we still had to get home somehow and he was not averse to having people find their own transportation home if they didn't handle themselves appropriately. (laughing) So we celebrated among ourselves as much as anything.

COACH MOEGLE:

I wasn't very superstitious. I always believed in being prepared – prepare the best and see what happens. In 1972, we go into the playoffs and I've got one of the outstanding pitchers in the state of Texas and several other kids and it really gives us a chance.

It never did happen again, but in that particular year when we went into the playoffs, I found an ol' copper penny laying around and put it in my pocket and didn't think anything of it. I go into the second ballgame and maybe on the parking lot at the school or somewhere I find another penny.

It goes on and here we are at Nelson Field in Austin and we're playing for the state championship and I've looked all day long for a penny. We are taking batting practice and I'm just going crazy trying to find a penny. And sure as the Lord helps me, I was wandering around on the old practice field west of the main ballpark and we're taking batting practice – I didn't even fungo because I was looking for that penny. I'm walking out by 2nd base on the skinned infield part and here's an old dark penny laying out there to the right of the bag. Somebody put that penny there, or I was very lucky.

I had found my penny and we went ahead and won the state championship. It was one of those real enlightening times. I think I've told the kids the story since then, and of course it registered with them that I was real superstitious. I wasn't superstitious. It was just that it happened in that year and it was the first time we won the state championship.

I was definitely trying to find that penny. To be truthful, I had given up on the fact I was going to find one. There was no chance on earth that I would find that penny on the infield. I still pick up pennies today.

MARK GRIFFIN '72:

During batting practice at the Reagan High School field before the ('72) state championship game, Coach Moegle was scrambling around. He was nervous as a cat. Now I know why. He couldn't find a penny. Well finally he was wandering around by 2nd base or somewhere and he found the penny. All of sudden things just kind of smoothed out after that.

JIMMY SHANKLE '74:

In the 1972 state championship game, we were up 1 run in the bottom of the 7th inning. It was going to be Coach Moegle's first state championship and Monterey's first state championship. The bases were loaded with two out. Donnie (Moore) looked over to Coach Moegle and motioned him to the mound. I'm thinking, "Oh my goodness," although back then I probably didn't think, "Oh my goodness." I thought we were in trouble.

During the conference at the mound, Donnie told Coach Moegle, "I'm nervous." Coach Moegle said, "Donnie, I'm nervous, too. Let's strike this guy out and win this thing." I was thinking to myself, "They think they're nervous." I was a sophomore so my tail was a little tight, too. As history would have it, Donnie struck him out and we won the state championship. The triple Griffin hit in the right-center gap to score Tommy McIntyre was huge, but my memory was about the three of us meeting on the mound. I've got news for you – we were all nervous. I can't believe Coach Moegle said he was nervous. (laughing)

MARK GRIFFIN '72:

He was an expert and he so overmatched his competition. Coach Knoblauch at Houston Bellaire and maybe Coach Blackburn at Abilene – those guys were true baseball men like Coach Moegle. The rest of the time, typically you'd have assistant football coaches coaching baseball. Coach Moegle was so far ahead of those guys that it wasn't even fair.

Coach Knoblauch and Coach Moegle were peers. They were in competition with each other. I had the chance to compare notes about Coach Moegle and Coach Knoblauch with Jim Gideon when we were roommates at Texas. He had played for Knoblauch at Bellaire and the similarities between the two coaches were dramatic – very disciplined, solid baseball men. They were idolized to a large degree. As the years went on, if you were interested in baseball, that was where you were going to play – Houston Bellaire or Lubbock Monterey.

JIMMY SHANKLE '74:

Mark Griffin hit the triple off Jim Gideon, and they would later be teammates on the 1975 UT national championship team. McIntyre was on 2nd base and he could fly, and Mark hit one that kept going and kept going and kept going. Right field at Nelson Park had a hill and they couldn't catch the ball. McIntyre scored. That was the first year Worth came out with the aluminum bat and it weighed about 39 ounces. If you got the head through, you could really hit it. But you had to get the head through.

I don't think that was an aluminum bat hit, because Mark hit that ball well. The difference in us winning that ballgame was the swing of the bat from Mark Griffin. His dad, Rip Griffin, was a prince of guy. He loved baseball. Rip couldn't be found if it was during the ballgame. He couldn't sit in the stands, so he would go waaaaaayyyyyyy down the foul line and watch.

MARK GRIFFIN '72:

The first aluminum bat was heavy and it made a real distinctive "PING!" when you hit it – not like what you hear from bats today. It had to be one of the first-generation aluminum bats out there. We were all enamored with the bat because we felt like the ball jumped off the bat a little better than wood. And we all used it. It had a rubber grip and I can remember day after day rubbing blisters off my thumb from the rubber.

Back then Coach Moegle didn't allow us to wear batting gloves, so we just had our bare hands on the bat. I can remember putting on Band-aids and salve and anything else I could think of. It was really funny because when we'd play a team that hadn't heard it, those catchers were in for an awakening when they first heard it "PING."

It was a heavier bat. I had to choke up. A really good fastball pitcher who could pitch inside to me would cause trouble for me because it had to be at least 34 to 36 ounces. It was a heavy bat, but when we made good, solid contact, that ball would jump.

I don't know if any other teams were using aluminum bats. I don't recall that any of our playoff opponents or, moving through the state tournament, anyone else used a metal bat. Obviously the UIL was OK with it, but I think predominantly everyone at that time was using wood bats. Frankly, when I went off to UT and played, it was probably my junior year before the NCAA allowed the metal bats.

COACH MOEGLE:

I had a rep call me and say, "They've got a new bat coming out and it's made of aluminum. Would you like to try one?" I said that I certainly would like to try one. I asked if the bats were legal and he said they were, but that nobody had one in Texas yet. He said it was called an "Instructo."

He told me he was going to Kansas City and would bring us a bat, the first aluminum bat in the state of Texas. It was just a piece of aluminum tubing that had a cap on the end. They had tapered the handle with a rubber sleeve over it. It was extremely heavy, and it made a tremendous "clank" when they hit it. We had been carrying 25 to 30 wood bats in a bag with us and we were now carrying 2 or 3 wood bats, the aluminum bat and a fungo.

GARY ASHBY '73:

We used the very first aluminum bat in Texas and boy, it would just go "PING!" And everywhere we'd go they'd say we couldn't use the bat and Coach Moegle would show them the rule that we could use it. That bat is down in Waco at the Texas Sports Hall of Fame now as part of Coach Moegle's exhibit. The bat weighed about 36 ounces. It was eight ounces heavier than what these kids use today. But we all had to use it. (laughing)

That was my junior year and I'd go up there with that big ol' gray bat. In fact, you might not even think it's a bat. We could set it on its end and it would just stand there. The fact that we had an aluminum bat and nobody else had one ... And why nobody else had one, I don't know, other than Coach Moegle was a "cutting edge, attention to detail guy."

We could use the bat, and we did use it. I guess everybody else didn't get the memo that they could use them. I think the bat definitely had some properties that helped. Because with aluminum we could get hits off our fists that we couldn't get with wood. And we could hit a lot of balls on cold days with aluminum, whereas with wood sometimes our hands would get what Mark Griffin would call "bees in the bat," because our hands would sting on cold days.

Anybody who plays ball in West Texas knows you'll play on some cold days.

COACH MOEGLE:

The aluminum bat had been such a big deal at the state tournament that by the time I got back to Lubbock my phone was ringing with folks wondering where they could get one. That was the introduction of the aluminum bat in the state of Texas. It is now in the Texas Sports Hall of Fame display in Waco.

MIKE CRUTCHER '68, ASSISTANT COACH 1973-'78, 1982-'85:

Most people don't remember this, but when I was student teaching at Monterey I umpired baseball for money because I wasn't getting paid to student teach. I umpired a bunch of the 1972 games when Donnie Moore pitched, and I was usually behind the plate. Moore loved me back there because when I was behind the plate you'd better be swinging. I'm still that way today – I want them swinging.

I had one complaint in '72 and it was by the coach at Hereford. His name was Mike Mitchell. After the game, Mitchell talked to Coach Moegle about my umpiring and Coach Moegle told him he should talk to me about it because he thought I would appreciate the constructive criticism. He wasn't after my rear or anything. He said to me, "I didn't think you gave my pitcher the same pitches as you gave Donnie Moore." I'll never forget what I said back to him. I'll never forget this. I said, "Coach, he wasn't throwing the same pitches that Donnie Moore was." Of course, the next day I was at school student teaching and Coach Moegle said, "Man, that was a good answer. Where did you come up with that?" I said, "I don't know. I just thought it was a good answer." (smiling)

MARK GRIFFIN '72:

That 1972 state championship game really began the process of Coach Moegle getting not only statewide but probably regional or national recognition. While he previously had teams that had been in the state tournament, they had always come up short. In fact, the year before in '71, Bellaire beat Monterey for the state championship, so he had been down that aisle a number of times. I think the state championship established once and for all the identity of the Monterey baseball program. I think from that point forward, the results speak for themselves. Not that they didn't beforehand, because they had excellent teams, but they just hadn't been lucky enough or fortunate enough to win the championship. My sense of it is that the dynamics of the program and the way it was perceived changed from that day forward.'

Coach Moegle - 1972

JIMMY SHANKLE '74:

The rival for Monterey High School baseball was Houston Bellaire and Ray Knoblauch. They started the Texas High School Baseball Association together and they were big buds. In 1971, Bellaire had beat Monterey in the state championship game, and in '72 we beat Ray Knoblauch and Houston Bellaire. So that was a huge rivalry between friends. The other one I remember from my era was Ernie Johnson and Midland Lee High School.

We used to play those guys every year, at least twice a year. They always had good teams and really good athletes. I'll never forget ... Ernie called a squeeze bunt with a left-handed hitter at the plate and a man on 3rd. We pitch out and I get the ball and tag the guy out and the ballgame's over. I'll never forget Coach Moegle, who really respected Coach Johnson. He said, "Shank, as good a baseball man as he is, I can't believe he tried to squeeze with a left-handed hitter." That was Coach Moegle – he played percentages and high-quality baseball. That disappointed him because he and Ernie were good friends and he really respected him. A squeeze with a left-handed hitter wasn't what you were supposed to do.

MIKE CRUTCHER '68, ASSISTANT COACH 1973-'78, 1982-'85:

In my first or second year of coaching, I think we were down at Permian. Of course, that was Shankle's group and they could really hit, plus they were swinging those early aluminum bats with the loud "PING." I used to throw batting practice before the games to those guys without an "L screen."

Shankle hit one back at me and it hit me in the throat. Everyone ran out there to check on me and I wasn't going to dare let on that I was hurt. I couldn't swallow and thought my windpipe was crushed! So the next day at school in the office Coach Moegle told me he had me fixed up. He went and got a hurdle and threw a net over it. (laughing) When we'd take it on the bus we'd tuck it in there somewhere. It would come up to my thighs so when I threw BP I'd throw one and duck to get behind that thing.

That was a group of big kids that could wear it out. In that '74 state championship team photo, I'm on the back row with those guys and I was 6'3" looking up at that group.

STEVE HARR '73:

I cried the day I pitched and lost our regional final game against Midland High in 1973. I apologized to Coach Moegle after the game for letting him down. He was gracious and simply said we win together and lose together and all you can do is leave it all on the field.

MIKE CRUTCHER '68, ASSISTANT COACH 1973-'78, 1982-'85:

Marlin Hamilton might be the best athlete I ever coached. He was a great athlete. When he was a senior he was our leadoff guy. We were in the playoffs in the Dudley Dome in El Paso and he crushed one on the road out there to start the game. He was a little guy but, boy, he could play. He lifted weights and had jacked-up arms. He hit that ball over 400 feet. That '74 group with Shankle and Alburtis could get it.

JIMMY SHANKLE '74:

In 1974 we won the state championship. It was a great moment for our team. We were 6-4 after 10 games, then we won 30 games in a row, including the state championship game. Richard Bowles, a sophomore, pinch hit a 3-run home run and we won the ballgame 4-3 over Spring Woods.

After the ballgame, we went back to the motel. We were all in our uniforms and everybody was gonna get in the pool. I looked at Coach Moegle and he looked at me and said, "Only you, Shank." We grabbed hands and bear hugged and went in the pool together. That was big. When he said, "Only you, Shank," that meant only I could've jerked him in that pool, because in 1972 he didn't go in the pool. But in 1974 he went in the pool with me, and with our other guys who were in there with us. It was a pretty special time for an 18-year-old kid to be able to go in the pool with someone we so highly respected.

COACH MOEGLE:

In 1974, we went back to the state tournament with a different group of kids than were there in 1972, although we still had a couple kids who started in '72. We won 30 games in a row in '74 to get back to Austin. In the 6th inning, I put in a 10th grader named Richard Bowles to pinch hit and he hit a 3-run homer to win the state championship.

JIMMY SHANKLE '74:

The thing that comes to mind the clearest and the brightest about the '74 state championship game is the 3-run homer that Richard Bowles pinch hit. He was a sophomore and wasn't a regular player. Coach Moegle pinch hit him I believe for Richard Holt, who was our 2nd baseman all year long and played steady defense and had done a good job at the plate. But Bowles was a good hitter and a really good athlete and good player who went on to play at Lubbock Christian for four years. He came in and pinch hit with two guys on. I don't remember the count but I remember where the ball ended up. He hit it over the left-center field fence. I've seen the tape of it and I'm coming out of the dugout in my shin guards and I'm doing somersaults as he's crossing home plate.

For us, he was the most unlikely guy to do that ... We had Larry Horn, myself and Rocky Alburtis as the 3-4-5 hole hitters who had combined for 30 home runs, which was an unheard of amount, and all of us played pro ball later on ... And we had a sophomore who won it for us. He hit the home run and we won the ballgame and the state championship. Coach Moegle made the right move at the right time with the right guy.

Did we question the move of putting Bowles in there? Not anybody I know of would've questioned the move. If you questioned his moves, you wouldn't play long. We knew we had the best guy on our side in the dugout, and hopefully we had the best players. When Coach Moegle said the sky was black, then the sky was black and that's pretty well the way it went. He had faith in us as players and we definitely had faith in him as our coach.

LARRY HAYS, LCU & TTU COACH '71-2008:

His teams in the early '70s had everything – great arms and hitters and all that. When he had Gardner, Moore, Shankle and Horn, I would go out there and think that if I had every one of them I could win a national championship. When he'd have a guy that couldn't do one thing, he could hide him and handle it and have success.

BOB FANNIN '78:

In our junior year, Coach Moegle didn't circulate a schedule for some reason. He used to tell us it didn't matter who we were playing if we took care of our business. One time, Derek Hatfield asked him who we were playing the next day. Coach told him, "It doesn't matter. You'll know when the bus pulls up." So, we would be out there at the ballpark taking pregame batting practice and a bus would pull into the parking lot off 66th Street. Somebody would run over to the corner and look out in the parking lot and see whose bus it was. "It's Hereford!" Imagine what it would've been like if the other team had known that we had no idea who we were playing?

RON REEVES '78:

In my junior year ('77), the core of the team was our class. We had a few good seniors, but we were taking the lead and we had a good, strong class.

JEFF HARP '78:

Dana Rieger was one of the best high school hitters I've ever seen. He had absolutely amazing hand-eye coordination. He wore it out one year at the Tournament of Champions in Midland. I was on 2nd base and he hit one that left the ballpark up at the top of the light pole. I stood there and watched it and got yelled at for gawking.

MIKE CRUTCHER '68, ASSISTANT COACH 1973-'78, 1982-'85:

I really respected Dana Rieger. He was just a tough kid and a great competitor. I mean unbelievable. The hardest ball I've ever seen hit in my life, and I've seen a bunch, was at the Midland Tournament. He hit it off that Marlboro Man out there and the ball just exploded off that sign ... BOOM!

RON REEVES '78:

In the region final my senior year, I had gotten beat early in the week down at Midland Lee. I finished the first game on Saturday and we won 5-4. Derek Hatfield started the final game and couldn't throw strikes. Coach Moegle pulled him and put me back in. Hatfield threw his glove into the dugout from way out on the field and was stomping around over there. Coach Moegle got on him, and Derek grabbed his stuff and walked out the gate and got in his car and left.

The game went along and in the bottom of the last inning Rieger doubled in two runs to tie it with two outs, then I got jammed and hit a grounder that the 2nd baseman booted. Rieger came around and scored with a beautiful slide at the plate to win the game. It was the most exciting athletic event of anything that I ever did, including starting as a freshman at quarterback at Texas Tech. That series was the essence of reward for our hard work.

Hatfield was supposedly off the team and we didn't really have anybody else other than me and him who could throw in a state tour-

Coach Moegle - 1978

nament game. Coach Moegle, in his own way of doing things, asked us what we thought about the way Derek had acted and if he should still be on the team. He was asking us like he knew the answer, but he also didn't want it to be his idea. He wanted us to want him back on the team. It was unanimous that we wanted him back. Coach Moegle told us to talk to him and deliver that message and make sure he came back with the right attitude. Derek came back to the team, and we won our first game in the state tournament. I pitched.

JEFF HARP '78:

In the semifinals in 1978, we were playing Corpus Christi Moody. We were up 6-1 and Ron (Reeves) walked the bases loaded. I was the catcher and I was peeking out the side of my mask at the dugout and sure enough, Coach Moegle was headed to the mound. I was hoping he wouldn't call me out there, but he pointed at me to get there. I was thinking, "Oh man." And with him, there was very little discussion. It was "yes sir" and "no sir."

On this day, Coach Moegle barked at Ron and Ron barked back. My eyes were like saucers. Coach Moegle then asked me if Ron was OK and I told him Ron was still throwing hard. He then told Reeves, "You got us into this – you get us out." I patted Ron on the back and I don't remember dropping any signs when I got back there. Ron was fired up. He got out of it with a strikeout and a pop-up on nothing but fastballs. Coach Moegle knew how to push buttons and he knew who he could push like that.

COACH MOEGLE:

We went back to the state tournament in 1978 and got beat in the finals on two errors in the 6th inning. We had a 4-0 lead and got beat 6-4, again by Houston Bellaire.

RON REEVES '78:

In the state championship game, we were ahead 4-0 early but made a couple errors and let them back in the game. It was tied 4-4 and I came in and relieved with two runners on and hung a slider and the guy lined it into left-center for two runs. We ended up losing 6-4. I had the feeling that we were about to win the state championship, but it was over like that.

A few minutes later we were in the locker room at Disch-Falk. We were all crying and I remember Coach Crutcher was crying with us. He came over and gave me a big hug and said, "I love you, you big ol' turd." (laughing) It was good stuff. Coach Moegle wasn't the kind of guy to come give you a big hug or do anything like that, but you just know that he cares. He's a lot more vocal about it now. He'll come up to my girls and tell them, "You know, I love your ol' dad." After he walks off, I tell them, "He never would've said that back when I was in school!"

BOB FANNIN '78:

The state tournament my senior year was a case of there never being a deal that was too big for us. We didn't treat it like it was different than any other day. Of course, we stopped at Underwood's Cafeteria in Brownwood.

Coach Hays was the same way in college. We were never going to be in a situation that was too big for us because of who "they" were. We talked about this in the office at Lubbock Christian. We went to a regional in Grand Junction, Colorado, in our first year in NCAA Division II. We were the 6 seed and were playing against the host, Mesa State. They were ranked #2 in the country at the time. Our guys were like, "So what – just go play." And it was like the state tournament my senior year.

NATHAN SWINDLE '81:

In my junior year ('80), the district schedule was divided in half and we won one half and Coronado won the other half. We had a one-game playoff out at Tech at the old ballpark and Coronado scored a bunch of runs early and hung on to win the game by one run. Coronado had a good team and advanced in the playoffs, eventually losing to R.L. Turner High School out of Carrollton. I always remember that because we had beaten Turner twice earlier in the season in the Midland Tournament. Beating Turner in the championship game was my first varsity win as a pitcher. We had made it to the championship game of the tournament and I was thinking, "I'm the only pitcher left in here."

And sure enough, Coach Moegle came walking down the dugout and flipped me the ball and said, "You're up." It scared me to death, but I had a good game and we won the tournament championship. Turner had a good left-handed pitcher named John Machin that everybody was fascinated with. Their coach was David Hall, who later was the head coach at Rice. Anyway, it always bugged me that Coronado got beat in the playoffs by a team that we had beat twice. But that fueled our fire the next year to make sure we didn't let that happen again.

JOHN DUDLEY '62, ASSISTANT COACH 1968-'72:

I think in the beginning when I first began to coach against Coach Moegle, I didn't realize what I was going to feel like personally, because I really felt a little bit of intimidation. I had played for him and coached for him and now all of a sudden I was across the diamond from him. I had to be very careful that I didn't let any of that bleed over into my players so they could sense it. There was a little of that, but at the same time there was this tremendous amount of respect for being able to be on the same field with him and have my team compete with him. Obviously, I tried to get our teams prepared, because I knew how he was going to prepare his ballclubs. And I needed to get my ballclub prepared on a level to be able to compete with him.

TRAVIS WALDEN '81, ASSISTANT COACH 1989-'94:

For the most part the 1981 season wasn't a grind. It was a pretty smooth season, except for the Midland Tournament. The year before, Coronado beat us in the 1-game playoff to get in the playoffs. We lost a couple games in a row down in Midland, and that was probably the 8th to 10th game of the season. I'll bet we reeled off 15 wins in a row after that. It was probably the best thing that happened to us because it woke us up. We didn't want a repeat of the previous year.

I know for a fact that the year before, he gave us some rope to be a little more loose with us. That next year it was tight and every day at practice was tough, because he knew that the team that won state wasn't as talented as the team the year before. That's why he stayed on us and pushed us. But I also think we were very fortunate that year.

COACH MOEGLE:

In '81, it was just one of those things that the Lord made in Heaven, because we didn't have a great team. We didn't have any outstanding or great players. We had one above-average player in Steve Coleman, the catcher. I had Travis Walden, left-handed pitcher, and Nathan Swindle, a left-handed pitcher. Both very good high school pitchers but nothing on the level you run into in Austin. I had good speed – Coleman could hit, and Mark Venable. I had a good ball club but not a state championship club.

Nathan that year went 14-0. He didn't lose a ballgame. He had great control, good movement, pitched smart, but not overpowering. Nothing fancy to where it would catch your eye. Travis was a great curve ball pitcher, had good location, competitive. Those kids just jelled together.

We happened to catch Pearland. They were the #1 team in the nation. They had won the state championship before. They just rocketed through the first game down there in Austin. We got into a rain situation – it started raining on Friday and we didn't complete that thing until Tuesday.

It rained until the water was about 3 feet below the 10-meter board at Barton Creek, Barton Springs. It rained 14 inches. It was so wet! We just hung in there.

NATHAN SWINDLE '81:

The way I've described our state championship team to people over the years is that we didn't have a lot of guys that played past high school. But in comparison to the '81 team, people will tell you our '80 team had better personnel, and I would agree with that. In '80, we had Randy Ledbetter and Rick Pinkerton and Kent Potts – a bunch of big, solid guys. But our '81 team was just a really good team. We were extremely consistent in what we did, game in and game out.

Steve Coleman had a huge year, all year long. I think his reputation preceded him later in the playoffs and everybody pitched around him. But Doug Hatch and Mark Venable got on fire batting behind Steve in the playoffs, especially at the state tournament. Scott Reid led off every game and he would get on base somehow – I think he set the single-season record for walks at the time. Darrell Kitten hit in the 2-hole and he would move Scott over, and Travis (Walden) hit in the 3-hole and he would hit a ball to left field and Scott would score, and then Steve would come up and it was off to the races after that. It was like clockwork every game.

We had solid defense. We had some things happen out of the ordinary prior to the season starting. We couldn't predict how it would affect the way things would go, but David Faulkner had started for two years in center field but got hurt in the fall playing football. Scott Reid moved to the center field spot, which put David in right field. But David was fast, and with the way Travis and I pitched to the outside corner, David could go get everything. And if they got around on it at all, they would hit it to center field, and Scott made some absolute circus catches out there. To this day, I love watching a center fielder that the pitchers have enough confidence in to throw it up there and let them hit it and let the center fielder go get it.

My focus all along in the playoffs was just to get to the state tournament. I never really thought about anything past that. We started the playoffs with Amarillo High. At that time, it was the classic matchup to run into Amarillo High somewhere along the way. The first game was at Lowrey, and we beat them 2-1 and all 3 runs were unearned. It was 1-1 in the bottom of the 6th, and somebody got on – it must've been Travis.

We had a sophomore courtesy runner named Fred Weathers on 2nd base and I was batting, I think with one out. I hit a routine fly ball to right field. Fred tagged up and the right fielder overthrew 3rd base and he scored. I was pitching and was really happy to have that run. I remember running out the fly ball and rounding 1st and could see the whole thing developing. I saw Fred tagging and saw the throw and thought it would get past the 3rd baseman. I started sprinting across the infield jumping up and down to meet Fred at home plate after he scored, and the picture on the front page of the sports section the next day was me congratulating Fred after he scored. So we beat them that first game, then we went up to Amarillo for the 2nd and 3rd games on that Saturday. They beat us in the next game 5-4, so it went to the 3rd game and I pitched that game. We just trounced them to advance. It was funny because later at Tech I became good friends with Ben Kohnle, the pitcher for Amarillo that day.

We moved on to face El Paso Bel Air. It was the same deal with us beating them here to start the series, then we beat them at Dudley Field, which was the AA park in El Paso. That was the same weekend of graduation so we went through the ceremony on Thursday night and I remember walking across the stage and getting to our principal, Mr. Snodgrass, and him telling me, "Good luck in El Paso."

We advanced to play Lewisville in the region finals. Again, we played them here on Tuesday and Coach Moegle stayed with our rotation of me pitching the first game and Travis pitching the second game. Maybe we were a little bit in awe of playing somebody from DFW and thinking that they would be really good. But when we got to the ballpark for the first game, they had guys laying out in the outfield during batting practice with their shirts off. It just rubbed us the wrong way and we decided quickly that they weren't so hot and that we could play with them. I was not a strikeout guy, but that day we had a big vocal crowd and I struck out the first three batters of the game. That energized everyone and we beat them 5-1.

Late in the game they started figuring me out a little bit and got some runners on base, but Doug Hatch threw one of their runners out at the plate. We were then headed to Lewisville to play there and it started raining. That spring it just rained and rained and rained. We never got to play there and started fretting over a place to play. The coaches called around and found a dry field in Abilene so we hopped on the bus and drove to Abilene and stayed at the La Quinta on I-20. To this day when we drive by there, I think about us staying there. (laughing)

We played at a ballpark that was kind of the equivalent to our Colt League ballpark (Hodges Field) – just a chain link city ballpark. But we beat them and Scott Reid made another circus catch in center field running one down over his shoulder. I can remember walking out of the ballpark after that game and walking up to my dad and saying, "We're going to Austin." And I'll never forget that, because it just sort of capped it for me. I had never thought past that.

When we left Lubbock for the state tournament, mom and dad were at work that day. I had my stuff packed and was walking out the front door when the phone rang. I had the door open and I remember thinking I needed to go, but I'd better answer the phone. I answered it and it was (Lubbock businessman) Dan Law. He said, "I've got one thing to tell you." I said, "What's that Dan?" He said, "When you get down there to Austin and you get on the field with those guys from Houston, you remember one thing for me. They put their pants on one leg at a time just like you." I said, "OK Dan. I'll remember that." And that's all he said. I hung up and left. We drove to Austin and practiced on Wednesday and played on Thursday.

In the state tournament, we were ready for the Nacogdoches pitcher. His name was Compton. He had a good breaking ball and we had hit breaking balls off the pitching machine all week. They had a little bitty catcher and Coach Moegle figured out that he couldn't throw anybody out, especially with the big leg kick from Compton. He wasn't very sharp that day, and neither was I, but we got a bunch of guys on base and stole a bunch of bases and won 11-4. My one regret was from the last out of the game, which was a pop-up between the mound and home plate. I caught it and I was more worried about going to shake Steve Coleman's hand than anything else, so I just flipped the ball back to the mound. I still think, "You dummy! Why didn't you keep the ball from your win at the state tournament?!" (smiling)

And then it started raining. It rained buckets and we couldn't play until late on Monday. All the other state championship games ahead of us were backed up so we started late and didn't finish until Monday.

Pearland had won state the year before and were coached by an old Monterey player named Bill Bratcher. Craig Smajstrala was a good player for them, and they had a good pitcher named John Dempsey. He was supposedly their "go-to guy." We didn't see him. I don't know why they didn't go to him. We'd seen him pitch in their semifinal game. He was very good – a big, tall guy and threw hard and they had all those days of rest, just like we did. But they started somebody else in the final game. We won 7-3 and Travis pitched most of the game. He came out in the 6th and Rick Dillman finished on the mound. Travis was a better 1st baseman than I was, so he moved to 1st base when Rick pitched. I was warming up in the bullpen when the game ended. They had runners on base but Rick got the last out.

Later I had some friends who listened to the game back in Lubbock and they taped the radio broadcast for me. I obviously didn't hear it live, but I tie this together with my memory of the game ending. I was in the bullpen and I was ready to go and wasn't throwing much. I was just throwing a pitch here and there to stay loose. But the radio broadcast is tied to my memory of this, and it went like this: "And the 3-2 pitch is ... swung on and missed and the side is retired. We have a new state champ!"

I'll never forget that. When I replay that in my mind, I can hear that radio call. It was very exciting.

TRAVIS WALDEN '81, ASSISTANT COACH 1989-'94:

We went down there not knowing what to expect. We were a bunch of kids who took our sack lunches out there like we did every Saturday at practice at Lowrey Field. We didn't know anything different.

He didn't build them up, other than building up the Nacogdoches pitcher and getting us ready for him. It just fell in place for us down there in Austin.

We knew Nathan Swindle was going to start the first game in Austin, and in his career I think he ended up 18-0. We knew he was going to give us a chance because he was going to throw strikes.

We got through Nacogdoches on a Thursday and then we had to wait until late on Monday night as we sat around and watched it rain. In those days, there wasn't all the indoor facilities we have now. Nowadays if we would've gotten rain like that, there are places that we could go practice. So we really didn't do much. All we did was change hotels until we finally ended up at the Chariot Inn in Austin. I can remember Coach saying that the UIL said if we didn't play that Monday night they would cancel the tournament and consider everyone co-champions. Estacado was down there at the same time as us and they were in the AAA state championship, so the Lubbock ISD was putting out some money for us to be down there so long.

We eventually got to play Pearland High School, and they were coached by Bill Bratcher who had played for Coach Moegle in the late '60s and early '70s. In fact, he had coached my brother so I had known him for a while. I think they had a few guys drafted, like most of those good Houston schools did. We got a few runs on them early, and they had a better pitcher that they didn't start. I think they were just going to try to stay in rotation. We got up on that guy and beat them 7-3.

That was Coach Moegle's 3rd state championship. I remember in the first inning hitting a ball over 3rd base like I always did. It hit barely fair and kicked over in foul territory and we ended up scoring 3 runs. We were fortunate to get up early on them because they were very good. Even though Pearland had won state the year before, we took the game to them and knocked them on their heels early. We had them playing uphill, so we had a better shot by doing that.

It didn't rain during the game. But it sure rained again late that night after the game. We had a little window of good weather for the final game. And I think after we left town the next day it rained some more. We played at Disch-Falk and they had Astroturf, plus they had the tarp on the infield so it dried off. We were lucky, because nobody wanted to be on a team that would've been that called a "co-champion," especially after Pearland had won it the year before. We just wanted to see how we could do against them.

One of the neatest memories I have of Coach Moegle came after the game that night. The game didn't start until after midnight. (His last state championship in '96 was rain delayed, too, so he's 2-0 after midnight!) Anyway, we went to eat at a steak house after the game. The rain hit again and we went back to the hotel. Nobody could sleep after being so wired up about playing. We were all standing out under this shelter thing at the hotel.

Coach Moegle stood over there and I guess that's about the first time I can remember him letting his guard down with anybody as he visited with everybody a little bit. That was a neat experience considering coming from my standpoint of getting to pitch the state championship game after dropping the ball the year before against Coronado. I don't think he ever trusted me again, to be honest with you. I know every time I went out there, he was always thinking it was going to happen. But it was just one of those days.

That is one of the first things I put on my resume – that I played for Coach Moegle and won a state championship in 1981. That was a pretty good experience. This was kind of a funny statement, but Coach Moegle said, "This is the worst team I won a state championship with." He said that when we were all standing around at the hotel that night after the game. We were telling him, "But coach, we still won it!"

We did a good job defensively. We just played good team baseball, and that's one thing I will say about that team. We had Steve Coleman hitting in the 4-hole and he probably still has the school record for batting average and probably RBIs and hits, and Scott Reid might have set the school record at the time for walks, and then Darrell Kitten hit behind him and moved Scott around, and I hit 3-hole. In Austin, Mark Venable and Doug Hatch, who both hit down in the lineup, really went off and made the all-tournament team, and that's pretty good for two 2 guys in the bottom of the order. Those guys carried us down there.

COACH MOEGLE:

We beat Nacogdoches in the semifinal that year. We had been told we couldn't beat them because they had a great pitcher, but we stole nine bases off him that night. He brought his foot and knee way up by his ear every time – he would not give in – he did it every time and we ran all night long. I had talked to Gerald Turner (head coach at Thomas Jefferson High School in Dallas), and he told me there was no way we could beat him because his breaking ball was too good. We set that Jugs machine up to throw that good breaking ball and we hit against it for four days. That tournament was made in heaven. Everything we did was right.

Coach Moegle - 1983

TRAVIS WALDEN '81, ASSISTANT COACH 1989-'94:

To get us ready for the state tournament my senior year, Coach Moegle set the pitching machine up to get us ready to hit the good breaking ball. Once we got to Austin and started playing, we were coming back to the dugout saying, "Coach Moegle doesn't know anything. That breaking ball is not very good." But he was trying to prepare us for what was ahead.

LARRY HAYS, LCU & TTU COACH '71-2008:

His 1981 team wasn't the same animal as those early '70s teams in terms of talent, but he won with them. That shows what a great coach he was.

COACH MOEGLE:

It was just a tremendous feat because here we were beating the previous year's state champions who had everybody back and were one of the top teams in the country. It proved to me that you didn't have to be the best team in Texas to win the state championship. You had to be at the right place at the right time and it had to be your turn. With this in mind, it became a lot easier to understand playing in the state tournament.

TRAVIS WALDEN '81, ASSISTANT COACH 1989-'94:

For the most part, 1981 was one of those seasons in which good things happened. It really wasn't a struggle. Even winning the state championship wasn't a struggle. Coach Moegle often says, "When it's your turn, it's your turn." I've also heard Bill Griffin down at Howard Junior College say that. He was an old-school coach, too. It was our turn in 1981, because everything that could go right for us did go right. We could play Pearland 100 times again and never beat them, but that night the stars were lined up and everything kind of fell in place for us and the ball bounced right. I remember our shortstop made a big play in one inning and we turned a double play. We probably hadn't turned a double play like that all year long.

BURLE PETTIT, LUBBOCK SPORTSWRITER:

As his success mounted, I don't think the other teams in the district ever got around to liking Bobby because they got tired of him wearing them out every year. But in Lubbock, he had a tremendous influence.

COACH MOEGLE:

In '84 and '85 we got back to the state tournament and lost in the first game. But our reputation was established in the state that we were a true powerhouse, because we had been to the state tournament in the '60s, '70s and '80s and were approaching a record for the number of appearances at the state tournament.

MIKE GUSTAFSON '85:

We played Abilene Cooper in the 1984 region final to see who went to the state tournament from out here. We had followed them in the newspaper all year long because they were in the next district to the south. They were beating people like we were, and they had a good record, like we did. Sure enough, we met them in the region finals.

The series opened on a Tuesday at Lowrey. We had a big crowd and the ballpark was tense. Kevin Short led off the bottom of the first with a walk, then I tripled to right-center and their shortstop threw the relay in our dugout. The ballpark exploded and we were up 2-0. Everything went our way and their starter, who was something like 10-0 coming into that game, didn't make it out of the first inning. I remember one of the hits was a bad-hop single that bounced over the shortstop's head.

We ended up beating them something like 11-4 and Short pitched great. One of our parents said the Cooper team was yelling at the umps out the bus window as they were leaving the parking lot. We all found out later that the umps were from Midland and were the same guys who were going to work our games in Abilene later that week. In the newspaper, their head coach said something like, "We're going to double-dip them at our place." The girls who shoe-polished our bus and decorated our lockers had double-dip ice cream cones on everything that week.

We played them on Saturday at their ballpark, which was behind the Abilene Cooper school building. The ballpark was jammed. Their #2 pitcher was a hard-throwing junior named Terry Suggs, who later pitched at Texas. He beat us with a score like the game in Lubbock earlier in the week, so we turned right around and played the series finale as part of the doubleheader.

It felt like the ballpark filled up even more as the word got out that the season was down to one final game. They brought their game-1 starter back, but this time he threw well. He and Kevin went back and forth until about the 5th inning when their 3rd baseman booted a ground ball with the bases loaded and 2 out. It was only a 1-0 game at that point, but it felt like a big lead as well as Kevin was pitching. In the top of the 7th we scored 3 more. It was capped by a long double to left-center by David Coleman. Kevin ended up throwing a 1-hitter and we beat them 4-0. The last out was a ground ball to me at shortstop. I bobbled it, threw the guy out on a close play, and we dogpiled near the mound.

We later heard stories about their fans popping off at our fans as the day grew hotter and more tense. Billy Lance played centerfield for us and supposedly he was getting abuse by all the people in pickup trucks surrounding the outfield fence. Billy was a tough kid and a great player, so I'm sure he was giving it back to them. (smiling)

As I look back on it now, the environment is probably something I've seen countless times in ballparks since then, but as a junior in high school playing the biggest game of my life, it felt like it was us against the world. I remember leaving the dogpile and walking toward home plate. I think I ended up standing on home plate yelling at their fans, "We're going to Austin! We're #1!" It was such a release at the time. I also remember Coach Crutcher grabbing me and saying, "That's enough. Let's go." (laughing)

We lost a 1-0 game in the state semifinal the next week. A guy named Gary Roberson pitched his tail off for Cypress Fairbanks and threw a 3-hit shutout. We had 3 hits and maybe 2 or 3 more guys reached via walk or error. In keeping with Coach Moegle's way of dialing up the pressure in big games, we stole 3 or 4 bases but just never got the big hit.

When it ended, we were all crushed and sitting in the dugout. I remember thinking how much work had gone into getting to that point, and that it was all over. I also remembered thinking about how hard it would be to get back. Little did I know that we would call up a bunch of guys from the JV and do it all over again the next year. I wish we would have won one of those years in Austin, but I sure am proud of having been part of back-to-back state tournament teams.

BRAD WALKER '85:

I personally went out on a high note – my last pitch was a swing and miss – a curve ball I loved to throw. I struck out one of Fort Worth Southwest's best players to save a playoff game and get us one step closer to the state tournament. I was literally pumping my fist and my catcher and good friend Jimmy Webster didn't shake my hand – he needed to hug me – and my teammates swarmed around me.

The postgame was the stuff of dreams, at least for a Monterey Plainsman. Playing in a college park at LCU, where I had watched some great college baseball including the NAIA World Series in previous years. The stands were packed. It was a home game for us, and the atmosphere was as close to Friday Night Lights as a high school baseball player could get.

The first question I got was from Michael Mann, Lubbock Avalanche-Journal sportswriter, who covered high school sports but by that time of the year he was practically our beat writer. He simply asked me, "First career save?" I confirmed and he walked away. Then it was time to face the cameras and be interviewed for local TV. Then I got the greatest compliment of my life from Coach Crutcher, who had pushed me much harder than Coach Moegle had since the day we met my sophomore year. He shook my hand and smiled and said, "We've come a long way."

We got home and I made some memories with my grandparents. One grandmother was on the phone with other relatives talking about the game and my TV interview she had just watched and, "Of course, he's so good with the press." That's hilarious. My dad's mother was laughing about how she thought it was a 9-inning game and wondered why everyone was going nuts when I finished the 7th inning. My dad was going on about how nervous he was. He was so happy for Mike Eckles and the job he had done for 6-plus innings before finally tiring in the 100+ degree heat, but then it dawned on him that his son was in charge of closing out the game.

The next morning was the best – I slept like a baby, or a teenage boy – and woke up late. There were my parents and grandparents waiting for me all with funny grins on their faces. They showed me the A-J banner headline on the sports section: "Walker Saves Day for MHS."

This story does not happen in Fort Worth if Southwest had beaten us. It wouldn't be the same in the weekly paper in Whitewright, where my dad was raised, or the 8-page Bonham Daily Favorite (my mom's hometown) with a sports page. The size of the city, with TV coverage and a large daily newspaper, played a part in making Monterey baseball what it is.

SHANE SALYER '85:

We played Fort Worth Arlington Heights at Hardin-Simmons in the region final our senior year ('85). The final two rounds of the 5A playoffs had been reduced to a 1-game series because we had been delayed for 10 days as a result of a "No Pass, No Play" lawsuit in Houston. Their pitcher was Tim Mauser and he was 15-0 coming into the game. He later pitched in the big leagues. We were sloppy early behind Mike Eckles and the game went back and forth all day. We took a 6-4 lead into the top of the 7th but Heights scored 1 and had runners on 1st and 3rd with 1 out. They had 13 hits on the day, but thankfully tried to suicide squeeze twice in their final at bat. They fouled off the first but popped up the next one a couple pitches later. Eckles caught it and flipped it to 3rd to double them up and end the game. Coach Moegle had us ready to handle the key situations and they had outcoached themselves.

MIKE CRUTCHER '68, ASSISTANT COACH 1973-'78, 1982-'85:

Coach Moegle would say this often after a tough playoff game. We might win a bi-district game or something and he would say, "That was our state championship." He knew if we had a team that was good enough to go much further.

I've been on the bus with him after winning the state championship, or losing the state championship, or after any other game in which the season had just ended. We would talk for a while and he would say, "What are we gonna do next year?" I'd say, "Coach, we just got through with this year." But that's just how he was. He was always thinking.

COACH MOEGLE:

I think the most interesting story that I have from 1994 happened with my family. We were playing Coronado in the region final to see who went to Austin. It was the only time in my 40 years that we had to play a Lubbock school in the playoffs. We were playing a 3-game playoff here in Lubbock, and Dr. Mike Moses, the Lubbock ISD superintendent at the time, told me we would play all 3 games at Texas Tech. I told Dr. Moses that there was no way Monterey was going to give up our field to play Coronado at Texas Tech. I told him that our field was big enough to go home and home. After some consultation on their part, they decided that we could have our home field at Lowrey Field but Coronado wanted Tech as their home field.

Coronado won the first game and we won the second, so we were going to play on Saturday afternoon. Saturday morning, I was sitting with my two daughters and my wife, and I'm going to tell you that flashes went through my mind that I had a 35-year old program that had been put on display with the idea that we would not be #1 in our district any longer if Coronado beat us. I put so much pressure on myself that I looked at my kids and said, "I'd rather be at our cabin in Ruidoso, New Mexico, than in Lubbock today, because of what can happen to us." We had over 3,000 at our ballgame and won to go to Austin, but going to Austin meant nothing like playing Coronado that year.

I'd been to the state tournament 10 times, but I had never felt the pressure of that '94 region final game against Coronado. John (Dudley) had as good a club as I did, or maybe a little better, because in '95 he went to the state finals with them. We were that even. I could see a reflection that the history of our whole program was going to be crumbled at this one meeting. We had finished 2nd a few times in district, but they never had the consequence like going to the state tournament or that we weren't top dog. That was going to be a killer.

SCOTT BRAND '94:

No one can ever forget the Monterey vs. Coronado series in the '94 region finals. It was huge for me, because I went to Coronado my sophomore year and all my best friends that I had grown up with played on that team. There were over 3,000 people at each game. I pitched in the second and third games in that series. As we celebrated on the field after the series, Coach Moegle came up to me and said, "Aren't you glad you came over here?"

It was such an awesome feeling. Unfortunately, we fell short at state against Corpus Christi, but that year was probably the most fun and memorable of my career, including college and pro ball. I was named all-state and had the privilege to pitch in the Texas High School All-Star game in the Astrodome, which was pretty cool.

JEFF HORN '96:

My junior year we were in the playoffs and we drew a pretty tough matchup to start. It was with Odessa Permian, and our first game got rained out. So it became a 1-game series at Lubbock Christian. We were also playing for his 1,000th win and Coach Moegle had a bunch of family in from everywhere to see the game. The team was tight, because if we lost the game, not only were we not going to get his 1,000th win, but we were going to be out of the playoffs. I hit a home run that day to pretty much put the game away and that was a thrill for me. Coach Moegle had a big smile on his face that day. That was a good moment.

COACH MOEGLE:

I returned in 1996 and brought back a good, big, strong ballclub. We won the state championship and Mark Martinez went 17-0 on the year.

JEFF HORN '96:

My senior year, the mood of the team was very confident. We had a lot of good athletes. Most of the key players on our '96 state championship team were on the team in '94 as sophomores that went to the tournament. And we had a monumental struggle just to get to the state tournament in '94. We were wide-eyed when we got there and got beat handily in the first game. A lot of us had played football and baseball. Our football team had come off a 10-0 season, and I believe our basketball team had gone 28-5. It was just a very, very strong senior class with a lot of good athletes in it.

Going into that year we had been building toward winning a state championship, not for three years but since we were 7 or 8 years old going to Coach Moegle's camp. When the playoffs started that year, we weren't hitting that well. A few of us seniors went to Coach Moegle and said we'd like to hit more live pitching and scrimmage more. We started doing that and started crushing the ball and built up a little momentum and it carried us all the way to the state championship.

The state championship game was unique in that it rained that morning. We did not know if we were going to play that evening. We went to the ballpark at 10 that night to see if we were going to play. They still had one more game to go before they would reach our title game. They used to go Class A, then 2A, then 3A, then 4A then 5A, and I believe the 3A game was finishing up when we got there. Coach Moegle pulled the seniors together and asked if we would rather play or come back in the morning. Being 18-year-old boys, we wanted to go ahead and play instead of coming back at 8 in the morning to play.

I can vividly remember looking at the scoreboard and the first pitch of our game was at 11:59 that night. When Mark Martinez struck the final guy out to end the game, it was 2:21 in the morning. It was a tough game.

In the state semifinals, we also had a really tough time. We were down most of the game and we won it in the top of the 7th inning. I hit a ground-rule double with the bases loaded and two outs to pull ahead, and then we got three outs and won that game. Then we got down early in the title game but inched our way back and held them scoreless. We got it to within one run, I believe at 4-3. In the bottom of the 5th inning we brought out Mark Martinez. He was our best pitcher and had pitched the night before. I believe we scored two runs in the 5th inning and two in the 6th inning to win the state title.

Coach Moegle knew we weren't out of the game, by any stretch. We had been swinging the bats well. A lot of us were hot at the right time. The key was to be patient and get a good pitch. We were facing a guy who was a good pitcher, but he was somebody who we could hit. I think it was about the 3rd or 4th inning that we got the bases loaded with no outs, and a couple guys got some key hits to get us back in the game. It was a total team victory.

When the game was over, we all ran out to the middle of the field and did the traditional pile that teams do when they win a state championship. For our group, it was a culmination of a lot of hard work. A lot of us had played together since we were 8 or 9 years old, and Coach Moegle was a legend by the time we were born. We had always gone to his baseball camps and he had told us from an early age that we had a chance to do something special if we worked hard. When we won it, it was the result of a lot of hard work. We had a bunch of good guys on that team.

In the state tournament, Mark Martinez had pitched a complete game the night before. I remember down there warming up for the state championship game that Mark wasn't happy. He wanted to pitch, but there was a 10-inning maximum rule in two days that a pitcher could pitch in high school. So Coach Moegle wasn't going to pitch him until the 5th inning. Mark wanted to start the game, but I don't know how his arm could have stood that. But he pitched three more innings that night and was quite effective.

I think our nerves stemmed from the fact that Mark Martinez wasn't starting the state championship game on the mound because he had pitched in the semifinal. There for several weeks, JR Mize, myself, Alex Garcia and several other guys had been pitching during practice, and Coach Moegle kept saying, "We're going to find out who wants to start the state championship game."

Nobody would admit it at the time, but we had a pretty good drop from Martinez to our #2 pitcher. Not that we didn't have anybody who could pitch – it was just that Mark was so dominating. And so I think that's what people were nervous about. Coach Moegle was just trying to piece four innings together to get to Martinez. I believe JR started the game and walked a few and hit one or something like that, and then we brought in Alex Garcia. Alex ended up settling them down and getting us through the 4th inning. I was nervous that game because I thought I was going to have to pitch, and I hadn't pitched much.

DUSTY BUCK '99:

In the 1997 playoffs my sophomore year, I got a two-out hit in the 7th inning to go ahead of Duncanville. They were ranked nationally and on paper outmatched us. We lost a close one the Friday night before and were facing elimination late in game two. We won game two and then won the deciding game to send Monterey to the state tournament for the second year in a row. We were picked to be 4th or 5th in district after losing many seniors from the state championship team the year before. We ended up going 33-6 and were state runners-up. I'm truly still so proud of that silver medal because of what we did.

TUEY RANKIN, ASSISTANT COACH 1997–'99:

When we won the state semifinal in '97, we stayed around to watch Round Rock play one of the Corpus Christi teams. Round Rock was really good with Ryan Langerhans and some other good players, and they were hammering the baseball. Coach Moegle finally said, "My ears are hurting – we've got to get out of here."

When we got on the bus, he told me that if we threw a right-hander with medium velocity, they were going to crush us. So he had Clark Mooty, who hadn't pitched much for us, start the state championship game. We really couldn't carry Round Rock's jocks, but it was a 1-1 game into the 4th inning before we made a couple mistakes and the game got away from us. Clark Mooty was probably the only shot we had.

DUSTY BUCK '99:

In 1997, I remember walking out of the locker room at Disch-Falk after beating Sugar Land Clements in the state semis and having so many fans chanting "Monterey Plainsmen" as we walked to the bus. It was one of the proudest moments of my life.

COACH MOEGLE:

Just by a stroke of luck in 1997, we go back to the state tournament and got beat in the finals. We probably didn't deserve to be there, because we weren't as good as Round Rock. But we got to play them in the state championship. And that was the last of our state tournament appearances. A lot of people say that those were our great years, but no, some of our greatest years were just years that we were able to win a district championship. It wasn't strictly that we were always playing for a state tournament. We were playing for the best that we could be.

One of those clubs was the first year that I coached in 1960. Those kids won the first district championship ever won at Monterey, and they really had to push because it was something new for them. But it was the most rewarding period of time, other than the state championship times. There were several years that we were able to win – the '94 team that went to Austin didn't deserve to be there. We had really done all we could do just playing Coronado here in town.

There were times that we didn't go to Austin but we should have. In '69 and '73, for example. Midland won it in '73, and they beat us by one run in the region final, and we were as good as anybody that year. Winning a state championship wasn't always the utmost, but having the kids perform at a level higher than I thought they could play was probably the biggest thrill that I got. But nothing would really replace the '72 state championship.

FRED OLIVER, MHS COACH 2000-'09:

Tradition, in any program in any sport, speaks for itself. You don't have to say a whole lot about it. Kids that come up through the program and have been raised in Lubbock and their fathers came through the program, know the expectations. I think what Coach Moegle started, each year built upon it. Sometimes we might call that a "monster." I think through the demands and expectations, that's what molds the team into the chemistry it has. The kids want to be a part of it. They want their name on that trophy and they want to be a part of something special.

GARY HUGHES '65:

I think the thing that sustained him over the years was every team after the first team had the success they did. Every team from then on realized that and wanted to do well and continue to carry the flag for Monterey baseball and not let the previous guys down. I think he used, very effectively, the kids who were coming back to cause the younger players to understand that they had a responsibility and that they were going to work hard. I think they learned quickly, as I did in my early years, that they did not want to let the older guys down. It carried forth from year to year and once that started it never stopped.

JEFF HORN '96:

Those 1960s guys probably took it the hardest from Coach Moegle. But after that, a guy didn't take the field in a Monterey uniform without taking a step back and looking at what all those teams had accomplished and making darn sure that they tried their very best. Again, credit Coach Moegle for creating a program that continued to reload year after year.

DUSTY BUCK '99:

Coach Moegle was already a legend when my time came around. All I wanted to do was play for Monterey. The feeling was unbelievable the day I walked into the locker room and got my bag with a varsity uniform in it. It seemed like the pressure to keep the tradition alive was already there years before I got to high school. When I finally got my time, there was nothing I wouldn't do for the man.

JIM BOB DARNELL '66:

We had moved to where my mother still lives on 57th Street when I was 10 years old, which would've been 1957. My dad had played baseball in the service before he'd gotten injured. I first remember hearing about Coach Moegle in about the 7th or 8th grade. We didn't have as much news media and such, because I always remember thinking it was funny when people told us they knew Coach "Moe-Gull" (pronouncing it wrong instead of "May-Gull"). My dad would tell me those stories and we would laugh about people saying they knew him well, but they didn't pronounce his name right.

Bill Dean and Bill Boyd are the people who really had a lot to do with me learning about Coach Moegle. I didn't realize this at the time, and wouldn't learn it until the late '90s, but Bill Boyd had been a member of Phi Delta Theta fraternity at Texas Tech. (Darnell would later be a Phi at Tech, as well.) Boyd didn't coach me as a kid, but he eventually coached my little brother. I was probably 13 or 14 when I remember him telling me about Monterey baseball.

NATHAN SWINDLE '81:

The first time I took notice of high school ball and the possibilities at Monterey was one day in Little League. We were practicing over at Hodges Elementary. This must've been about 1975. At the time, Duncanville was one of the teams that was always a playoff contender. They were in town, and from Hodges I could see them piling off the bus at their hotel fired up after they had won a game. I remember thinking it would be cool someday to be on a high school team and get to play in the playoffs and experience all that. That was when I started paying attention to Monterey baseball. I remember being really excited about the 1978 team. I went to their playoff games at Lowrey and listened to their state tournament games on the radio.

TRAVIS WALDEN '81, ASSISTANT COACH 1989-'94:

All I really wanted to do when I was growing up was play for Coach Moegle. Every year we would hear rumors that he was going to retire. Everybody all the way through our Little League years was hoping we'd get the opportunity to play for him. I remember him coming over to watch us pitch. We were playing Southwest and when he showed up everybody in the ballpark knew he was there and he made his presence known. Every year around All-Stars he would come around to see who the best players were.

GARY ASHBY '73:

In the early '70s, either Monterey or the team that beat Monterey by one run won the state championship. We were this close to five straight state championships. That's hard to even comprehend nowadays that somebody could possibly go through and win five straight championships. But it was because of the guys in the '60s, who built the tradition.

If you've seen the Monterey baseball locker room, every year was detailed on a poster on the wall. It told the record of the team, the statistics of the starters and the pitchers' records. When we got to Monterey, there were only 10 or so posters. Now they circle the entire locker room. We knew everything about the guys who came ahead of us. I knew that my doctor's son was on Coach Moegle's very first team. I knew that Danny MacDougall was the best pitcher on the first team to go to the state tournament.

But we also knew the players on the team who were on the first team that did not win district. And there had only been one team that hadn't won district at the time. We almost noticed the names on that team more than the teams that went to the state tournament because they stood out like a sore thumb. (laughing) We never had that problem, but a few years after us, there was a team that didn't win district and they stood out, too. That tradition was what we drew on.

COACH MOEGLE

I put the banners up in my locker room and I don't really know why I did it other than to establish it as a memorial to the kids who had gone through our program. I'd seen the Celtics do it with their banners hanging, and lots of teams had a ring of honor thing like the Cowboys have in their stadium. I thought it was something really nice to look back on and reminisce on how dedicated and how good the kids were that played for me. The later groups came in and saw the progress of players from their sophomore to junior to senior years. Plus, kids could look back later and see their dad or people they'd heard about, and it instilled a lot of pride in being part of it.

It means a lot to the kids who played to know that they were recognized and were part of the program. It was a status symbol for them to get their name on that board, especially if they could get their name up there for three years.

I just think of all the ones who put up so much sacrifice. The numbers don't really tell what the individual was. When I look at those posters and I'm around that stuff, I think of the dedication and hard work those kids put in. It wasn't easy playing for me because I was so demanding, but the rewards were great for the kids. They made men out of themselves, even though they were still boys. They reached another level in their lives.

FRED OLIVER, MHS COACH 2000-'09:

The locker room signs were a real smart move. I think most kids see those and they want to be up there, too. They want their names to be on those posters for years to come. We have special moments in there in which fathers come up with their sons and point to a name of someone in their family or someone they're close to and it gets into their heart and mind about the expectations of Monterey baseball.

BOB FANNIN '78:

My family moved here from Florida before my sophomore year. I didn't know all the stories like the guys who grew up here and went to his baseball school. Everybody was a little standoffish and scared of him, but I didn't know any better. A couple days before school started, my dad took me up to the school to meet the coaches. I remember it like it was yesterday because Coach Crutcher turned to Coach Moegle and said, "We've never had one from Florida before." (laughing)

I was a little hobbit at that point, but after my sophomore year I just kept growing, and even kept growing into college. We didn't know at that age if we were any good. We were just trying to play baseball and survive. He brought me up to the varsity at the very end of the season. I wasn't getting called up to play or anything, but just to be around the varsity. Tim Leslie and Mark Morgan made me stand in the dugout with one leg on the third step the whole game. They told me, "Don't jinx it." My mom asked me that night why I stood in the same spot all game. (laughing)

RON REEVES '78:

You know those posters that hung around the locker room? Every one of those names on those posters, right now if you read them to me, I could probably place them with the years they played. That's tradition. It definitely made a difference. If you can ever get that going in your business or whatever, you've got it made.

BOB FANNIN '78:

I had no idea who those guys were and I didn't know anything about the tradition. But I learned quick. I remember that it didn't take long for me to realize that we did things in a different way and that there were expectations on winning.

I heard somebody say to Nick Saban that the upcoming SEC championship game "really doesn't matter." Saban replied, "What do you mean it doesn't matter?" When he said that, I thought about Coach Moegle. There was NEVER a day that it was OK to go out and just play ho-hum. I know that has stuck with all of us, in everything we do. I mean, things have happened to guys in life, but there's some fight in Coach Moegle's guys. They're going to land on their feet somehow and find a way to make life work.

JEFF HORN '96:

I was fortunate enough that my father played for him and won two state championships for him. So it was a big goal of mine to win the state championship. I'd always been somewhat of a historian, and I knew that this was probably his best and last shot at winning the state championship. It had been 15 years since the '81 bunch had won it. I knew that he had really looked forward to us. I don't want to say that he stayed on just for my group, because he stayed on for a few more years after we left. I knew that he really felt like we had a shot, especially with Martinez on the mound. It meant a lot to us players to try to get that 4th state championship for him and kind of cap his career. We were very proud to win that one for him.

DUSTY BUCK '99:

No one pushed me to want to succeed more than Coach Moegle. I bought into the MHS lore and mystic at a very young age. I grew up watching teams from the early '90s and idolized Clint Bryant, Greg Cushman and later Monty Ward, Scott Brand, JR Mize, and Mark Martinez.

RON REEVES '78:

Marlin Hamilton, Gary Ashby, Mark Griffin and Jimmy Shankle ... Mark Griffin invited a bunch of his Monterey teammates to his house one night after a reunion or something. I was the only one hanging around from my era so Mark must've felt sorry for me and invited me to join them. I had so much fun sitting there listening to them. I thought I might feel like an outsider because I wasn't about to chime in about our accomplishments from my time. That night I felt like I was part of a club when I got included with them.

BRAD WALKER '85:

Coach Moegle built something special that could only have happened in Lubbock, and we aspired to be a part of it.

JIMMY WEBSTER '85:

One thing I find a little sad now is that my players don't know who Coach Moegle is. I understand it, because there's no reason why a 17- or 18-year-old high school boy should know him when he hadn't coached in their lifetime. But it's still sad to me.

MARK GRIFFIN '72:

I feel sorry for a generation of kids. I wish my son would have been able to play for him. I think it would have been a significant part of his life, just as it was in mine. So from that standpoint, selfishly, I feel bad for those who never had a chance to experience what some of us did, which was the honor to be in a relationship with him and to play for him.

DUSTY BUCK '99:

As you can tell with most of his former players, my time at MHS under his watch truly was some of the most influential and special years of my life. That "M" on my hat still means something to me.

TUEY RANKIN, ASSISTANT COACH 1997-'99:

I've been through more sports banquets than I can count – football banquets, golf banquets, baseball banquets. There were more kids who sobbed at the baseball banquet than any of the others. Every banquet has a few kids like that, but at his, there were always more. He had that other side to him that kids really connected to. I think Jimmy Webster said it best, something like, "We didn't like him back then, but we still wanted to send him a Christmas card."

JIMMY WEBSTER '85:

He coached from the '60s to the '90s. He coached guys who went to Vietnam to guys who were playing video games, and everything in between. And he knew how to handle all of them. Certainly, there was some adjusting for guys who came into the program, but he adjusted to the times, too.

TRAVIS WALDEN '81, ASSISTANT COACH 1989-'94:

I can remember the thing he said to me one day coming back from Amarillo. He rarely said anything about himself, but he said something about the win that day being the 35th year in a row that he'd won 20 games. He said he was prouder of that than the state championships because it spoke to developing a program and a tradition. There are guys who are trying to win 20 games in one year and he'd done it so many years in a row.

COACH MOEGLE:

When I first started, 20 wins was a standard. We only scheduled 22 games, I believe. So, 20 wins was going to be difficult. My personal goal was to win 20 of those 22. Of course, if we went to the playoffs, we added games to that. This was a selfish thing on my part, but I always wanted it. After we'd done it for 10 years, it became obvious that we were going to have a good program. In my 40 years, we did it 39 times and we only missed in my last year in 1999.

TRAVIS WALDEN '81, ASSISTANT COACH 1989-'94:

When you win 20 games for 40 years, it means you've built a program that's not built around one player. He had someone to step in every year and keep it rolling.

COACH MOEGLE:

I was contacted by the National Federation of State High School Associations in the 1990s to say that I had established a record for career wins in the nation. I was in the record book listed as the #1 baseball coach in America and was recognized for that in a lot of different articles and stuff. I was still coaching and wasn't paying attention, but over a period of a few years after that, a new record book came out and they listed two men from the state of Iowa that were the new record holders. Being very competitive, my daughter confronted the Federation and they informed her that Iowa has a different circumstance and that their season runs after the school year is over.

Coach Moegle - 1999

Consequently, these men were receiving recognition for their wins in the summertime and they were playing in a system that allowed them to play 60 games a year as opposed to the 30 games we were allowed in a normal school year. They had contacted the Federation and got their games recognized in the same way ours were. It should be like the Barry Bonds situation that has an asterisk that explains the difference. I'm sure by now that somebody has surpassed what I did.

FRED OLIVER, MHS COACH 2000–'09:

To be the winningest coach in the United States at one time is phenomenal. It's a number beyond recognition. I can't comprehend it. For people who don't understand what goes into 1,100 wins – yes, it's longevity. But over a 40-year period, they had to do things right and win all those ballgames. He averaged 20-plus wins a season for all those years. That number is unbelievable. No matter how many years he coached, he did the job and his teams did the job and he would be the first to say he wouldn't have those wins without those players. But somebody had to lead them and put them in the right place. And he did that for 40 years.

GARY ASHBY '73:

To go to Austin takes a whole lot of ability and it takes luck, but it also takes cockiness and knowing you belong down there. There's never been a team since the '60s at Monterey that didn't have that, and it's because of those guys in the '60s. To me, it all falls back on leadership and motivation and all the intangibles that go into being the winningest high school baseball coach ever. You don't have 40 years of exceptional kids come along – you might have a few years and a pitcher here or a pitcher there – but you don't have 40 years of talent to do what he did year in and year out. So I think we have to give him credit for being a pretty durn good coach. (smiling)

JIMMY SHANKLE '74:

He coached Monterey baseball for 40 years. I would challenge anyone, anywhere in the United States to come up with number one, a better coach and man, and number two, a better program.

Thanks Coach Moegle.

CHAPTER 7

Friend, Mentor and Family Man

Coach Moegle taught us about life. He taught us how to be a man and how life isn't always easy. He taught us how to look a person in the eye and compete every day. That's a big takeaway. He's a straight shooter. He's going to tell you exactly what he feels, and you aren't necessarily going to like it.

— Clint Bryant '92

GARY HUGHES '65:

That fact that he's a strong Christian man and that those qualities came through is why his players are so close to him today. I know that he cares deeply for his players, because I know he's made trips around the state and around the country for some of his players who have had illnesses and other problems. He's been deeply involved in their lives. In my case, 40-something years after I played, he's been a caring person and wanted to be sure that I was doing well, just as when I was playing for him. I have a special regard for him as a person, not just as the winningest high school coach of all time, and my coach, but as an individual. I have a special and high regard for him.

BOB FANNIN '78:

There were a few guys who really struggled with Coach Moegle, but we ended up loving him like a dad. We don't realize until we're done playing for him how much he really cares for us.

JOHN DUDLEY '62, ASSISTANT COACH 1968–'72:

When I played for him I saw him in one way. But when I coached with or against him, I saw him in a different light. He is such a gentleman and a guy who really cares about people.

BURLE PETTIT, LUBBOCK SPORTSWRITER:

I think the bottom line about Bobby is that he doesn't take himself too seriously. Despite all that he accomplished, I don't see a difference in him when I run into him today than I did the first time I ever saw him. He seemed nonchalant about his success. I know a lot of guys who have done a lot less that pop buttons every time they walk out the door. He's never taken himself too seriously, and he's not real good at accepting praise. He'll change the subject.

JOHN DUDLEY '62, ASSISTANT COACH 1968–'72:

I think he developed a close relationship with players over the years and he really has a deep concern for them. There were a couple guys from the class of '63 facing cancer and a life-threatening illness, and Coach Moegle got on a plane and flew to visit those guys and spend some time with them. He was reassuring to them, and it just points out how important his players were to him, despite when they played for him.

JIM BOB DARNELL '66:

I grew up with a dad who was harder on me and my brother than Coach Moegle ever thought about being. My dad came out to every practice from probably the 7th grade on – football practice ... anything. He was always out there. When I was a sophomore, I used to hear people say, "Your dad is out here trying to brown nose Coach Moegle." I just laughed and said, "I guarantee you there is not anybody out here who is going to brown nose Coach Moegle."

There were parents that hated him and there were some that liked him. When my dad died, Coach Moegle went to the funeral. The man who did the funeral was a friend of ours – a lawyer up in Plainview. He talked to Coach Moegle and said, "Why did you come to Mr. Darnell's funeral?" Coach Moegle said, "He was the best parent I ever had."

It's hard for me to talk about this. My dad cared a lot about his kids. He was very hard-headed. I tell people all the time that I didn't realize how hard-headed he was until he died, but he wanted to make sure that we grew up to be good people. And anything Coach Moegle wanted him to do, he would do. He worked his butt off helping get Dixie Little League started.

I had three Monterey letter jackets and after I graduated I might have worn them once. I gave them to dad. Mom took the letters off them and dad wore the jackets to go hunting. After my brother graduated from Monterey, dad started asking Coach Moegle to go fishing and hunting with him. He never did that during the time when we were in school.

I had quit going hunting and fishing with my dad when we were kids. When I was about 6 or 7 years old, we went hunting near a creek in Childress. We went down a turn row near a cotton farm and dad fired his gun at my feet. Unbeknownst to me there was a rattlesnake there. So my desire to be a hunter and a fisherman after that sort of waned. But my little brother was just as addicted to it as my dad. I was always glad that Dad and Coach Moegle developed a close relationship after we got out of high school. Dad never did try to cross that barrier when we were in school. He wanted us to earn it on our own, and I think we did.

JIMMY WEBSTER '85:

My mom was a special education teacher so she viewed this experience through a unique, incredible lens. She didn't take to Coach Moegle's treatment of us at the time, because she thought he was manipulating us.

Probably to a person, the guys in my class would sit here and say, "My mother and father had the most impact on my life ... I'm a product of watching them ... I'm a product of their upbringing ... I learned a work ethic and right and wrong from them." After them, it was Coach Moegle – certainly in my case, it was.

That said, I've always thought my mother felt like Coach Moegle at that time was a little more authoritarian and manipulative to get people to do what he wanted them to do. After I got out, my parents and Coach Moegle would talk very highly of each other. My parents thought very highly of him. At some point later in my life, they looked up and I was OK and wasn't a detriment to society. So there had to be some mutual gratitude in there somewhere.

And that's what we all learned from him – if we were going to be a salesman, a CIA agent, the President, a house painter or a ditch digger ... dadgummit, we were going to do it right.

MIKE CRUTCHER '68, ASSISTANT COACH 1973-'78, 1982-'85:

When Coach Moegle retired, he said something that really bothered me at the time, but it's also the best compliment I've ever had. We were at his retirement banquet and he was talking about his assistants. He praised all of them – Coach Dudley, Travis and all of them. He saved me for last, and I was with him longer than anyone else. When he got to me, he said, "Let me tell you something about Mike Crutcher. If I was hanging over a cliff, I'd want him to hold the rope." I thought it wasn't much of a compliment at the time, but I know that it was the greatest thing he could say about me.

COACH MOEGLE IN 1972:

Mike Crutcher just graduated from Tech. He is an exceptional person.

JIMMY WEBSTER '85:

Everything came down to guts with Coach Crutcher, which made it a great marriage between him and Coach Moegle.

BOB FANNIN '78:

Several of us had played JV football for Coach Crutcher our sophomore and junior years. Crutcher had Moegle's heart. He had played for him and had been through the tough times in the '60s. We were talking about the "Junction Boys" book and movie the other day in the office. We sort of wondered how somebody didn't die in that deal. There were days that kids nowadays wouldn't imagine.

JIMMY WEBSTER '85:

I was sitting in Coach Crutcher's American History class – not athletics, but in his classroom – and he was telling stories about how he loved Dana Rieger because the guy would puke and roll around in it because he was so tired after running. I remember thinking Coach Crutcher was wired a little differently because he was telling stories to the students in his history class about running kids and them puking. And that was early in the school year.

The rest of the class reacted with, "Ewwwwww, that's gross." But I remember thinking that it was cool because number one, somebody (Rieger) worked that hard, and number two, somebody else (Crutcher) noticed it. I was just getting to a stage of maturity that I wasn't the one saying, "Ewwwwww," but I was getting the idea that there was a bigger story there than that a guy had puked.

JEFF HARP '78:

Early in my senior year, we were working on baserunning and sliding. Coach Crutcher took a position like he was going to tag us and we would slide into the base. Being a senior and having a relationship with him after becoming a catcher, I decided to take a chance. So I slid headfirst but wrapped my arms around him and took him down.

About the time he said, "What are you doing," the rest of the team dogpiled him and wrestled around with him. He was mad as it happened, but after it was over he loved it. I never would've dreamed about doing that my junior year, but in my senior year after all the work we'd put in, I felt like I had that trust. I'd watched Jimmy Shankle come back and work out and he and Crutcher would end up wrestling and beating on each other. I remember thinking that I didn't want to catch if I was going to end up like those two. (smiling)

JIMMY WEBSTER '85:

When I was cut from the team my sophomore year, Coach Moegle didn't do it immediately. It was at the end of the fall semester and I had gone to buy some spikes because I thought I might make the team. I bought white spikes, and my older brother had gone through Monterey and knew about the baseball program and he told me, "That's not going to work. You can't wear white spikes there." So we dyed them black. But that all came tumbling down on me quickly when Coach Crutcher called Shane Horton and me into the office. He said, "Webster, you and Lance come here," only there wasn't a "Lance." He had called Shane by his older brother's name, which was Lance. I had a pretty good idea that my fate had just been sealed. (laughing) The silver lining was that he knew my name.

It was good fortune that I was in Coach Crutcher's class as a junior. After being cut, I had gone on to play on the soccer team. One day Coach Crutcher was talking to Coach Jones, the soccer coach, while we ran in the school halls for conditioning on a bad weather day. I was getting it (running hard) because Coach Crutcher was there and I thought in some way it might be a baseball tryout with him there watching.

There was a long list of fortunate things that went my way in a short period of time, because I certainly had a lack of talent. Some guys hadn't panned out on the JV our junior year and it appeared they were short a catcher. So, I went to Coach Crutcher in class and asked if I could try out again. He said he would ask Coach Moegle. The very next day he said he had asked and Coach Moegle had said no. I could read his body language that he was disappointed because he was a tough guy and could be very intimidating and loud and brash.

I loved Coach Crutcher but I could tell in his face that he was disappointed. And then about two weeks later he asked me when our last soccer game was. I told him it was the next day, and he asked, "Are you coming out after that?" I told him he had said not to come out, but he told me to come out and asked what position I had played. I told him I had played everywhere but catcher. He told me he would see me in a couple days.

From day one I was a catcher. I remember putting the shin guards on the wrong legs on the very first day. I didn't know. And then I put the chest protector on backwards with the wide part on the wrong shoulder. I caught on the JV that year and we went undefeated, but with a bunch of ugly scores. We had a bunch of juniors on the JV that year and several of those guys started on a state tournament team that next year. I was as happy as I could be. I got to play ... I got a uniform ... I was fired up. Coach Moegle didn't interact with me much that year. It was all Coach Crutcher. My skill level was not good enough for Coach Moegle to spend his time watching me.

That varsity team our junior year won 35 ballgames and lost in the state semifinals. They had an established catcher in Jimmy Simpson, and David Coleman was a year behind me and he was the heir apparent. David was starting on that team as a sophomore at third base, so I would've been an insurance policy for the team my senior year, at best.

I probably had Coach Crutcher in my corner. In fact, I remember vividly Coach Moegle and Coach Crutcher both telling me to varying degrees saying the exact same thing. As a coach now, I can respect this. (Smiling) Coach Crutcher's version was, "Every day after practice ... Every day, Webster! We go up there in that little office and Coach Moegle asks me, 'Who is the best catcher?' And I tell him you are, and you make me look like that!" This is while they're hitting fungo, so I was up there with them by the backstop and nobody else would hear this.

Coach Moegle's version was, "Everyday, Webster – I ask Coach Crutcher who the best catcher is. And for some reason he says you are. You can't even throw it to 2nd base in the air. I don't know what he sees in you." It was just talk – just matter of fact conversation while he hit infield.

MIKE CRUTCHER '68, ASSISTANT COACH 1973-'78, 1982-'85):

I was used to being treated tough as a kid. My dad insisted on me being tough. That's what I thought was the right thing to do. My senior year in the next-to-last-pitch of our district season at Palo Duro High School, I took a foul tip off the index finger of my throwing hand. Back then catchers didn't put their throwing hands behind their back so my hand was exposed.

The bone was hanging out the end and the fingernail was peeled back. I went to the dugout to show it to Coach Moegle. We didn't have a trainer back then like we do now. He got a pair of pliers and pulled the fingernail up and covered the bone. I ended up having surgery later to fix it. I went back out there and caught one more pitch to finish the game. I didn't think anything about it, but I knew my finger was broken.

You'll never believe what he did, and I played like this the rest of the year, and we ended up losing in the regional finals. We were in Furr's after the game at Palo Duro, like we always did, and we were in line. Coach Moegle asked one of the workers, "Can I go back in the kitchen, please?" The worker said yes and he told me to come with him. If I'm lying, I'm dying about this. He always had a pocketknife and he took it out and asked if they had a lemon in the kitchen. They got him a lemon and he sliced it in half and he drilled a little hole in it and stuck my finger in it. It burned ... It was miserable ... It was miserable!

Every day the rest of the season I would go in the office and he would stick my finger in a lemon. And I'd go home with that bone sticking out the end of my finger with no fingernail and you know what my dad said? He said, "Well, hell, boy, are you going to play or not?" And Coach Moegle was basically saying the same thing. He would change that lemon and I'd put an ace bandage on it and would wear a lemon on my finger in school. I asked him about the lemon and it was basically an old wives' tale about reducing the pain or something. I played the rest of the season with that finger sticking out and tried to hit with my finger off the bat.

I always thought about wanting to be tough ... to be that type of kid. My parents were both uneducated. My dad quit school to go in the army during World War II. He lied about his age to get in, then went to the Pacific. My mother was young when they got married. They weren't upper middle class and didn't understand the full value of education and sports. But Daddy always told me, "You're going to be the best you can."

JIMMY SHANKLE '74:

Coach Moegle meant a lot to me in my life – more than people would ever know. Our senior year in 1974, it was right before the season started, I had a pair of old worn out Riddell baseball shoes with holes in the soles and holes in the toes. Everybody wore them. I couldn't afford them, and I didn't have the opportunity to work in the summer because I was playing ball and doing things. My dad drove a cattle truck for a living at that time.

About three days before the season started there was a new pair of Riddell cleats in my locker. I asked Coach Moegle what the deal was with the shoes. He told me my dad came by in his cattle truck and dropped the cleats off in time for the game. My dad would be gone for periods of time driving his truck. He used to come to the games out of town or at Lowrey Field in his cattle truck. He would pull in, watch the game, give me a kiss and say, "Way to go" and then leave to haul cattle again.

So when Coach Moegle told me my dad dropped them by, I believed him. Ten years later I found out that my dad didn't bring me those shoes. Coach Moegle bought me those shoes because he knew I needed them, so I'd have a good pair of shoes to play the season in. That's the kind of guy he was that hardly anybody got to see. And I was one of the few to have that benefit.

COACH MOEGLE:

There was a scout with the Boston Red Sox named Danny Doyle. Danny drafted Jimmy (Shankle) in the 2nd round. Jimmy had been selected to play in our first State High School Coaches Association All-Star Game in the Astrodome. He called me and said that Doyle was in town to sign him. I told him that Doyle could sign him anytime and to go ahead and play in Houston.

He said that Doyle had offered him $40,000 and that he wouldn't offer it again. I asked him if $40,000 was worth it to him, and he said, "Yes, $40,000 is a LOT of money." I said OK, and he asked me to come to his signing. I told him he should have his family there, but he told me he would rather have me. So, I went and watched Danny do the contract. That was pretty neat.

JIMMY SHANKLE '74:

For all the years of knowing and playing for Coach Moegle, it's been a pleasure and a labor of love. When we were at Monterey High School together and later when I played pro ball I came back and worked out with his teams. I loved being around the guy. He's like a second father to me. He was to a lot of kids who didn't know it at the time. Maybe I let him in a little more than others did, because there was a need there for me. He's meant a lot to a lot of kids – a tremendous amount to a lot of kids. He's made men out of a lot of boys. To that, my hat is off to him, to his wife and daughters who lived through it all, too. He's got a great supporting cast.

TUEY RANKIN, ASSISTANT COACH 1997-'99:

I believe Coach Moegle coached against my dad when Dad played at Midland High. He was a young coach at the time. And he remembered my dad. So, when Coach Moegle and I started coaching together, he and my dad kind of became buddies. Every time they saw each other, they loved talking. They were both old-school and my dad thought the world of Coach Moegle. As a matter of fact, if my dad were still alive, I promise you he would tell me that I need to call Coach Moegle and go have lunch with him. They had a lot in common. They were both "men's men" kind of guys.

CLINT BRYANT '92:

My parents loved Coach Moegle. With my dad having grown up a farm boy outside of San Antonio, there hadn't exactly been a silver spoon in his mouth as a kid. It was all about hard work and earning what he kept. Parents tend to side with their children these days, but my parents never did. If I came home and complained about Coach Moegle, that was not going to go over well. They loved his coaching style and loved the way he pushed us. They saw what he was trying to do and bought into that same message. It wasn't always roses, but looking back, it was exactly what most kids needed.

JIMMY WEBSTER '85:

My dad was proud when I made the team. He took me to get a haircut – the Coach Moegle haircut" – over the ears. It was at his barber shop, with his guys – the mail carriers and his friends. I remember the tone in his voice and the look on his face.

JEFF HORN '96:

I will say that toward the end of my senior year when we were making our run, Coach Moegle, for the first time in all the years that I had known him, became more of a friend to us seniors. I don't know if he thought we needed that, but he became almost more like a friend than a coach. That was really cool and I'll always remember it. I had heard all the horror stories, but I really believe Coach Moegle had a lot of fun going along for the ride that we took that season.

JIMMY WEBSTER '85:

I coached at Lubbock High his last three or four years at Monterey and was obviously in the same district coaching against him. When I first got to Lubbock High, I had asked him how he taught his cur-

1999 retirement reunion

veball because he had a group of pitchers at that time that threw a hammer (a really good curveball). He told me to ask him when he retired and I kept that in mind.

In the summer of 1999 at his retirement celebration, I asked him again and he said to come see him. Mike Gustafson and Brad Walker went along with me and we went to his house for an afternoon. He went to his garage and grabbed some baseballs. We sat on his couch and he talked about the grip and how he had played against a guy in minor league ball who had a good curve. He said he hunted the guy down after the game and the guy showed him how he threw it.

It's like a lot of the things we talked about – the life-altering stuff. I'm not saying that alone changed his life, but my gosh did he have some guys who could throw that pitch. They would tuck that thumb back and just fire it. That day he told me some guys could get it immediately, some guys could get it with some work, and some guys would never get it.

When I saw it at its best, he had Alex Garcia and Mark Martinez and Robert Castilleja and those guys were throwing hard, heavy curve balls that just disappeared. They were all mid-80s with their fastballs. Martinez had the edge on those guys, but all of them were decent pitchers. That run he had right there was one of the best ever. He was piecing those guys together masterfully. They won a state championship game, and then lost the state championship game the year after Martinez graduated.

But it all went back to years earlier when he met a guy after a game and asked him about his breaking ball.

JOHN DUDLEY '62, ASSISTANT COACH 1968-'72:

One of the neat things for me personally is having had the opportunity to play for him, to coach with him and to coach against him, and now to claim him as a friend. It is extremely gratifying for me, and I wouldn't trade it for anything. To be fortunate enough to play in his program, then to have the opportunity to coach with him for five years and to see him as a coach instead of the way I saw him as a player, I got a better understanding of what motivated him and why we did certain things. It was interesting as his assistant coach, that the players didn't want to approach him, but they would come to me to ask Coach Moegle certain things. I was the "go-between" and that was fun to be able to do that.

TRAVIS WALDEN '81, ASSISTANT COACH 1989-'94:

The 2007 Western Little League all-star team that went to Williamsport for the Little League World Series had Gerald Arredondo as a coach. Gerald went to Monterey and had tried to play baseball but quit. He later went to wrestling and then played football for Coach Moegle his senior year. He doesn't have the baseball side of the Coach Moegle stories, but he's got the football side of the stories.

Before the team left for Williamsport, they had a big send-off and Coach Moegle spoke to the team. When the team got back, Coach Moegle mailed a letter to Gerald and told him he was proud of him. Gerald showed it to me. He told me out of everything that happened, that letter meant the most because he had finally gotten Coach Moegle's respect. Everybody wants to earn respect. It shouldn't be given – it should be earned. Gerald had earned Coach's respect.

When I was there, we had a very good relationship. It was a friendship. He wrote me a letter later on and told me I'd turned into a good coach and that he appreciated my friendship. Like Gerald, I kept that letter. His approval meant so much.

TUEY RANKIN, ASSISTANT COACH 1997-'99:

We sort of knew each other from my time at Lee, plus I had coached against Coach Moegle when I was at Tascosa. I had student taught at Monterey so he knew me and always said that when he had an opening, he would get me back there. He knew I had baseball in my background, so I was going to be the baseball assistant. I was a little bit intimidated because I was going to work with Coach Moegle. At that time, I didn't know if my coaching track was going to be football or baseball. Baseball was probably my favorite sport.

One of my first experiences with Coach Moegle involved him asking me what I had coached at Tascosa. I told him I had been the varsity assistant and that I had coached outfielders. He said, "A monkey can coach outfielders. I'm going to teach you to coach my infielders." (smiling) And he taught me to coach infielders.

GARY ASHBY '73:

He was brutally honest. That might be why parents didn't confront him, because they really didn't want to know the truth. If you didn't want to know the truth, don't ask the question. Because you were going to get the truth.

I was doing my student teaching under (MHS basketball) Coach (Joe) Michalka and Coach Moegle. A kid came in with a slip and he was a little rotund. Coach Moegle said, "What's that?" The kid said, "Miss Jones says I'm supposed to take your PE class." Coach Moegle looked at him and said, "No. Son, we do 100 pushups and 100 situps and a bunch of running. You take that slip back to Miss Jones and you tell her you're too fat to take my PE course." The kid turned around and went back to Miss Jones and I never saw him again. Coach Moegle was BRUTALLY honest.

TUEY RANKIN, ASSISTANT COACH 1997-'99:

I would come over to football from baseball and we would be

talking about a football player and I would say something like, "This kid tries hard, but he can't run a lick." And Coach Morton, in a kidding sort of way would say, "There you are, going all 'Coach Moegle' on me."

JEFF HORN '96:

If you ask Coach Moegle a question, you're going to get the truth. You may not like it, but it's the truth. That's just another strong quality of his.

CLINT BRYANT '92:

Coach Moegle taught us about life. He taught us about how to be a man and how life isn't always easy. He taught us how to look a person in the eye and compete every day. That's a big takeaway. He's a straight shooter. He's going to tell you exactly what he feels, and you aren't necessarily going to like it. As I think about my career after baseball ... in my management style, I try to be up front and honest with people. They aren't always going to like it, but it makes them better people.

TUEY RANKIN, ASSISTANT COACH 1997-'99:

One thing he would say to kids who did everything right – they worked hard and tried hard but just couldn't play – was "Son, you've got skill but you just don't have any talent." (laughing)

NATHAN SWINDLE '81:

Right before Christmas break, he would tell each of us where we stood with him in the program. It was usually on a cold, gray day when we were practicing in the locker room. We would all be sitting there and he'd go around and point at each guy and tell us what we needed to work on to get some playing time the next spring. And he was completely honest. He told my friend Roy Horton, "You're a good kid and you work hard, but you just don't have any talent. You need to get your schedule changed." Right there in front of everybody. We were all sitting there thinking, "Whoa!" And we all hoped we wouldn't hear something like that when he got to us. Roy ended up being our equipment manager for the state championship team.

TRAVIS WALDEN '81, ASSISTANT COACH 1989-'94:

As a player, I thought he just didn't like me. But on the other side as a coach, I would sit in the office and talk with him every day after practice and listen to why he did things and how he handled players. There was a "method to his madness."

NATHAN SWINDLE '81:

With the glass door and the glass walls in his office, we knew he saw us when we came in the locker room door. I would hustle past his office as quick as I could my first two years, but as a senior, I had some down time between my last class and the start of practice. I finally decided I would go in there and talk with him. We would just shoot the bull before practice, and I liked it. I found out engaging him in conversation was a good thing. I looked forward to seeing what was on his mind every day, because he'd tell me.

TUEY RANKIN, ASSISTANT COACH 1997-'99:

The very best times I had with him were in his office. We had baseball after lunch, because we ate lunch really late. I officed with the football coaches, but I would go up to his office about 15 to 20 minutes before practice. We would talk about the stock market, and he loved to talk college football and college basketball. And we would talk about what was wrong with the school. He would say, "If corporations ran their businesses like the school system, we'd all be broke." (laughing) We would just sit there and talk, and I value that as much as anything. He had such a system set up. He told me several times, "This thing runs itself." The kids would be out there warming up and they would be ready to practice when we got out there.

JEFF CHASE '90:

My family moved across town to the Monterey district in 1989, between my junior and senior year. The school boundary lines had been re-drawn around that time and my parents wanted my younger brother to stay with his group and go to Evans and Monterey.

During off-season baseball I was issued my gray t-shirt and a pair of shorts, like everyone else had for so many years. I didn't have a Monterey hat so I asked Coach Moegle about it. He told me I would get a hat when I made the team. That was an eye-opening moment for me because I had been an all-district pitcher at Coronado the year before. I knew right then that this was going to be a no-nonsense situation.

Coach Moegle - 1989

Later in the semester he caught me as I was coming in the locker room. He called me into the office and asked me how school was going. He knew that I was the new kid. We talked about stuff that had nothing to do with baseball. I had seen him from across town, so my view of him was like most people in the opposing dugout, which was that he was intimidating and tough and never said a nice word to anyone. On that day in his office I learned who he really was. To this day I appreciate him carving out some time just to talk to me in the office that afternoon.

JEFF HARP '78:

I can't tell you how many times in my 34 years of coaching that I've thought, "What would Coach Moegle have done?" Would he have cut all of them? (laughing) Would he have pulled one to the side? Would he find that leader?

What would MY mentor ... What would MY coach have done? When I first started coaching, I tried coaching like him but that wasn't me. He was the only guy who could do that.

LARRY HAYS, LCU & TTU COACH '71-2008:

Guys who wanted to coach like him can get in trouble. They were smart, intelligent guys but they would copy him and get in trouble.

COACH MOEGLE:

Several of my players went on to coach. John Dudley was the first to coach at any level. Mike Crutcher, Bart Bratcher, Steve Mims, Dick Jones in 1969. Later on, Gary Ashby, Shankle, Jeff Harp, Steve and David Coleman, Travis Walden, Doug Welch, Jimmy Webster, Mike Eckles and Dusty Hart.

I've had a lot of kids who played for me that tried to coach like I coached them. And they've had no success whatsoever. I don't know exactly why. Maybe the caliber of kids they are working with isn't used to that kind of stuff and they won't perform for them.

I tell my players who go on to coach to take what they learned from us, but to build their programs their own way. They'd come by and tell me about their new job, and I'd tell every one of them, "Don't be like me. Be yourself." The worst thing he could do was emulate me and it not be a part of his makeup. They could see the firmness and toughness that I had, and if they tried to imitate it and it wasn't really a part of their personality, their kids could see through that. Kids are really smart and they know when you're bluffing and don't know what you're talking about. You can't bluff your way with kids. You just can't do it.

LARRY HAYS, LCU & TTU COACH '71-2008:

When I started the baseball program at Lubbock Christian, I didn't know anything or anybody. I just knew I probably shouldn't be doing it. (smiling) Coach Moegle took care of all the high school kids in this area for me. If he ever told me to take a kid, I took him if I could get him. A few times I took a kid that he told me not to. And maybe once it turned out all right. But if he ever did this, (a choking gesture with his hand to his neck) I knew. I'd be out at the ballpark watching the kid and he would do something and Coach Moegle would catch my eye from the 3rd base coaches box and make the choking sign to me. I took two or three kids he told me not to, and I regretted it most of the time. One of them worked out OK. He would say, "That kid can play for you, but you don't want him out there. You'd have to chase him off and it wouldn't do you or him any good." He would just give me the honest, bottom line assessment.

Between him and Coach (Julian) Pressly at Odessa Junior College and Ernie Johnson down at Midland Lee, I had good baseball men who respected each other and would let me bounce names off of them.

Why he decided to help me, I don't know. But I'll always appreciate it. The first couple kids he sent to me were Robert Vittitow and Glen Palmer, guys who hadn't worked out at other places. He told me Palmer would burn up a lot of innings for me. I didn't know what that meant, but I found out. If he was on, he would beat a good team. And Vittitow was a competing dog. He came over and was a clutch hitter. Coach Moegle had told me he would hit but might make me mad on defense. And he did hit. Several of those guys early on did well.

He really helped me. I think a lot of people in my situation would've been intimidated by him, but I wasn't. He knew who I was, and I knew who he was, and he was OK with me. He didn't come out with a bunch of "You need to do this and you need to do that," because he knew I wasn't coming at it from the same direction as him. But, I had the same expectations. That's where we were the same.

COACH MOEGLE:

When I first started coaching, I didn't know anybody in the coaching business. We had an opportunity to go to the state tournament in 1961 and this was when I first ran into the people from Houston. I got to know some of them, but it still wasn't with Bellaire and Coach Ray Knoblauch. That didn't happen until 1963. In '61 we were playing Lufkin and Baytown, and Houston didn't come into play until '63 when Bellaire beat us 3-1.

That was my first interaction with Coach Knoblauch. He had come out of pro baseball just like I had. He had played at a little higher level of pro ball than I had – he had played in the Texas League. At Bellaire they had a unique situation in that they were the only school in the Houston school district that offered Russian, so he recruited from all over Houston to come there to play baseball and take Russian. At Monterey, we were dependent on the local kid living within our district and having to compete against Bellaire for state championships.

In 1970, Knoblauch was there but we lost to Aldine in the semifinal. Bellaire beat us for the state championship in 1971, 5-4, and it felt like we would never beat them. Then in '72 the tide turned, and we could offset his good pitcher with our good pitcher, Donnie Moore. I also had a group of kids that just would not give up. I had the chance to play them again in '78 and we had a 4-0 lead but committed a couple errors late and lost 6-4.

That was the last chance I had to compete against Ray. He's since passed away, but to be 600 miles apart we really had an intense rivalry in the '60s and '70s. We started the first High School Baseball Coaches Association. He started as the president and I was the vice president. I did all the work and he took all the rewards for it. (smiling) We started the association in 1973. It's up to 2,250 members now. We started with 27.

FRED OLIVER, MHS COACH 2000-'09:

He is definitely a leader. He's a founding father and charter member of the Texas High School Baseball Coaches Association. He was an original member in 1973. Because I am heavily involved in it and have been a past president of the organization, I know about the charter members. It took some courage to start this association for baseball coaches only.

MIKE CRUTCHER '68, ASSISTANT COACH 1973-'78, 1982-'85:

I was a charter of member of the Texas High School Baseball Coaches Association, because I was with Coach Moegle when all of that was starting. At the big meeting every year I was in charge of getting the donuts.

Coach Moegle would give me $3 or whatever and I would go get a couple dozen donuts. I got some Jack 'n' Jill donuts one year and Coach Moegle loved them. The next year I got the same donuts and there was a sign that said something like "Now Selling Franchises." So I told Coach Moegle about it.

Now, he will probably deny this and tell you he didn't do it. I told him they were franchising and that we should go into the doughnut business. He said, "Let's do it." So he and I applied for a doughnut franchise. (laughing) We were going in the doughnut business! He said he would keep coaching and would be the "silent partner" and I was going to run the doughnut business. I said no thanks. We were going to be "doughnut guys." Yeah right! (laughing)

FRED OLIVER, MHS COACH 2000-'09:

The view that most coaches around the state have of Coach Moegle is of greatness. Again, I was fortunate to be president of the association from 2002-2004. I invited all the charter members back for a luncheon and our banquet. They all came back, including Coach Moegle.

The stories that were told that weekend were unbelievable. They knew if they faced him in the playoffs, they were going to have a hard time winning and they'd better be prepared. They knew they weren't going to face a sloppy team that didn't know how to do the routine things. They knew they would face a very competitive team. While we're stuck out here on the South Plains, Houston Bellaire knew Bobby Moegle.

I use Bellaire because Coach Knoblauch, who was Bellaire's coach during all those years, had some real head-knockers with Coach Moegle in baseball. Ernie Johnson at Midland Lee did, too. They knew the caliber of baseball that was going to come from the Plainsmen. Coaches thought well of him, and they continued to ask him questions about certain situations in baseball. He was very highly thought of.

COACH MOEGLE:

High school baseball coaches are paid a whole lot better now and can be hired just to coach baseball, not football assistants, too.

JEFF HARP '78:

I saw Coach Moegle in Waco at the baseball coaches convention. It might've been his last year to coach. We started talking and walking like he was the mentor and I was the student. I was looking around at everybody thinking, "Do y'all see who I'm with? That's right ... I'm with the man."

JIMMY WEBSTER '85:

All the coaches wear jeans and sweats at coaching school in Waco, but in the '90s Coach Moegle would wear khakis and a button-down shirt. I still wear khakis down there.

JEFF HARP '78:

I'll be at coaching school and guys will come up to me and say, "Hey, tell us a Moegle story."

TRAVIS WALDEN '81, ASSISTANT COACH 1989-'94:

When I used to go to coaching school in Waco with Coach, so many players who had played for him were now coaching. They would come to him and it was "Coach this" and "Coach that." It was amazing. They were asking for his advice, because they knew he had that passion. What was amazing to me was that he held it for as long as he did.

I coached at five different places and he coached for 40 years in the same building and on the same field. I could see that his passion had died off a little bit, but I guarantee that if he had taken another job somewhere later on, he would've kicked it right back in where he was earlier. But for him to get the kind of effort from everybody over 40 years, those type leaders don't come along very often.

MARK GRIFFIN '72:

We call him "Coach" because that was our relationship with him. The time does not affect that at all. He'll always be "Coach Moegle" to me. I don't think I'm man enough to ever call him anything but that, because that's who he was to me and that's what he was for me. Because of him, a lot of us have achieved some things later in our lives. And if we're truthful and candid, we go back to those days with Coach Moegle because he was instrumental in taking young men and causing us to be good, quality grown men.

JOHN DUDLEY '62, ASSISTANT COACH 1968-'72:

One of the things indicative of the respect that Coach Moegle commands is that I don't know of a player in all those years who called him or calls him by his first name. For me, he is "Coach Moegle" and he will always be "Coach Moegle." I can talk about some other coaches that I have worked with or played for, and I may call them by their first name. But when it comes to him, he is "Coach Moegle." I think when you talk to the majority of guys who have played for him, they'll never address him by his first name. It's always "Coach Moegle."

JIMMY WEBSTER '85:

I was back in town one summer when I was still coaching down in Devine. I was probably 28 years old and my wife, Kelly, and I were at dinner with Daren Hays and his wife, Kristi. I ordered a beer, and Coach Moegle walked into the restaurant. I didn't want to disappoint him, so I looked around to find the waiter to cancel the drink order. I couldn't find the waiter, so I got up and went to the kitchen and opened the door and yelled to the waiter to cancel the order. I was a grown man, not 16 years old, but I didn't want to disappoint him. That's how much I thought of him.

For years after I got out of high school, I would see him and would have to wipe my palms on my jeans because I still got nervous at 28, 30 years old.

MARK GRIFFIN '72:

A lot of people don't know this, but he was really a good football coach, too. Now that I look back at it, his passion was teaching. He was a good teacher. Whether it was football or baseball, he was just a very good instructor. You sensed that passion early on, and if you didn't appropriate that into your being and into your spirit, then you weren't going to be as successful with him and understand and appreciate what he was doing and why he was doing it.

RON REEVES '78:

He was a good football coach. He was the same in football as he was in baseball. He was hard all the time. I played linebacker, too. He was intense and very aggressive. We did stunting and twisting and blitzing. We wreaked havoc because we'd have guys running in the backfield that never got touched because they never knew where we were coming from. We had great defenses. In fact, if we hadn't had good defenses we would've been in trouble. We won a lot of games 10-3 and 7-0.

JEFF HORN '96:

My dad played football for him and he talks about what a great coach he was. He said, "If you thought he had piss and vinegar in him in baseball, you should've seen him on the football field where it was OK to be nastier." (laughing)

JOHN DUDLEY '62, ASSISTANT COACH 1968-'72:

I think it was about 1976 that we were going through a football coaching change at Coronado. Coach Moegle and I were traveling to Waco at the time for the baseball clinic. With me being a coach at Coronado, and with Coach Moegle being interested in the football job over there, all we did was talk football down there and back. He wanted to know all about the football position. When we got home, he told me he was going to apply for the job.

I think it's good that he didn't get that job because of everything that has transpired and all the decades beyond that at Monterey and the championships and things. Nobody is going to equal his number of wins given the longevity he had.

COACH MOEGLE:

I put in an application for the Coronado football job. I felt like I had put my time in at Monterey and had been there for 20 years and had coached a good level of football during that time. I did apply and was actually told that I had the job. This is a true story and it may hurt somebody's feelings, but I was told when I left the athletic office that I had the football job.

I was very prepared to handle the job, but by the time the superintendent and principal found out that I was the choice, they didn't want me as their coach at Coronado. They hired another guy. A lot of people who told me I was the new coach at Coronado had to apologize to me because they were overruled by the superintendent and principal at the time. I always had a hard feeling because I thought I'd be a very good football coach. I felt that being with James Odom and Bill DuBose that I had a good background and I felt that I could've done the same thing in football that I was doing in baseball.

But God works in funny ways, and He threw up a barrier and said that I was going to stay on this path. And consequently, as I look back on it, it really became a good thing because I built a good reputation here and statewide, but at that time I didn't understand it.

MARK GRIFFIN '72:

He was the defensive coordinator for Coach Odom and I had played against him at Lubbock High. His coaching style in football was no different. He was a student of the game. If he was going to engage in the process of instruction, he was going to make sure he knew everything he could about the game.

Interestingly enough, a couple years after we won the state championship, he actually applied for the Coronado head football coaching job and the principal at Coronado at that time had a son named Scott who was my age and had not made it through the baseball program at Monterey. I think Coach Moegle had cut him or something. Mr. (Max) O'Banion still had hard feelings about that and wouldn't hire him as football coach.

So who knows what would have happened if he had been hired as football coach at Coronado. I doubt Coach Moegle appreciated it at the time, but it was probably the very best thing that could've happened for him to not get the job.

GARY ASHBY '73:

He was a great football coach. He tried to get the Coronado football coaching job, and had he gotten it we wouldn't be doing this interview today.

TRAVIS WALDEN '81, ASSISTANT COACH 1989-'94:

I think he was a quality football coach. I know there was a time when the Coronado football job opened when Coach Quarles left and Coach Moegle applied for the job. We were about the age to get to Monterey and were hoping he was going to be around. We were afraid he was going to take that football job. He was a solid football coach. I've got a lot of friends who are football coaches now who talk about what Coach Moegle taught them that they still use as coaches.

If he had wanted to be a great football coach or basketball coach, he would've been successful. His discipline, the structure of his practices, the toughness in everything he did and being ready and knowledgeable about what he was doing would have made him successful at anything he wanted to do.

MIKE CRUTCHER '68, ASSISTANT COACH 1973-'78, 1982-'85):

When I was his assistant coach, we had a million hours of discussion about family stuff, mainly about raising girls, because he and I both had two daughters. When I was young, I would say, "By golly I'll NEVER do that" when talking about the girls and what they would do later on. And he would say, "Don't say that, because at some point you're going to do it." And sure enough, it happened the way he said it would. (laughing)

JIMMY WEBSTER '85:

I have two daughters, just like Coach Moegle. When the girls were little and I was at Lubbock High in the late '90s, I remember telling him I was having a hard time balancing everything, because I wanted to be the best I could be at coaching. I wanted to know how he had balanced his marriage, his daughters and coaching football and baseball. His answer was simple – it was that Coach Odom had been great to them.

That was a rough time for me because I was a young coach and full of piss and vinegar and climbing the football ranks and trying to be good at coaching baseball AND be a good father and a good husband. He was the only person I knew to talk to about it. The other similarity between Coach Moegle and me is that we both married a good person who was able to balance our absence from the home. And they were not only able to handle it, they were understanding of the job.

MIKE CRUTCHER '68, ASSISTANT COACH 1973-'78, 1982-'85:

When we would talk about our daughters, his were older and were dating and mine were still little. We talked about them dating and he would say, "Don't be too tough, and be considerate." I had dated a girl in high school who lived next door to Coach Moegle and Carolyn. Carolyn would come over and take a picture of us before prom or whatever. But Coach Moegle would never come over. And the next day at school he would gig me about the tuxedo I was wearing or something like that.

As we got older, he would watch his money closely while I never watched mine. And he would gripe a little about having to pay for the girl's sorority. And I would always tell him, "My daughters will NEVER be in a sorority." He would say, "Don't you say that." And I would tell him, "You don't understand – they will NEVER be in a sorority. I'm telling you they will never be in a sorority." Sure enough, in her first year at Tech, my daughter Amy came to me and said, "Dad, I want to be in a sorority." Coach Moegle always wore me out about that.

TUEY RANKIN, ASSISTANT COACH 1997-'99:

He treated his assistants well. With some coaches it can be a beating, but on one of my first days with Coach Moegle I grabbed a rake after practice and started raking the foul lines. He asked me what I was doing and I told him I was raking the lines. He told me I was paid to coach and not paid to work on the field, and that was that.

And on spring break, a lot of coaches don't give the kids time off. But we would get a few days off. He would say that the coaches needed a break and the kids needed a break, and that I wasn't paid to work on spring break. We would come back and practice once or twice before our next game. He pointed out that the kids needed time away if we were going to make a long run. He really knew when to back off. The good coaches know when to back off a little bit.

I remember going to scout our next opponent in El Paso, maybe when we would have a bye. He would tell me to take my wife with me and enjoy El Paso when I wasn't scouting the games. He was real good about the family thing and giving his assistants time off.

MIKE CRUTCHER '68, ASSISTANT COACH 1973-'78, 1982-'85:

We didn't socialize with Coach and Mrs. Moegle a lot because we were different ages. Think about that staff at Monterey at the time. Coach Moegle, Gus Wilson, Coach Odom were all from the same generation. And now here at Wylie East, the shoe is on the other foot. I'm the old guy.

JIMMY WEBSTER '85:

Most 16-year-old kids think a 50-year-old coach is old, which is about the age Coach Moegle was when we were in school. Now I'm the 50-year-old coaching high school kids, and I see my kids reacting to me the way we did to Coach Moegle. When I tell them something, I can see them cutting their eyes to each other, just like we did.

MARK GRIFFIN '72:

I think the records are important to him – they would be for anybody. Who wouldn't say, "I'm proud of what I accomplished?" But just as importantly if not more so, quite frankly, I think he's as proud of the men who played for him and what they've done with their lives since then. Those records speak for themselves – there was nobody any better. I know he genuinely takes pride in his players and what they've gone on to do in life since they played for him.

JOHN DUDLEY '62, ASSISTANT COACH 1968–'72:

I'm sure he is proud of his players, but what he is most proud of his is relationships with players and coaches from over the years. The conversations that he and I have had are about the people and how they're doing now.

CHAPTER 8

The Funny Stuff

If he had some doubts about a prospect, he'd go ahead and tell you.

I never will forget one time when Frank (Anderson, Hays' pitching coach at Texas Tech from 1991-1999) said we really needed a specific kid.

I'd seen the kid and I didn't see what Frank was seeing.

So I called Coach Moegle and told him, "Frank says we need him."

Coach Moegle said, "You tell Frank he needs glasses." (laughing)

— *Larry Hays*

BOB FANNIN '78:

One thing I remember that I was in awe of was in BP somebody would be out there feeding that pitching machine and he would cut across the infield from 1st to 3rd base with guys just crushing balls all over the place. It was like he was saying, "Go ahead and try to hit me." He was sort of immortal at that point. (smiling)

LARRY HAYS, LCU & TTU COACH '71-2008:

If he had some doubts about a prospect, he'd go ahead and tell you. I never will forget one time when Frank (Anderson, Hays' pitching coach at Texas Tech from 1991-1999) said we really needed a specific kid. I'd seen the kid and I didn't see what Frank was seeing.

So I called Coach Moegle and told him, "Frank says we need him." Coach Moegle said, "You tell Frank he needs glasses." (laughing)

BURLE PETTIT, LUBBOCK SPORTSWRITER:

We became good friends. I don't think Bobby ever realized he was talking to a sportswriter, because he was going to say what he was going to say anyway. You see coaches change the pitch of their voice when the interview starts. Bobby would give the media the same answer that he'd give one of the parents or one of the players. He just said what he felt.

I went with him to scout a team for the playoffs one time. We were on our way back and he said, "You know what? If we don't beat those ragamuffins, they ought to fire me." How many coaches say that? Most coaches say that the next team they play is the best team that ever existed and that they'd be lucky to even be on the field with them. Bobby didn't play that game.

GARY ASHBY '73:

He kept me out after practice one day. It was me and Shankle and it was my senior year, and I hadn't pitched up until then. We must've been a little short of pitching. He said, "All right, let's see your fastball." I threw one or maybe two fastballs. He said, "Let's see your curveball." I threw one curve ball. He said, "OK, let's go home." So that was my Monterey pitching career. It didn't take him long to evaluate talent. (laughing)

JIMMY SHANKLE '74:

The players' perception of the weather was if Coach Moegle's nose got cold, we would go in. He had a fairly good-sized nose, so we thought that was it.

TUEY RANKIN, ASSISTANT COACH 1997-'99:

We always, no matter what, took infield and outfield first at practice. And the JV and the varsity would take infield together. Early in the year, it would be terrible because the JV players would be throwing it all over. But what would happen is that the JV players would start to raise their play because the expectations were different. I was the JV coach and the varsity assistant, plus I was a varsity assistant for (MHS football) Coach (James) Morton.

I coached 60-something baseball games, plus all the spring football meetings. I wanted some more time with the JV kids one day to be sure they were ready for a game the next day. I told Coach Moegle that I was going to keep the JV kids late one day and do a little extra infield work. He kind of laughed and said "OK." We did it and it was horrible – balls were flying everywhere and we weren't sharp. I went up to the office afterward and I was mad at the kids. He said, "Do you see why I do it at the start of practice?" (laughing)

BOB FANNIN '78:

There was a story on a daily basis when we played for him. Something happened every day. That was the fun thing about playing for him – we just hoped we weren't going to be on the receiving end of what was going to happen that day. One time, Derek Hatfield ran across a water spigot somewhere at practice, which was at the school. Hatfield was real skinny – had a great arm, though. He could lay in the outfield during practice and we would cover him in those clovers out there. He could lay there for an hour and not get seen.

Anyway, Hatfield got hold of a spigot and he plugged it in out there in the outfield one time and it exploded on him with water going everywhere. Coach Moegle noticed because Hatfield was soaking wet. We all had to run for that.

LARRY HAYS, LCU & TTU COACH '71-2008:

My dad went to a game once and he was so glad to meet Coach Moegle. He said, "Coach Moegle, I'm Shanon's granddad."

Coach Moegle said, "Are you the reason why he can't do so and so?" Dad didn't like that. (laughing)

JIMMY WEBSTER '85:

One day we were taking infield at practice, and Coach Moegle was hitting. We had two balls going, as we always did. For some reason, a ball got loose around home plate. I don't remember if I'd dropped it or if it was a bad throw. But it rattled around and ended up to my left under Coach Moegle's feet. I should have said something to let him know it was there. But I was peddling as fast as I could and I didn't speak unless I was spoken to. He stepped on it as he was hitting infield and he went down to the ground. Naturally, everyone in the field was facing us and everybody started laughing into their gloves. I could see them laughing and so I got tickled myself and smiled.

He got up and wore me out. I just took it. (laughing)

JOHN DUDLEY '62, ASSISTANT COACH 1968-'72:

There were some guys in that '63 class who were real close to each other and to Coach Moegle. They were a year behind me in school. When they had a class reunion, they called Coach Moegle and had him hit them infield and then they wanted him to run them in 4-4-4. He told them they couldn't still do that and they said that they could. I didn't see it, but I'm told they went up to school and got their gear out and took infield and outfield, and they did run the 4-4-4. I was told that Buddy Hampton just barely made it. But he was going to make that last sprint.

KELLER SMITH '63:

You learned to never drink milk or eat Frito pie in the cafeteria on Wednesday, because if you did, there was a good chance you were going to lose it.

JIMMY WEBSTER '85:

One day after practice he asked me if I had brought the list of Dixie Little League kids yet. He had asked me for it a couple days earlier because he knew my dad was still involved in the league. He wanted it so he could mail his baseball school information to everyone. I had completely forgotten it, and instead of just saying, "'I'm sorry, Coach. I'll do it tonight," I panicked and started in with this excuse-filled saga about my dog eating the list and a bunch of other nonsense. He finally looked at Mike (Gustafson), who was sitting next to me, and said, "What did he just say? That didn't make a lick of sense." (Gus) laughed, and Coach Moegle just walked off.

LARRY HAYS, LCU & TTU COACH '71-2008:

One of the funniest things I ever saw him do was he had a kid out there who had thrown well and I'd read about him in the paper. They had a few days off for some reason and I had just gotten back from a road trip or something. So I called Coach Moegle. He told me that they would be scrimmaging out at Lowrey Field the next day, and he also told me about a couple kids who were like some others that had done well for me. I was wanting to see this one pitcher throw so I asked if all his pitchers would work in the scrimmage. He told me they would, so I headed out there the next day.

When I got there, I looked down the left field line where the pitchers usually warmed up. The kid I wanted to see was down there with about 20 baseballs in a pile. He was just winding up and throwing the balls into the fence. I saw his assistant coach and asked about the schedule for the scrimmage. He had the list of who would be pitching, and they had divided the scrimmage into three short games. The kid I wanted to see wasn't on there.

I looked down the left field line and the kid was still throwing the balls into the fence. I asked Coach Moegle, "Is he going to throw today?" He said, "He's throwing right now." I said, "Coach, you aren't going to let him throw in the scrimmage?" He said, "I'm not going to let him hit OUR guys. I don't mind him killing the other teams because he's going to hit two or three a game. But I'm not going to let him hit our guys." (laughing)

The kid would wind up and throw it against the fence, then he'd pick up another ball and wind up and throw another one. When he was out of balls, he'd go pick them up and bring them back and throw some more. That was his practice.

MARK GRIFFIN '72:

In the top of the 7th when we scored the winning run (in the '72 state championship game), my mother and father were fortunate to be there. My mother must've been sitting on the end of the bleacher seats. She got up and started jumping up and down, screaming, and she fell out of her seat and down to a concrete embankment. I think the joy overcame any bruises or pain that she had. It was a fantastic moment and one that, of course, we'll never forget.

MIKE CRUTCHER '68, ASSISTANT COACH 1973-'78, 1982-'85:

When I was coaching the JV, we were in a tournament out in Levelland. Dickie Jones, who was a former teammate of mine at Monterey and later coached at Amarillo High, was the head coach at Levelland. We got beat in a game out there, and we should've won the tournament. I punished those kids unmercifully right there on that field. Dickie came over to me and said, "Mike, you've got to get off the field. We've got another game." I told him, "We're not leaving this field until I punish these kids. Just don't invite us back next year if this is a problem."

I punished those kids and Dickie was over there telling me, "You're worse than Moegle!" (laughing)

LARRY HAYS, LCU & TTU COACH '71-2008:

I don't remember what time of the season it was, but I hadn't seen them (Plainsmen) because we (Lubbock Christian) had been playing. Coach Moegle had one kid, maybe David Coleman, that I wanted to go out and see, plus there were two other kids in the district that I wanted to ask him about. So I went out early and had a great visit with him. Ray Coleman came out during our visit, and Ray knew Coach Moegle well because his son Steve had already been through the program. We discussed the kids that I wanted to ask about and practice was about to start so I thought I would watch a little bit.

David was the first hitter and (Coach Hays' son) Shanon was next. We were behind the backstop watching him hit at the practice field, so we were very close to the hitter. Ray, Coach Moegle and I were back there and David was doing a pretty good job, I thought.

Coach Moegle stopped David and asked him, "Coleman, have you ever gone to my baseball school?" David said "Yessir."

"Have you been to my camp more than once?" "Yessir." He kept quizzing him and David kept saying, "Yessir."

Finally, Coach Moegle said, "Well you haven't learned anything." And then he quizzed him even more about what he was doing at the plate that day. David got back in there to hit and he was so flustered that he missed the next three or four.

Then he said, "I'll tell you something, Coleman. I will kiss your rear end down at the county courthouse at that gazebo if you ever get to play college ball. You aren't even close, and if you think you're a college hitter..." and kept going on David like he would.

Ray was standing right there with me during all of this.

Knowing that Shanon was coming up next, I told him, "I'll see you later, Ray." I wasn't going to let him tear into Shanon with me standing there so I left. (laughing)

RON REEVES '78:

In my senior year, we were in Austin at the state tournament. Coach Moegle's baseball school was still going on back in Lubbock. I don't remember the exact days of the week, but we went down on the bus with Coach Crutcher in charge, while Coach Moegle stayed back and finished the last day of baseball school. Coach Crutcher was strong and fully capable of taking care of us, but he was a young coach and was so afraid that something bad was going to happen. I remember him being nervous about being in charge of everybody because Coach Moegle wasn't there.

Anyway, we had bused down there and practiced and had eaten dinner and were back at the hotel that evening. There were five or six of us older guys in our room, and we were playing cards. Coach Crutcher came by our room and said, "Want me to show you some card tricks?" He had his big ol' eyes flashing, and he grabbed a towel and wrapped it around his head like a swami. We had a blast, and he was caught up in having fun with us. All of a sudden there was a knock on the door. Whoever it was at the door said, "Have y'all seen Coach Crutcher?" Coach Crutcher said, "Yes, I'm right here." The guy said, "Coach, Kelly Smith just got hit by a car." Coach Crutcher said, "He got hit by a whaaaaaaaaat?!?!" You know how his voice would go up when he got excited. (smiling) And he was talking to nobody in particular as he left the room, saying "Moegle leaves me in charge one time and Kelly Smith gets hit by a car..."

As it turned out, we were staying right by I-35 and Kelly and a couple other guys tried to cross the road to get a Coke or something at a convenience store. I mean, Kelly didn't get hit "bad" by a car, but he did get hit by a car. (laughing)

It's just one of those stories that when a few of us are together and we're talking about baseball, somebody will say, "He got hit by a whaaaaaaaat?!" And then we all start laughing.

STEVE HARR '73:

I was on the '72 and '73 teams. I was a left-handed pitcher who only pitched, both starting and closing. As a result, I had very few plate appearances. We had travelled to play Big Spring High School and it was my day to pitch. By some miracle I hit a ball hard in the left center gap.

As I rounded second and picked up Coach Moegle in the 3rd base coaching box, he was waving me on to 3rd. I had seen the left fielder stop at the fence and raise his hands to indicate some kind of ground rule double situation. It looked like the ball had gone under the fence. Coach Moegle waved me to 3rd and when I got there, he told me to go home. I didn't question him so off I went.

The umpire told me to go back to 2nd and Coach Moegle went into "discussion" mode with the umpire. Coach Moegle insisted that the outfielder had reached down for the ball first and then backed off and raised his hands.

The discussion went on for some time and Coach Moegle was not backing off. I waited at the plate and eventually they waved me back to 3rd. He said he reached a compromise with the umpire. I think it's the only ground rule triple in school history!

TRAVIS WALDEN '81, ASSISTANT COACH 1989-'94:

We played at Midland Lee my junior year. It was a good game, but we'd lost 4-3. We were in the locker room showering and some guys were doing something around the corner and they were laughing about something.

I happened to walk around the corner at the same time. Coach Moegle saw me there so he got all over me and said he was going to put me back on the JV. He told me that I thought everything was so funny and I needed my own TV show. It just caught me off guard because I had just walked around the corner.

When we got on the bus, it was bad news. Whenever somebody got in trouble, we all ragged each other about it. To this day they still rag me about having my own TV show. It was funny. It was never funny at the time, but once everything had settled down, those stories are hilarious.

TUEY RANKIN, ASSISTANT COACH 1997-'99:

We were out at Moegle Field on one of those long Saturday scrimmage days. We had two little chairs and were sitting out there watching the scrimmage and Coach Moegle had a Dallas Morning News that he was reading as we were talking about college basketball. I would see a kid doing something wrong and would go over and work with him. Coach Moegle said, "First thing, you need to sit down. You're making me nervous. It's just February. Second thing, he isn't going to play anyway."

JIMMY WEBSTER '85:

The first time I coached against him, the game was at Lowrey Field. I'm walking out of the dugout to the plate meeting and he was standing there facing me. He sticks his hand out and he was looking right at me. Just as I got there and stuck my hand out, he turned to the umpire. He left me standing there at home plate with my hand sticking out with nobody to shake it. It was like he said, "Hey little boy, I coached you and now I'm about to OUTcoach you." He put me in my place again. (laughing)

JEFF HARP '78:

One of my former players went to play at Hardin-Simmons for Steve Coleman. The player called me and told me that Coach Coleman knew me. I told him that Steve and I had gone way back together. He then told me, "He says some things that sound an awful lot like you."

I laughed and told him that we learned those things from the same man. I also told him not to make Steve mad, and he told me, "Kind of like you?" I said, "Exactly!" (laughing)

HUNTER LANKFORD '87:

As a sophomore, one of my early humbling experiences came during our appearance in the state tournament where, as the backup catcher to Jimmy Webster, I went out to warm up Mike Eckles between innings. I remember approaching home plate, looking up at the stands at Disch-Falk and turning toward the field, and immediately thinking, "This place is huge ... Mike looks tiny out there ... here comes the first pitch ... clean catch ... OK, throw it back, firm, hit him in the chest ... ooooof!"

I launched it straight into center field as if I were trying to throw out a runner at second base. I immediately received complimentary heckling from the stands and got to enjoy those all the way back to the dugout as Jimmy resumed his position.

MIKE CRUTCHER '68, ASSISTANT COACH 1973-'78, 1982-'85:

Coach Moegle and I often went fishing and hunting together. He really liked that. Bill Loper printed our team media guides for us and he had two sons go through the program. Bill had access through Piggly Wiggly to a hunting lease and a fishing lease near Post. One time I was walking behind him when Coach Moegle was casting. He hooked my ear and just ripped it to pieces. He had to get that fish hook out of my ear and I told him, "You are killing me!" (Laughing) Those are some good memories.

CHAPTER 9

The Impact

We've all had Coach Moegle in our minds later in life, still pushing us. It's paying our bills.

It's rocking the crying baby to sleep in the middle of the night when you can't keep your eyes open.

It's life.

— Jimmy Webster '85

COACH MOEGLE:

In 1998, Greg Sherwood told me there was a new policy where coaches no longer had to teach class. I liked that. In 1999, Wayne Havens called and said there was a problem and the rule had been changed and that I would have to teach. I didn't want to go back into the classroom, so I decided to retire. I was 65.

JACK DALE, BROADCASTER:

One thing I appreciated about Coach Moegle was that he thought about me and my radio program when it came time for him to retire. People in the media are always looking for the big story or the scoop. In the spring of '99, Gary Ashby was on the program with me on a Wednesday morning, as he normally was back then. We invited Coach Moegle to be on the show and we talked baseball, but then out of the clear blue sky he announced his retirement on our show. So I'll always appreciate him for giving us that big story right there on our little ol' radio show. It was big news in the city because people were wondering how long he would continue. He gave Monterey baseball 40 years, and that's a pretty good career right there.

JEFF HORN '96:

I think retirement was bittersweet for him. He never lost that zeal for competing and pushing to win and accomplishing a task as a team. I think the intensity as he had grown older had changed a little. But it was a sad day for Monterey because he was the common denominator for 40 years, with unquestioned success. To have success over so many generations was unheard of. It was totally shocking when he hung it up.

TRAVIS WALDEN '81, ASSISTANT COACH 1989-'94:

He went to the state tournament in the 1960s, '70s, '80s and '90s. When he retired, I didn't look at the era ending, but rather all the things he did and all that he accomplished. Eventually it was going to have to end.

I was glad to see the way he did it, as opposed to somebody just going through the motions no longer coaching and just being a figurehead. That wouldn't be Coach Moegle. If he wasn't over there coaching 3rd base and getting after us and flipping rocks at the ground from his knee and throwing his hands in the air and getting on the umpires and being himself, that would've been a travesty. He still had some toughness and was still getting after people at the end. He knew it was time, and I respect that.

I see too many people who wait too many years to retire as a player or coach and it kind of diminishes their legacy. Coach Moegle went out on top. He did it his way and he did it the right way. He knew it was time and he walked away the way he should have. And he was as mean as he ever was, and that was the way it was supposed to be.

FRED OLIVER, MHS COACH 2000-'09:

It's always hard to give up coaching, for anybody. Maybe you don't miss the long practices and some of the things that go along with it. But the games, you truly miss. He is admired throughout the United States. Many people know him. For me to take the reins of Monterey baseball after him was quite an honor. He remains a friend and a great guy. He is one of those who will be remembered forever along baseball lines.

JOHN DUDLEY '62, ASSISTANT COACH 1968-'72:

His retirement was a bittersweet situation. Obviously, there has to be an end at some point. But at the same time, you hate to see that era end. I think when he retired it probably didn't hit most of us that he was not going to be there anymore. Until we got to the next baseball season and he wasn't on the field – particularly in my case as a competing coach across town, I expected to see him out there.

When we celebrated his retirement, we went out to the field. Players from every decade were there. During that day, he hit infield and outfield to us by decade. One of the interesting things was that more guys were there from the '60s and '70s than the later decades. Somebody remarked that the memories of us older guys had faded more than those guys that had just finished playing for him. But I think it's also indicative that he had such a major impact on everybody.

Guys came from all over the country. Then at the banquet that night, there were so many people who wanted to be there – not only players but also townspeople who knew Coach Moegle – that it had to be held at the Civic Center just to be able to house that many people.

COACH MOEGLE:

I've had kids who have gone into the business world and it has really been a competitive situation. They'll reach back on the period of time when they played here and it was hard and they had to compete against another individual at a real young age, not knowing exactly what it would entail or where it would lead them. They reach back on this fundamental background that they had as just a youngster of maybe 15-years-old and learning how to compete against a senior and trying to beat him or compete with him on a real high level.

They can go into this business or maybe a family situation and reach back and pull from this experience. It's kind of like our religious background. We get into a situation and we always go back to our basic fundamentals and our roots. There are a lot of kids who have told me over the years that they have been in tougher situations as an adult and how much they appreciated what they learned at that time in high school.

The work they did that they thought was extremely hard at that time probably laid a format for them to be successful in life. It's just a testament to the fact that they were all contributors to a very successful program.

BOB FANNIN '78:

I still do this today … The Moegles used to live on 62nd Street, a couple houses in on the north side of the street. Even to this day, if I'm going north on Indiana I look over there to see if he's out there. He hasn't lived there in 30 years, but I'm just making sure he's not out there looking at me as I drive by. (laughing) People don't realize the effect he had on us, and still has today.

The one thing that we're all looking for from him is a compliment or approval. Just something that says, "You're OK with me." I ran into him one morning in the last few years over at Home Depot. It was after we won the national championship at Lubbock Christian in 2009. We started talking and he told me he was proud of me. We started talking over by the toolboxes on aisle three and we ended up on aisle 12. (laughing) He had finally told me he was proud of me, and it was great.

BURLE PETTIT, LUBBOCK SPORTSWRITER:

The success of his teams is reflected in the success of his players afterward. As trite as it is ... for kids who are coached properly, sports is a great preparation for life – a great education in itself.

COACH MOEGLE:

I think sports is a real indication of how life will be. You're going to have ups and downs and you'll win some and lose some and have good times and hard times. But in the end, it's the record that you make and it's the way that you feel about yourself and the way you confront problems. It's the way you run your family and live your life.

Whether it's the military or sports ... by being in the military and playing professional baseball and having a commitment there, the foundation for me as a person was established way before I entered coaching. And when I came into coaching, I only knew one way to do it and that was what I considered the right way. I changed the philosophy on thinking in this part of the country about the way we went about our business.

There were few baseball coaches and very few knew anything about baseball, and most were football coaches. By having strong discipline and hard work and never feeling like we were inferior to anyone was a carry-on to life. I think nearly every one of my players will tell me to this day that their situation was difficult, but once they run quarters or run bleachers and had gone through off-season, they could face the difficult situation.

This is one of the real rewards that I have as an ex-coach – that I look back on the success that a lot of kids had that are prominent and they still haven't changed one bit. They developed a pride about themselves that carried on to their children. I see a lot of daughters of my former players who tell me their dads ran things just like I did, and that makes me feel good.

JIMMY WEBSTER '85:

Sal Maldonado played for me in my first couple years at Lubbock High. He was an average player, but he could fly. And he was dirt tough. You couldn't do enough to him. He went to the military in some sort of special program that was tougher than the regular training.

He came back and told me that because he had made it through our program in those early years at Lubbock High, he knew he could make it. Russ Lawson said the same thing. He had been pushed at age 16 or 17 and drew on that later in the military.

We've all had Coach Moegle in our minds later in life, still pushing us. It's paying our bills. It's rocking the crying baby to sleep in the middle of the night when you can't keep your eyes open. It's life.

BOB FANNIN '78:

There are so many times, even as adults today, that we want to say, "I'm tired of this. I just want to be done." But we say no, and we find a way to give a little more and get it done. In everything we do, there's somebody watching. It's going to filter down in a good way or a bad way. And we're so indebted to guys like Coach Moegle and Coach Hays.

COACH MOEGLE:

I was tough on kids because somewhere in their lifetime they're going to run into a situation in which they've got to be tough. They've got to be able to know they've experienced something just as bad as what they were about to go through.

MARK GRIFFIN '72:

I think he had a profound effect on men. The true measure of his influence probably didn't manifest itself when they played for him. It was later in life. They had handled his coaching and his program and there was very little short of physical harm that they couldn't handle from a mental aspect.

DONNIE BUMPASS '61:

As I age, the physical conditioning memories from Coach Moegle remain with me. In Wednesday's practice, we would run four sets of 25-yard dashes, four sets of 50-yard dashes and, finally, four sets of 100-yard dashes. We pushed ourselves, under his guidance, to limits we didn't fully understand. Pushing ourselves to the limit is a memory that I draw on regularly as I reach my older age. I am currently 76. In a way, it's a small memory, but I draw on it to accomplish other tasks – some physical, some mental.

TRAVIS WALDEN '81, ASSISTANT COACH 1989-'94:

One day I was sitting in the coaches' office after practice and I told him that one of the players had hurt his leg that day. He said he had noticed, then said that there's a price to pay sometimes. He said to look at the kids when they walk out after they've done something they didn't think they could do. They have a sense of pride about them and that carries over to the baseball field. Because those guys know that they've worked hard together, they've got a better product than if they hadn't done the work.

GARY HUGHES '65:

I learned a great deal from Coach Moegle in those three years: how to compete and how to be aggressive and to not give up – some life traits that have served me well. I appreciate those lessons very much.

DUSTY BUCK '99:

I was scared as hell going in as a sophomore on the heels of the 1996 state championship with several key contributors coming back. He pushed me harder and beyond what I thought I could do because I refused to let him down. He taught us about being good people and instilled a mindset to compete at everything – games, practice, competition quarters or sprints. At the time it all seemed to be about baseball, but he was really teaching us about competing in life.

Sure, winning games was important, but teaching us to be good people who gave it their all was what he really did. He didn't accept lack of effort, period. We all knew exactly what was expected of us. He would tell us "effort doesn't require talent" and then in Coach Moegle fashion, he'd tell us that we didn't have any talent either. Like every other team that came through MHS, we worked harder and milked more out of our ability than everyone else. Ultimately, he was hard on us because he knew there would be adversity on the field and in life. Some hated it and it wasn't for everyone, but those who bought in would do anything for him.

FRED OLIVER, MHS COACH 2000-'09:

Coach Moegle had high expectations for all his teams and all his players. I think every coach should do that. If a coach doesn't have expectations and goals, what's the use of going out there and competing? I think his style set the tone for his expectations. He was a winner. He wanted them to win. He wanted them to understand how they should go about winning.

He set an expectation that just winning wasn't good enough. He wanted them expecting to go deep in the playoffs. That's why he holds all the records he has. The high expectations between the lines was what he was after. Those kids who could handle the expectations were going to produce for him, and I think that influenced them later in life.

COACH MOEGLE:

As I look back on my 40 years of coaching kids – and I've had them from the big leagues to Little League and from every walk of life – the great thing is the camaraderie of the family atmosphere that we developed over a long period of time. I can have a kid from the 1960s talk to a kid from the 1970s or '80s and they went through

Coach Moegle - 1979

the same thing. It probably wasn't as severe in 1980 as it was in 1960.

But as I look back over the years, I've got people who have been the face of cancer research at MD Anderson, I've got guys who have been in the Senate, Federal Judges, pediatricians, and this "family" can look back and see that I had something to do with their lives. The idea that I took a youngster and through competition, discipline and caring for him – maybe the only family life he had was in our program – made him better, I've experienced that quite often since I retired.

I'll get a phone call from guys who say they'd been thinking about me. I had lunch not long ago with two guys from the 1972 state championship team. I played golf with one the other day who played for me in the '60s. That family atmosphere and the idea that these kids went through tough times with me and learned how to win and were affected by me is a real highlight of being a coach.

KELLER SMITH '63:

The sustenance that was provided in the baseball world went way beyond that in life. Even though I couldn't play a lick of baseball today, I still carry with me the lessons that he provided me during the three years I was so intimate with him. Ninety percent of the guys who played baseball for him – I would venture – would tell you that exact same thing, perhaps in other words or more articulate than I've been able to say.

Coach Moegle will tell you his proudest accomplishment is not the 1,100-plus victories, it's the impact he had on hundreds of young men, who in turn had a positive impact on others, their families, etc. If a man or woman can extend themselves through the behavior of others, they are a successful human being. And he is at the top of that list.

BURLE PETTIT, LUBBOCK SPORTSWRITER:

He loved kids and he loved baseball. He had so much respect for the game and so much respect for the kids who played for him that he wanted both of them served well. When you have Bobby Moegle working with kids, there's no greater compliment to academic education; because there was a practical application of life.

MARK GRIFFIN '72:

He saw what you could be, while you just saw who you were and what you thought you could do. He could say, "I see you as being able to do this," when you could never ever dream of being able to do that. That was one of his secrets to success. He saw you as you could be, not as you saw yourself.

BOB FANNIN '78:

He saw things in us that nobody else could see. I didn't go to college out of high school. Me and Ron Reeves and a few others played in a summer tournament down in Austin. We played pretty good there and were coming back to Lubbock. We had borrowed Reeves' stepdad's motor home. There's an exit sign on I-20 – we see it all the time on the way to Dallas – it's down toward Abilene and it says, "Noodle Dome Road."

Reeves saw it and said, "Fannin, we need to call somebody and get you in college at Noodle Dome next year." (laughing) He said, "I'm serious, we need to call Coach Moegle when we get home."

We went to see Coach Moegle, and he called Jack Allen at Ranger Junior College and told him I would make a good hand. Jack said, "Tell him to come on." All it took was a call from Coach Moegle. And now as a college coach we have guys we trust like Coach Moegle. When David Coleman calls and says we need to take a guy, we take him. I got to play for Coach Moegle, Jack Allen and Larry Hays. One day I looked up and realized how lucky I had been.

MARK GRIFFIN '72:

He never called me and asked me to come over from Lubbock

High. I called him and told him I was going to be at Monterey. I think I may have called him on a Friday and told him school starts on Monday and that we had rented an apartment and that I would be over there. He said, "Great, come on." Frankly, but for him I would not have had the opportunity to go play baseball at Texas.

When the season was over, there were only four seniors – Donnie Moore, Jimmy Killion, Jeff Minor and myself. Donnie was going to get drafted, and Jimmy and Jeff were going to college and weren't going to pursue baseball. I still wanted to play and he thought I could. He asked me where I wanted to go and told me he could help me at Texas or Oklahoma. I told him I'd like to try Texas first. I had no idea.

Donnie Moore and I flew down there together. Coach Gustafson thought if he could offer me a little bit of a scholarship, he would get Donnie, too. Donnie went to Ranger Junior College for a year and then on to pro ball. Without Coach Moegle, there was no way that Coach Gus was going to recruit me from Lubbock. I owe that to Coach Moegle, and I'll always be indebted and grateful to him for being willing to speak for me and put his reputation on the line.

JIMMY SHANKLE '74:

When I was a young kid he was everything to me. He was a great baseball guy. He and I had a real special relationship. I got no favors in high school, other than going in his office every day for three years to talk about life – not about baseball all the time, but mostly about life. For that hour while I had study hall, I went up there and talked to him and Coach Crutcher about God or life or how to get out of the poverty hole we were in. Whatever it was, I got a good lecture on life every day during baseball season and every day during off-season because they were there.

When I take all that and roll it together – the lessons of life I got from him, as well as his system – I realize he was a great educator of young men and not just a great baseball coach. He made a lot of men out of young, rebellious guys. The older I get, the smarter I realize he was.

BURLE PETTIT, LUBBOCK SPORTSWRITER:

I would be surprised if he didn't have contact with players from 40 years ago, because the kind of mentoring they got 40 years ago, they still need today. I would imagine that even the successful bankers and other professional guys would call and talk to Bobby when they have a problem or a quandary. That kind of relationship never dies, and I don't believe it ever wanes.

KELLER SMITH '63:

Make no mistake about it, as there is in any time frame or age group, there was always an element of potential troublemakers. Most of those, he ran off quickly. By the way, it didn't make any different how talented they were. As sophomores, people who didn't fit the system were sniffed out and were gone. And I'm telling you, we had some kids in our school who could've been fine ballplayers. But they didn't fit the mold and never got a chance.

Among those of us who were lucky enough to make the cut, there were some who could've strayed off the road. But we didn't get much chance to do that. Fortunately, for those of us who might've strayed, he kept us on the road long enough that we concluded we were where we were supposed to be. There are some successful guys out in the world today who played ball for Coach Moegle and would tell you if it hadn't been for him, they don't know where they might've ended up.

JEFF HORN '96:

He was interested in not only winning baseball games but producing quality people. His players have gone on to be successful in life. There are a lot of bank presidents, attorneys, doctors and coaches. He's had a very far-reaching effect.

KELLER SMITH '63:

When you really put it under the microscope, it goes way beyond baseball. It was about life and how to conduct yourself.

DUSTY BUCK '99:

It is hard to explain to people what playing for Coach Moegle and being a Monterey Plainsmen baseball player meant, then and now. Most people who played high school sports are proud of their respective program, but there was something special and rare about being a small piece in the 40-year tapestry of Coach Moegle and Monterey that still fills my heart with pride.

It's a brotherhood that spans multiple generations, bound by one man and a tradition of winning. I think we all wear playing for him and MHS as a badge of honor that was definitely earned. Needless to say, few have had the resonating impact on my life that he and that program have had. There's not much I wouldn't give to relive any day playing for him.

FRED OLIVER, MHS COACH 2000–'09:

I know all good coaches take advantage of the opportunities to teach things other than just baseball skills. We teach life skills every day. Coach Moegle took advantage of those opportunities like most of us do by having the kids be responsible and accountable for their own actions on and off the field. They were going to be in class, they were going to make good grades, they were going to be on time.

If they weren't doing those things, then there was punishment and they were held accountable. If they did it too many times, they were off the team. That's why many players point to a specific practice or game as something that Coach Moegle did that made them successful in life or in their occupation or marriage. Many things in life have been taught through the skills of Coach Moegle.

All of us can go back and determine who has been the most influential person in our lives. And the reason we pick somebody that's been influential is because they were stern and they didn't give in. They weren't your buddy and they weren't necessarily your most favorite person. I remember one of my teachers in high school was one of the most difficult teachers in the school. Nobody would say they really liked her because she was so tough. And yet she was a history teacher and I turned out to be a history teacher and I loved what she did for me. I can say that now.

I think many kids at the time they played for Coach Moegle might say they played in fear of him, but they come back years later and understand he was wanting them to do the right thing, and demanding that they do the right thing. He knew deep down that years later his players would be successful because they lasted three years with him and his program, and they couldn't help but be successful.

GARY ASHBY '73:

If you didn't fit into his plan to win baseball games, he didn't keep you just to keep you. He didn't find another jersey for that senior to wear and be a part of the squad – he wasn't going to help the squad so he didn't have a uniform anymore. Believe me – I'm not saying that's right, I'm just saying that's the way it was. I think there's probably some gray area there and you could probably find that guy a jersey and let him suit up and ride on the bus and let him throw batting practice or something. But nope, if you weren't going to contribute you weren't part of it. We left Monterey way more prepared for life than kids do nowadays, or at least I think so. That doesn't mean we're any more successful than those kids are going to be. But we were prepared.

Life is like that – if you aren't going to help the company, the company isn't going to keep you. If you aren't going to do what it takes to make the sales and reach the quotas in whatever business you're in, they aren't going to keep you on the squad. It prepared you for life. Work, get better and achieve, or you weren't going to be a part of it.

Coach Moegle gets a lot of credit for all the people who have gone on to bigger and better things when they've left his program. It's amazing how many bank presidents, heads of corporations, state politicians, local politicians – most people that come out of there are successful people. But I almost take the other side of it – most people that survive making the team and not quitting the team are going to be people who are "survivors." He ran off enough kids to fill a roster that could win district. So I really think a lot of the success that the people who came through his regime had is that they were "strung well" and were capable of enduring. A lot of people, for various reasons – either they were mentally beaten down or physically couldn't handle it – never saw their senior year (on the team).

When push came to shove, I didn't quit. I probably thought about it, but I didn't. But the ones who didn't would get pushed mentally and physically as much as we were ever going to get pushed in the real world. When I went into a job where it took a little extra work and all, that wasn't a problem. Outworking a guy wasn't going to be the problem. Now being smarter than him might've been a problem but outworking him was not going to be a problem, because the work ethic was there. So for what success I have on this earth, I'll give him more credit than anybody else.

MARK GRIFFIN '72:

He wanted us to carry some things with us into college, our family life and our business life – a strong character, work ethic and a commitment to do things the right way. His influence went beyond the baseball field, and I think to a large number of those guys, while they may not have thoroughly enjoyed the experience at that point in time, today look back on it with very fond memories and a debt of gratitude.

GARY HUGHES '65:

Large numbers went on to play in college and earned a scholarship. A few went on to play professional baseball, which could be attributed right back to his demanding personality. Coach Moegle had a profound effect on our careers. I think we all realize that had it not been for him and the lessons he taught us, we would not have been as successful in our work and family endeavors.

JIMMY SHANKLE '74:

We didn't always have the smartest guys in class but look at the guys who played on that '72 team – doctors, lawyers and guys who have been successful down the line. It is the same way with the '74 team – successful people with successful families and successful kids afterwards. He taught us a lifestyle. Some of the guys rebelled against it because it was tough. It was the famous, "You can do it my way or you can go to PE class." Well, I didn't want to go to PE class.

His program was the vehicle and not the destination. He is so proud of what his players have done later in life. I've coached, and when I think it's all said and done, that's where the prize is. How did the guys who played for me turn out? I'll bet 90% of Coach Moegle's guys are successful with a good life and good relationships between themselves and their parents, their wives, their kids and their lord. And that's what makes him the happiest.

Believe it or not, at the time we only thought it was wins and losses that he cared about because that was what was important at the time, but he was doing it so later in life we were disciplined people and disciplined fathers and disciplined husbands. He was trying to make us better people and to make us men, and I think he did that.

HUNTER LANKFORD '87:

As part of the 1987 class, we were also friends and classmates with Coach Moegle's youngest daughter. So being a Moegle player was also family. For me, and for a few others who had experienced a broken home through divorce or other disruptions, being a Moegle man served as a compass.

Being accountable to his program provided motivation to study, to be groomed, to be respectful, to work hard and to stay out of trouble. By default, when parents are split, the inherent co-parenting function is disintegrated. As such, not only was Coach Moegle a coach, but he also became a father. He provided guidance, accountability and fear during times of adolescent need. Winning baseball games, throwing out baserunners and slapping base hits are absolute great memories.

But being one of Moegle's men includes DNA that never leaves – DNA that emerges through life's trials and tribulations.

JACK DALE, BROADCASTER:

There can be boys playing high school baseball who can be made into young men, just like in almost any sport. It can be something really outstanding for the individual youngster that's playing if it's done in the right way. And I think with Coach Moegle, that's what you got. You can talk to so many of his former players and they'll tell you that they wouldn't be where they are today if it wasn't for him, because he made them what they are today through baseball. Take all the fluff away and break it down to just the high school players playing baseball under the right leadership with the right coaching and so forth, and you have a program that makes boys into men.

GARY HUGHES '65:

Years later, we realized that those lessons and that discipline was what we needed at that age.

JEFF HARP '78:

I did my student teaching for him. The academic advisor at Tech had assigned me to Coach Moegle and he knew that I had played for him at Monterey. He told me, "You can NOT help him at baseball practice." I said OK and went to school. On the first day Coach Moegle handed his PE class over to me and left and I led the class in weight training. After class I told him that I couldn't believe he handed the class over to me. He told me, "I knew you had it." And then he asked me, "Are you coming to baseball practice today?" I told him, "Yes sir." (laughing) There was no way I was going to tell him no. He had such an impact on me it was ridiculous.

JOHN DUDLEY '62, ASSISTANT COACH 1968-'72:

Coach Moegle had a major impact on me as a player and a coach. When I was in college at Texas Tech I made a decision that I wanted to be a teacher and a coach. He was the first guy I reflected on and wanted to, hopefully, be as successful as he was. I realized how much work was going to be involved to be able to do that.

What I knew about baseball in the very beginning, I had learned from him. I began to pick up a little more along the way, but I can guarantee that what I knew about baseball came from having played for him. He probably shaped my attitude as a coach for a lot of years. Probably after a period of time, each one of us develops our own personality, but when we get started, we carry a lot of his personality into our coaching style.

JIMMY WEBSTER '85:

When we hear stories about Vince Lombardi, they fit our experiences with Coach Moegle. He changed our lives like Lombardi changed theirs. I think I would've been OK without Monterey baseball, but I definitely would not have played college baseball. At another place I might've made the team sooner and played more, but my teammates wouldn't have been good enough to carry me. But there also wouldn't have been a high mark to shoot for. And when you don't have that, the status quo and selfishness sneaks in. And "selfishness" was never a word you heard at Monterey ... EVER. It was never an issue. On a lot of teams that are average-to-poor, that's an issue.

My life would have been a lot different ... a lot. It's hard for me to even wonder and think about, because when I didn't have something, I wasn't the best kid around. It wasn't like I was committing crimes, but there was a time that I could've gone either way.

STEVE HARR '73:

I would not have had a career in law had I not played for Coach Moegle. He taught me to set a goal and never walk away from it until I had given my all. My discipline to take on any task and unwillingness to quit or just slip by with a minimal effort all came from him. I was never his friend or favorite, but he made me want to be the best.

SCOTT BRAND '94:

I was selected in the 8th round out of Monterey by Cincinnati and turned down their offer to go to junior college for a year. The next year I was drafted in the 8th round again by the Yankees and took their offer because they doubled the signing bonus and paid for four years of school at Texas Tech during the off-season. If it wasn't for Coach Moegle, I would have never signed with the Yankees.

TRAVIS WALDEN '81, ASSISTANT COACH 1989-'94:

I look at guys I later coached with or against that went through Monterey and they basically all have the same kind of philosophy of outworking people and being tougher than people. And even in the Little Leagues ... I've helped out in the Little Leagues when my son was playing, and I see a lot of guys coaching youth baseball and YFL football who played for him and talk about how Coach Moegle influenced them.

JOHN DUDLEY '62, ASSISTANT COACH 1968-'72:

When we played for him, because he pushed us so hard it felt like we were just trying to survive. I don't think we appreciated what he had done for us until we finished our playing career and looked back and saw that he did, in fact, push me to be as good as I could possibly be and that he brought the best out of me. Having been a coach, I wish I could've coached first, and then go be a player, because I would have understood better what he was trying to get out of us and get out of me personally.

MIKE CRUTCHER '68, ASSISTANT COACH 1973-'78, 1982-'85:

When I started coaching, he was really ... to use the word "patient" with Bobby Moegle might be a misnomer. But he was real patient with me as a young coach. He tried to teach me coaching concepts more so than baseball things like throwing the curve ball and stuff like that.

CLINT BRYANT '92:

When we played for him, he was a father figure. We talked with him, but we didn't really consider him a friend or a peer at the time. After I finished at Tech, I had my number retired. He showed up that day and felt more like a family member than a former baseball coach. He really did care that day and was asking about me in a way that was far different than in high school.

I think if you play for him and miss out on having a relationship with him later, you miss out on something. A lot of the guys who played for him hated him, and that's sad because the person he is beyond baseball is one that I look up to more than I did when I played for him.

SCOTT BRAND '94:

We either loved Coach Moegle or hated him. I loved him! The guys who hated him were usually the guys who couldn't take it. He was a big influence in my life and showed me what it took to have mental toughness.

LARRY HAYS, LCU & TTU COACH '71-2008:

I think every year I would take one of his players. I would hear all these Coach Moegle stories on the bus. He was a big part of our conversations. We'd have four or five kids there that had played for him. One would play like he hated him. After being around the kid for four years, I figured out the kid didn't hate Coach Moegle. He may have thought he did. But Coach Moegle had given him a reason to exist and to bow up and play and get past whatever hang-ups he had, whether he knew it or not. But there wasn't a one of them who wouldn't talk about him and start smiling. They knew what he'd done for him.

JIMMY WEBSTER '85:

Our 1985 group was a group of good kids. We weren't out doing stuff we shouldn't have been doing. We didn't want to disappoint him, our parents or the program. He didn't have to mop up after us or check our grades or worry about curfew – we were going to take care of that stuff. If he was concerned about anything, it was probably that he needed to get us tougher. When we were done, he might've said that we played a little over our heads. But he still worked us and ran us. He knew what he was doing. Instead of being surprised by our success, he still worked us.

It sounds cheesy, but I can't say it forcefully enough how life-altering it was. Our parents were our parents – if we screwed up at home, they would love us because they had to. He had some leverage on us that they didn't have and that changed people's lives. The more

Coach Moegle - 1985

we talk to people around the program, the more they mention that part. They can't imagine where they'd be without that experience.

JEFF HORN '96:

Once we got out of the program and went into life, we learned that maybe we've already faced some of our toughest battles. It made us think that he knew what he was doing after all. The feeling I have after I got through playing is one of sincere appreciation. He's someone who still cares about us. I remember playing in a golf tournament with him a few years ago. I had the time of my life riding around in the cart listening to his opinions about certain guys that had played for him, because now we talk one-on-one. It was no more player-coach but more friend-to-friend. I think that's why we've stayed in contact with him.

JIMMY SHANKLE '74:

At his retirement dinner, one of the last things I said was that Coach Moegle made a man out of me. I truly believe that. And anybody that was his player and allowed him to do that during that time in their lives, or later in their lives, might feel the same way. Gary Ashby is a great example. He was a great player and even better in college and as a professional player and was almost a big leaguer. During the time in high school, he fought it a little bit, but now he and Coach Moegle and Mark Griffin and I go eat together when we can all get together.

Coach Moegle really made a difference in people's lives, and maybe they didn't know it at the time. In my particular situation, I knew it.

KELLER SMITH '63:

The passion went beyond baseball. If it had just been a passion for a sport, the results would've never been as spectacular as they were. He loved the game, he knew the game, and he was the best with what he had. But there was an equal if not greater passion for helping young men get off on the right foot with their lives, and to mature quickly and understand the difference between right and wrong, to understand what discipline could bring you, and to leave Monterey High School with that instilled in you.

That was the real passion. The baseball was the vehicle to deliver that. The affection came later. The affection didn't occur out there on the practice field behind Monterey High School. The affection came 5 years, 10 years, 20 years, or 40 years later, when we grew up, matured, reflected and thought, "My God, how blessed I was to have been part of that."

And that has led to these examples that now are the rule, and that is the reunions, the retirement celebration, the telephone calls, the emails going both ways. And now the subject of those is the gratitude, appreciation and love that was never expressed back when we were running 4-4-4.

MARK GRIFFIN '72:

Hard work, diligent preparation, and you weren't going to make any excuses as to why we weren't successful – those are great traits to have beyond the baseball field. I think the legacy of this gentleman was not only what he did on the field but also what instilled within the souls and hearts of his players that they would take into the next station of their lives and prepare them for whatever came later.

My understanding and appreciation of the Moegle formula would be hard work, diligent preparation and no excuses. Then we'll let the chips fall where they may. He would have his guys ready to play, and if they didn't perform to that level he would either find someone else or do a better job instructing them the next time. Any time we went into a game, those ingredients that made up that formula manifested themselves more often than not. Those were non-negotiables.

Those are great traits beyond the baseball field. I think that's really the legacy of this gentleman – not only what he did on the field but what he instilled in the souls and hearts of his players that would take them into the next station of their lives and prepare for whatever came their way.

NATHAN SWINDLE '81:

Playing for Coach Moegle was a very positive thing in my life. I've talked to a lot of people about playing for him and I'll get a lot of different opinions about this. It was all positive for me and I attribute a lot of that to deciding in my senior year that he wasn't so scary after all and that I was going to go in there and talk to him. I found out he was a good guy. Now, he was totally honest with everybody and people didn't want to hear that sometimes, but it gave us some direction on what we needed to work on.

I'll always appreciate being a part of the program. It was something I looked forward to well in advance of me getting there.

TRAVIS WALDEN '81, ASSISTANT COACH 1989-'94:

There was a guy who told me one time that you can't teach your own son toughness – somebody else has to do it because if you try to teach your son toughness he'll resent you. I think there are a lot of men who are thankful that Coach Moegle had a big part in teaching their sons how to be tough and to be young men and to be accountable.

Coach Moegle told me once that the worst thing that happened to our country was doing away with the draft. He said that because everybody went away for two or three years and got some discipline and toughness, whether they wanted it or not. People who played for him have that. My brother says if you meet a guy who was a Marine, you'll know within 5 minutes that he was a Marine.

If a guy played baseball for Coach Moegle, you'll know within 5 or 10 minutes of a conversation, because something will happen and the guy will tell a story about playing baseball for him. To me, that's where he becomes a legend. He helped develop young men and taught them some toughness and gave them discipline.

JOHN DUDLEY '62, ASSISTANT COACH 1968-'72:

We look back through the eyes of a player, and we recognize that he made decisions that were based on the team and not on an individual, and as the result we were part of something special.

Coach Moegle's Record

YEAR	WINS	LOSSES	
1960	22	7	
1961	26	8	State Runner-Up
1962	25	9	
1963	34	6	State Tournament
1964	25	11	
1965	27	9	
1966	22	9	
1967	24	11	
1968	26	9	
1969	27	4	
1970	28	7	State Tournament
1971	33	3	State Runner-Up
1972	30	6	State Champion
1973	33	6	
1974	36	4	State Champion
1975	28	8	
1976	26	7	
1977	30	5	
1978	33	6	State Runner-Up
1979	27	8	
1980	28	5	
1981	38	4	State Champion
1982	25	6	
1983	27	8	
1984	34	5	State Tournament
1985	30	4	State Tournament
1986	25	4	
1987	27	5	
1988	22	5	
1989	27	7	
1990	24	5	

YEAR	WINS	LOSSES	
1991	26	8	
1992	23	5	
1993	27	4	
1994	33	10	State Tournament
1995	24	7	
1996	36	3	State Champion
1997	33	8	State Runner-Up
1998	29	8	
1999	15	12	
TOTAL	1115	266	

Monterey Baseball Assistant Coaches Under Moegle:

1968-1972	John Dudley
1973-1978	Mike Crutcher
1979-1981	Wyman Raper
1982-1985	Mike Crutcher
1986-1988	David Walden
1989-1994	Travis Walden
1995-1996	Greg Hogue
1997-1999	Tuey Rankin

About the Author

MIKE GUSTAFSON Ed.D.

Dr. Mike Gustafson has served as the President/CEO of the College Baseball Foundation since June 2009. His connection to baseball goes back to his playing career in which he performed on consecutive state tournament teams in 1984 and 1985 under Coach Bobby Moegle at Lubbock Monterey High School. A two-time all-city and all-district middle infielder in high school, he attended Texas Tech and played baseball from 1986-89. After graduating from Tech, he attended the University of Texas and obtained a master's degree in Sports Management. In 2005, he completed his doctorate at Texas Tech in Higher Education Administration.

Mike has served as radio and television analyst for Texas Tech Baseball since 2010. His wife, Dana, is a middle school science teacher and they have two children - Brooks and Savannah.